Solace
A Correspondence of Gardening, Friendship and Healing

"...highlights not only the power of friendship but also of the spirit to survive illness and death."—*The Ottawa Citizen*

"Thus began a correspondence that evolved into a discussion of the garden as a metaphor for the human spirit, told in the language of plants, and then into this book. It reminds me of the published letters between Virginia Woolf and Harold Nicholson discussing their garden, seemingly a code for something larger."—*Literary Review of Canada*

"A testament of faith in the power of the spirit to heal through love."—*Two Chairs* magazine

"We have the good fortune to be able to share the record of an exploration into the gardens of their souls."—*Northern Life*

"Diane and Marla, in their correspondence and in their friendship, remind us that loving and healing must be nurtured as carefully as we nurture our gardens. Indeed, seeing love and healing as something we nourish and cherish and grow helps us rediscover the connections between all of us, connections which draw energy from the earth itself. In reading this book, I have come to know myself and those around me in new ways, and Diane and Marla have rekindled my own desire to use my work and my life in service to healing and to love."—Dr. Douglass St. Christian, Department of Anthropology, University of Western Ontario

"A very lovely and heartwarming book."—Dr. Robert Nelson, former director of the multiple sclerosis clinic at the Ottawa Hospital

"A book for all seasons, a book for all reasons."—Ivan Wheale, artist

"[This] is not a how-to book for gardeners. Nor is it, strictly speaking, a philosophical work. It is a poetic blending of practical information and reflection on the strength of the human spirit."—*The Common Reader*

Diane Sims and Marla Fletcher

Solace
A Correspondence of Gardening, Friendship and Healing

NOVALIS

© 2005 Novalis, Saint Paul University, Ottawa, Canada
Cover design and layout: Pascale Turmel
Cover artwork: Christopher Broadhurst, selection of work from the Wallflower
series, oil on canvas (Images courtesy Edward Day Gallery, Toronto)
Interior photos: Jupiter Images

Business Office:
Novalis
49 Front Street East, 2nd Floor
Toronto, Ontario, Canada M5E 1B3
Phone: 1-800-387-7164
Fax: (514) 278-3030
E-mail: cservice@novalis-inc.com
www.novalis.ca

Library and Archives Canada Cataloguing in Publication

Sims, Diane
    Solace : a correspondence of gardening, friendship and healing /
Diane Sims & Marla Fletcher.

Previous ed. had title: Gardens of our souls : a correspondence of friendship
    and healing.
Includes bibliographical references and index.
ISBN 2-89507-571-9

    1. Fletcher, Marla—Correspondence. 2. Sims, Diane—Correspondence.
3. Gardens—Psychological aspects. 4. Grief. I. Fletcher, Marla II. Title.
III. Title: Gardens of our souls.

BF353.5.N37S55 2005   155.9'37'092   C2005-901091-6

Printed in Canada.

DISCLAIMER
The information in this book is true and complete, to the best of our knowledge. The healing information presented is for interest and information only
and is not to be construed as medical advice. Please do not self-diagnose or
attempt any treatment of illness without consulting your physician.

Originally published by Macmillan Canada in 1998 under the title
Gardens of Our Souls: A Correspondence of Friendship and Healing.

We acknowledge the financial support of the Government of Canada through
the Book Publishing Industry Development Program (BPIDP) for our publishing activities.

5 4 3 2 1   09 08 07 06 05

Contents

Acknowledgments

My deepest thanks and appreciation go to:

- Ian and Emma, who delighted and inspired with their laughter, their wonderful drawings and Emma's one-of-a-kind birthday book;
- Becky, the original best buddy, leaning post and loving sister;
- David, who taught me how to really listen to music, and who kept the paper flowing;
- Don, for solid support and his achingly beautiful fiddle tunes;
- Dad, who willingly shares the colour and wonder he sees around him;
- Paul, my faithful listening post and computer guru; and
- Mom, who imparted a strong spirit and a lifelong love of well-chosen words.

Marla Fletcher, Ottawa, Ontario, 2005

Together, we sincerely thank all those close friends, family members, horticultural pals, colleagues and others who listened, encouraged, advised, encouraged, shared expertise, encouraged, provided plants, contacts and resource materials – and, above all,

Acknowledgments

encouraged! Marlene Wehrle and staff at the National Library of Canada's Music Division were especially helpful. Yvon Renaud advised us with such wise counsel. Our deep appreciation unfailingly goes to Anne Louise Mahoney, a gentle and superb editor at Novalis. Thank you for the love and exceptional advice you gave in making this project happen.

Marla and Diane

For Harvey
Wherever I have gone, whatever I have done, my heart untravel'd fondly turns to thee/still to my brother I turn...[1]

Diane

My personal love and gratitude, as always, go to family and friends. I mention a few but know you are many. Without you I could not be – you have fed me body and soul: Harvey Sims and Janet Sabourin, Nancy Drayer, Ruthmarie and Don Schroeder, Chris Samson, Bob Allen and Ed Welker, Cynthia Howard, David and Sharon Wadley, Douglass and Stephen St. Christian, Yvonne Yoerger and Bern Murphy, Lee Pridham and Paul Hansford, Robyn and Eric Harris, Beulah Patterson, Joanne Hunsberger, Karen and Martin Davies, Maril Crabtree, the only Old Bear, Therese Webster; and Bizzie and Gracie – my dearest forever "paws and claws."

Of course, this work would or could not have reappeared but for the spirit of my faithful friend, Marla Fletcher. Thank you, Mar.

My medical appreciation is unlimited. Truly, the list is endless. As one team member paraphrased, "Sometimes it takes a village to care for one person." You do that.

---

1   Paraphrase of a verse from *The Traveller*, by Oliver Goldsmith, Act 1, st. 7 (1764).

I could not heal, nor cope, without your support for my daily battles with multiple sclerosis (MS) and ovarian cancer: Dr. Sean Blaine, Joan Ritsma, Shanna Core; Dr. Angus Maciver, Joan Mottola, Irene Kaufman; Dr. Brian Hasegawa and Marcia Bender; Dr. Andrew Hussey and Amy Dale; my homecare team, including, Connie, Linda L., Lynda C., Brenda, Trudy, Linda F., Marg H-P, Marjorie, Sandra, June, Ruthanne; staff at the Stratford General Hospital; the Stratford chapter of the Multiple Sclerosis Society of Canada; and the cancer and neurological clinics at The Ottawa Hospital.

A portion of royalties from the sale of this book will be donated to the Stratford MS chapter. These marvellous members are dedicated to raising awareness and research funding on behalf of those of us with MS.

Finally, a note about biblical references. I used three translations: The King James Version (KJB), the Jerusalem Bible (JB) and the New International Version (NIV). Each is rich in interpretation – I hope you enjoy the variety.

Merci beaucoup, mes amis. Que Dieu vous protège.

Diane Sims, Stratford, Ontario, 2005

On Our Kneepads

I t began, as many worthy life endeavours do, almost accidentally. My closest friend, Diane, had suffered the sudden, wrenching loss of her sister through illness, and I wanted to comfort her. Diane and I met through our work on a national magazine; because I lived some distance away, my modest efforts were largely restricted to letters, faxes and telephone calls. It wasn't enough, and the words never seemed to fully express what I was trying to say. I had to do better.

I am most at peace in a garden, so it was natural to mull this over one fine spring day as I started preparing for a new season outdoors. At once the answer presented itself – right at my fingertips. I'd send one of my garden plants appropriate to the situation, something that would distract my friend from her grief while speaking directly to the pain she was feeling.

She and I share a deep passion for the natural world, and have spent long hours exploring how that ardour is expressed in our gardens. As I tucked a frost-heaved primula firmly back into the ground, I revelled once again in the rich sensation of soft, rippling new growth and loose, warm soil. It was the right way to go – I just knew it!

And so our journey began. With that first plant, I sent a detailed letter explaining why I'd chosen that particular species and citing all the relevant meanings and references I could find. The research was a delight for me, because healing with plants has been a recognized option since at least 3400 B.C. The earliest records date from Chinese and Egyptian civilizations, as revered practices, with variations and refinements, made their way through Greek, Roman, Arab and Indian cultures. Today we have the Indian Ayurvedic healing system, traditional Chinese medicine, native healing practised by indigenous peoples on every continent, and widespread interest in naturopathy and herbal medicine.

Diane was deeply touched and, to my surprise, she responded in kind. The gardens of our souls were on their way – in a flurry of faxes, letters, packages, telephone calls, e-mails, even snail mail! The gardens are living testament to age-old traditions, and to a firm friendship that continues to defy any obstacle or distance, whether in years, miles or twists of fate.

Some facts have been changed, protecting privacy where necessary and allowing us to create scenarios and compress the time sequence to cover plants with which we haven't necessarily worked. We have also changed personal names, including our own, allowing us to shape the correspondence. I sign my letters as Anne; Diane uses the name Elizabeth. The feelings are real, though, and the spiritual and horticultural references are all factual. We've researched carefully to give fellow gardeners and spiritual travellers solid information we hope they can use. You won't find the latest "hot" plants or amazing hybrids here; most of the plants we've explored are time-honoured and well loved. These wildflowers and herbs, trees and shrubs, annuals and perennials can be found in most temperate climates.

> And what is it to work with love?... It is to sow seeds with tenderness and reap the harvest with joy, even as if your beloved were to eat the fruit.

(Kahlil Gibran, *The Prophet*)
Marla Fletcher, Ottawa, Ontario, 1998

So much is changed, so much the same, some seven years later. Both marriages have ended. The outer trappings of our lives are different, but our close bond endures and the inner quests continue.

Marla Fletcher, Ottawa, Ontario, 2005

* * *

Fifty years ago, a contemporary and mentor of Mohandas Gandhi wrote, "I have kissed this world with my eyes." Poet Rabindranath Tagore had suffered greatly during India's struggle for independence before he could articulate that thought. It comforts me time and again as I struggle with my own pain. What peace Tagore must have found, to speak those words! Now, I humbly tailor Tagore's sentiment, saying, "I have kissed this garden with my hands and my soul."

My dear friend Marla came to my rescue during a year of intense personal loss. My only sister, Karen, and my beloved mom had both died. Then, after twenty years of coping with mobility and visual impairments from multiple sclerosis, I was diagnosed with ovarian cancer. This was eight months after the same cancer consumed Karen, and four months after my mom died from a massive stroke. The markers along my road were slipping into the shadows and the way ahead seemed shorter, and oh, so much darker.

Reaching out, Marla began to share the joy she had found in gardening. Over the months, the letters, petals, clippings and information accumulated as Marla and I explored our gardens. I became determined to write myself into wellness.

Then something wonderful happened – the cutting that had been spirited aboard an Air Canada flight from Ottawa to Sault Ste. Marie in the dead of winter sprouted. We had life! From that time forward we knew this was about hope, about affirmation of life in the midst of adversity, and about the ridiculously simple pleasure a garden gives.

We hope this work offers some comfort or peace along your road, whether it be one of loss, of pain, or of loneliness. We know that the road to health is not linear. Pain, like a wolf, circles around our flanks. It is this cyclical experience we hope our letters convey; it is okay to cry with grief the day you first feel some joy. Like a warm hug, our friendship has encircled this correspondence and interspaced our plants.

This isn't a garden how-to book; there are many excellent books of that type available. And it isn't a spiritual how-to book. Again, those abound by much more qualified authors. (Please check our bibliography for some of the superb references on the market.)

Rather, this is a testimonial of how one gardening friendship blossomed into healthier bodies, souls and gardens. If you find comfort in any letter, idea or favourite plant, Marla and I will be delighted!

Come then, my love, my lovely one, come.
For see, winter is past, the rains are over and gone.
The flowers appear on the earth.
The season of glad songs has come,
the cooing of the turtledove is heard in our land.

(Song of Songs 2:10-12, JB)
with hope, Diane Sims, Sault Ste. Marie, Ontario, 1998

Seven years, eight surgeries and six moves. Despite these events, Marla and I remain firm friends. We have had some rough times, but the testimony of enduring love has worked. While Marla and I engaged in the final phases of publication of this book, I was introduced to the late Californian poet Eugene Ruggles. I hope his words comfort you as you open the covers of this book: "Come in, there is no lock, hang your coat beside the fire and pull up a chair to its edge. / We shall drink tea and clear the path leading back to the heart's first address."

Diane Sims, Stratford, Ontario, 2005

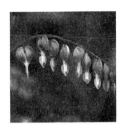

Loss and Pain

L oss and pain are four-letter words. In that context, both are damning and damaging.

The *Concise Oxford Dictionary* defines loss as being deprived of something, a detriment to our being. Pain is similarly summarized as suffering or distress of body or mind.

Whether we suffer from physical pain or the intense ache of emotional pain – such as the heartbreaking loss of a loved one, the sudden collapse of a long-standing relationship or the demoralizing sorrow of shattered illusions – there is anguish that we must work through. There is no escaping loss if we want to participate in the life experience; we cannot, then, escape pain.

Clearly, loss and pain hurt. "My suffering teaches me about my disease. My pain teaches me about my life," reminds an entry in Anne Wilson Schaef's *Meditations for Women Who Do Too Much.*

While medicine and meditation help soothe physical pain, the consolation of time and the comfort of love ease the wounded spirit.

The plants in this chapter speak of the time and the love needed to sustain our soul through pain. As it takes time to grow and nurture a garden, so it takes time to heal body and soul. And the love found in a deep, abiding friendship helps console our soul through the dark days of despair.

Solace

The Psalmist, in describing his suffering, wrote that "now darkness is my one companion" (Psalm 88:18, JB). May this exchange of thoughts and garden comforts help fringe your darkness with an edge of light – and of life. May the damaged heart of today be the lighthearted spirit of tomorrow.

* * *

Dear Elizabeth:

I have enclosed in this package a slip from my garden that I hope will be a living expression of my sympathy. It's lemon balm, *Melissa officinalis*.

Nicolas Culpeper, a seventeenth-century English herbalist, considered lemon balm a very valuable plant. In his writings promoting the use of herbs and other plants for medicinal use, he says this aromatic herb "driveth away all troublesome care and thoughts out of the mind, arising from melancholy and black choler." May it work its magic on you!

Here's what I found out. The Latin word for "balm" comes from the Greek word for "bee"; it is said bees will never leave a garden where balm is growing. For centuries the plant has been considered a tonic for the heart, and its antidepressant effect has been documented in more recent times. Tea is made from the leaves as a refreshing drink or cold remedy, and fresh leaves are added to jellies and fruit cups. Crush the leaves and you'll discover its sweet, lemony scent – reminiscent of lemon meringue pie, to my mind.

Lemon balm is welcome in my garden because it is a no-maintenance perennial that dependably fills a half-shaded corner. It's a rangy, round, shrub-like plant that remains lush and fragrant throughout the growing season. Balm is a spreader, but is easily plucked out when unwanted. The serrated edges of downy leaves seem to make them dance in a breeze, and the scent is particularly noticeable in the evening. Tiny clusters of white flowers appear on mine in midsummer.

A member of the mint family, lemon balm is native to various parts of Europe, western Asia and North Africa. It has been naturalized to the south of England, too, and grows throughout temperate North America. According to my reference sources, lemon balm can stand some shade and isn't too particular about the quality of the soil. It is easily spread by seed, slip or root division. To revive sagging spirits, one herb book suggests infusing a large handful of clean, fresh lemon balm in a bottle of mild white wine for several hours. Excuse me now; I have to slip out to the liquor store before it closes.

Anne

Dear Anne:
Your lemon balm has comfortably edged its way into my life: I searched my old perennial garden and found a struggling shrub tucked under a pink rosebush amidst some shasta daisies and bee balm. And lemon balm is one of the cooling ingredients in the face tonic you sent me. Here, in return, is a flower you and I both love – the cornflower.

"When we look into the heart of a flower, we see clouds, sunshine, minerals, time, the earth, and everything else in the cosmos in it. Without clouds, there could be no rain, and there would be no flower." As I work through my pain, the simple blue *Centaurea montana* embodies that thought from renowned thinker and scholar Thich Nhat Hanh. Annie, I don't wish this physical or emotional pain on anyone, but it has shaped much of who I am. I have to focus on today, as tomorrow sometimes seems overwhelming. With your help, I am learning day by day about my garden, including these happy cornflowers. Now, here's what I've discovered.

These sentinel perennials acquired their generic name from Chiron, the wise and gentle centaur accidentally wounded by Hercules' poisonous arrows. In Greek mythology these stately garden guards helped treat the wounded centaur. Alas, the immortal Chiron suffered sorely. Prometheus looked kindly on Chiron and took on his mantle of immortality, thereby allowing the centaur to die. Then, in 288 B.C., a Greek philosopher identified the wild knapweed as a *Centaurea*, and that name took root, notes

Laura C. Martin in *Wildflower Folklore*.

There's an equally sad story associated with another member of the *Centaurea* family. This deep-blue wildflower is apparently named for Cyanus, a young woman who made floral garlands for festivals in Roman times. The woman was devoted to Flora, the goddess of flowers. When Flora found her friend dead in a field one day, she transformed her into a cornflower in heartfelt tribute.

The popular "cornflower" moniker comes from England, where the plants were abundant in grain fields. Then, the English Victorians associated the cornflower with purity and delicacy.

In our part of the country, the three-foot stalks of *Centaurea* send up long, silvery leaves in early June. Their thin petals barely hint at the telltale blue disks that will open by July. It is that sky-blue hue that captures the essence of the cosmos in Thich Nhat Hanh's quote. But pink and white varieties also exist.

These fringed flowers enjoy my dry, sunny garden and make grand companions for the poppies, day lilies and irises. As well, there's a showier annual type called bachelor's button that does well from May-sown seeds. (I have not tried these.)

The *Centaurea* is easy to grow and flowers throughout the summer, with long-lasting blooms. It will stay fresh for quite a while when cut, and the bud resembles a button. According to *Wildflower Folklore*, it thus became known as bachelor's button – a handsome boutonniere. Cutting back after the first flowering will usually bring new blooms in fall, a bonus!

When I see the cornflower's feathery fingers reaching upward, my soul stirs with hope – for I know that next year these faithful pompons will again grace my garden.

Elizabeth

Dear Elizabeth:

Thank you for the cornflower; I'll treasure it. It's a good thing we do most of our gardening in private: you never know what it's going to bring out. One day I'm hanging whimsical wind chimes; the next I'm sobbing among the shrubbery.

Loss and Pain

Yes, sobbing. I'm thankful there was no one around to see. It happened yesterday, when I went out very early to plant my sweet pea seeds. Maybe it's menopause creeping up, or maybe I'm just lonely. Who knows? It was a visit from my neighbour's lovely little calico cat that set me off. She's a playful young thing who comes over often and loves to climb into my lap for scratches behind the ears – especially when it's not convenient.

Anyway, I was carefully placing presoaked seeds the prescribed eight inches apart, in a zigzag pattern down the length of the trench I had dug along the back fence last fall. I was just beginning to cover them with a light layer of compost and bone meal when I saw the cat gleefully digging and pouncing at the far end. She was tossing my poor seeds around like miniature volleyballs!

My yelp of outrage didn't bother her in the least, and her defiance reminded me of my dear, departed Angus. Tears started streaming down my face. I crouched like that, knees soggy in the morning dew, for at least ten minutes before collecting myself enough to finish the job and retreat.

Do you remember Angus, my beautiful grey tabby? He was just as mischievous – especially in the garden – and just as disdainful in his youth. I still miss both him and my round, orange Jasper-cat terribly, two and three years after their deaths. Why do you suppose it's so much easier to forge deep, unconditional links with our animal companions than it is with other humans?

With Angus and Jasper gone, I can safely enjoy a bouquet of gloriously scented sweet peas without fearing they'll be toppled from their vases; it seems a pretty poor bargain most days.

Sweet peas are another of those "old-fashioned" flowers you and I seem to favour. They've been in cultivation since the late 1600s, crossing the Atlantic from Italy and England about one hundred years later. There's a perennial type, *Lathyrus latifolius*, that twines its way up fences and trellises to produce white or rose-tinted prow-like blossoms, but the scented annual *Lathyrus odoratus* is the one I love. It comes in purple, blue, pink, red, white, cream, mauve, salmon and some bicolours, blooming from early summer through fall. These wonderful plants love to be appreciated; picking the flowers actually encourages more blossoms.

If you try them, choose a sheltered spot where there's a support system – such as a fence – that the tendrils can grasp. Sweet peas like cool weather and a sunny location; keep their roots moist with a layer of mulch. Start filling in the trench with more soil after the plants are two inches tall. Fertilize them regularly, and remove spent blooms to keep the show going all summer.

Some people grow dwarf types in containers, but take care not to let the soil dry out. Daily watering is probably necessary. Other gardeners use sweet peas as screens to hide unattractive sheds, fences or walls, or to make a porch more private. I like the heat-tolerant and heavily scented climbing variety 'Old Spice Mixture', which has a generous colour range.

Sweet peas speak of both lasting pleasure and departure. The pleasure is obvious: these flowers are around all summer and are good for at least a week when picked. But poet John Keats noted their temporary nature. He described the airy blossoms as "on tiptoe for a flight / With wings of gentle flush o'er delicate white." And, of course, sweet pea is an annual so it won't be back next season unless you replant.

I've read that scent often triggers memory and can bring on joyous recollection or a spasm of bitter grief about what's been lost. For me, the sight of a frolicking feline sent me back years, to something I've missed more than I can say. I guess the experience has helped me deal with the hurt, but I'll know better when I cut my first nosegay of sweet peas later this summer. They should be opening just in time for your next visit, so I'll have some on the bureau for you.

Anne

Dear Anne:

I'm looking forward to those sweet peas! But this June morning my heart is heavy. I miss my mom so much! "Why is my suffering continual?" lamented Jeremiah (Jeremiah 15:18, JB). "How much longer must I endure grief in my soul, and sorrow in my heart by day and by night?" asked the Psalmist (Psalm 13:2, JB).

As I walked in the garden with my first cup of coffee today, I saw my bleeding hearts tucked in and around the still-closed tulips. Their delicate, drooping blooms captured my heart. I picked a dozen pink blossoms and pressed them – quickly, as they wilt easily – to make notepaper for you. In the meantime, here's what I've discovered.

The popular, bushy *Dicentra spectabilis* is originally from Japan and does well in sun or partial shade. The soil needs to be well-drained – as my sandy soil is – and the plant blooms for about a month between March and June (depending on location).

The common name, bleeding heart, comes from the heart-shaped blossom; its white-tipped heart is usually pink with tiny, deeper pink inner petals forming a "drop of blood." The Latin name, *Dicentra*, comes from the Greek words *dis* for "twice" and *kentron* for "spur," and describes the fanciful hearts, notes Patrick Lima in *The Harrowsmith Perennial Garden*.

While *spectabilis* dies back by August, *Dicentra eximia* grows throughout the summer. This is a shade perennial that spreads well.

Both species have finely cut, blue-green leaves. (In the West, *Dicentra formosa* is common. It is similar to *eximia* but has more greyish leaves.) While these clumps need two to three feet of space each, it is space well spent, as the mounds are delightful – with or without blooms. Like mine, they make lovely border plants. Tall perennials – but not floppy ones that could snap the bleeding hearts' delicate stems – should be grown around them to cover dying foliage in mid- to late summer.

Look for them in old homestead gardens – by the early 1900s they were considered too quaint for planting. I think they carry their age well and they remind me of Shakespeare's verse in *Othello*: "But I will wear my heart upon my sleeve." My forget-me-nots make soft-coloured companions to the gentle hearts.

My favourite common name is "Dutchman's breeches," for *Dicentra cucullaria*. This winsome moniker describes twin white blossoms that look like puffed-out pantaloons waving upside down from the stem. It's a wildflower variety that thrives in rich woods. Also known as "blue staggers," they harbour poisonous alkaloids that can kill cows that eat the plant, notes *Wildflower Folklore.* Bumblebees, too, get short shrift from these plants: their tongues can reach the pollen, but not the nectar!

Until next time, dear friend. My heart is lighter, having shared this with you. I close with a lovely quote from Lucy Maud Montgomery as she remembered her grandmother's garden: "There was one very old-fashioned bed full of bleeding hearts.... We liked this bed best, because we might always pluck the flowers in it whenever we pleased."

Elizabeth

Dearest Elizabeth:

Whenever I'm hurting and want to be alone, or feel like I've lost my best friend, I head for water – preferably a place where there's a weeping willow tree nearby. There's something about the dramatic sweep of those drooping branches and the whisper of silky leaves at the slightest tremor.... The tree seems to echo my sorrow and, somehow, comfort me. It looks as sad as I sometimes feel. You're so lucky to have one by the stream that cuts through your property! Since you already have the old willow as a place to do your deepest thinking, I'm sending along angels – of the gentle wind-chime variety – to watch over you. Maybe you can hang them from one of its branches.

References to willows abound in Christian literature, but I like what Connie Kaldor said in a song she wrote in memory of a dear, departed friend: "I'll go down to a river and plant a tree. Something strong, wild and living – those are my memories." And in the 1971 rock musical *Godspell*, there was also a reference in "On the Willows," sung during the crucifixion scene.

The weeping willow stands for melancholy, of course, but the water willow is said to represent freedom. Biblical scholars disagree about which species of the genus *Salix* was meant in the many citations in each Testament. Some even say "willow" and "poplar" were used interchangeably, according to Allan A. Swenson in *Your Biblical Garden: Plants of the Bible and How to Grow Them*, since both are common to the old Palestine area. Both also grow quickly, and need plenty of water to survive.

Willows are airy trees that owe much of their grace to their long, slim, silver-tinged leaves. They are classic tall shade trees that grow easily in areas that get at least a few hours of daily sunlight. The more upright form seen in parks and on lawns is usually white willow, *Salix alba*. A smaller weeping type is *Salix babylonica*. The pussy willows we collect in spring are the fluffy grey catkins that become the seeds of the trees.

As you well know, willow lovers put up with a lot to make a home for their trees. The brittle branches break easily in wind and winter storms. Water-seeking roots often invade sewer pipes and septic beds, and they're always dropping leaves. That said, willow bark has been valued medicinally for centuries. It reputedly lowers fever and reduces pain and inflammation; medieval witches were believed to have used willow to treat rheumatism. Scientists identified the bitter crystalline compound from its bark as salicin in the 1820s, and it later became synthesized into salicylic acid, the active ingredient in many pain remedies. The astringent tannins in willow bark have been used to treat heartburn, too.

One last charming attribute – the bark of new growth shoots is bright yellow, and signals the sap flowing within each spring. So, are you feeling willowy yet?

Anne

Grief and Bitterness

Grief leaves us frightened, angry and lonely – encumbering us with an anguish from which there seems no deliverance. "I not only live each endless day in grief, but live each day thinking about living each day in grief," wrote C.S. Lewis of the loss of his wife.

Grief is long-term pain. Like pain, grief is sudden, shocking and sharp. But grief is more; it is a cortège that crawls through time. There's no use pretending we can skirt the procession; at some point we will be dragged into the parade to inch along the route with fellow mourners.

In the aloneness of grief we need to listen to our surviving souls. They whisper a place where we can find a connection to all that continues to flourish – in our gardens. As the haunting old hymn "In the Garden" attests, "I come to the garden alone/ While the dew is still on the roses/ And the voice I hear/ Falling on my ear/ The Son of God discloses/ And He walks with me, and He talks with me/ And He tells me I am his own/ And the joy we share/ As we tarry there/ None other has ever known."

In our gardens we can weep with bitterness, or laugh that we're still alive; our fists can pummel the earth with anger, or we can forget for a few hours the responsibilities of coping and carrying on.

Spending time in a garden is a tonic for the grieving body as well as the aching soul. The exercise tightens muscles, boosts blood circulation and causes the brain to release endorphins – the body's own mood enhancers.

But it's the closeness, the interaction and the sense of creation we experience in a garden that renews our soul. In an amazing enigma, grief will give birth to something unexpected – the wonder of life that Lewis called joy.

As Lewis trudged the road of grief, he began to see his loved one like a garden. Eventually, his soul turned from gazing after his lost garden of love up to the one who created the garden. "Thus up from the garden to the Gardener, from the sword to the Smith. To the life-giving Life and the Beauty that makes beautiful."

We can be surprised by joy, made to wonder anew at life, and we can explore unmapped territories of our souls – with the help of our gardens.

The trees and plants encountered in this chapter have something in common with grief. They may crop up by happenstance in our gardens or be planted as ceremonial markers. Some make our gardens hardier by creating pockets of shelter, even as grief can gird the soul. Others are winsome surprises, as the fruits of grief always are.

As we take our sorrow to the garden, we'll find it offers time and a place where we can claw away at the bitterness of our heartache.

Bitterness. The very word is like something to be spat out, a nasty taste that must be eradicated before any other flavour can be admitted or savoured.

Everyone knows that bitterness is a negative emotion, something that must be overcome, but what is it, exactly? How does it work? Dictionary and encyclopedia definitions make it sound as bad for the mind as for the mouth; they talk about mental pain, misery, resentment, virulent feelings, harshness, sharpness and piercing cold. Two phrases seem to capture its bite: "unwelcome to the mind" and "hard to admit or bear." A psychological counsellor might add that bitterness results from any wrong, whether real or perceived, that is aimed at oneself or a loved one. If it is taken in and accepted as part of the psyche, deep, permanent scars can develop.

Bitterness is like a scream unscreamed, something acrid and sinister blocking the throat. Yet this powerful emotion is essential to our lives: pleasure is all the more real and wonderful for the memory of how it felt to be bitter and miserable.

In the Bible, long-suffering Job maintains his faith despite many misfortunes and disappointments. Perhaps it is because he gives voice to the bitterness in his soul that his spirit survives: "No wonder then if I cannot keep silence; in the anguish of my spirit I must speak, lament in the bitterness of my soul" (Job 7:11, JB).

In *Creating Eden: The Garden as a Healing Space*, psychotherapist Marilyn Barrett describes in beautiful terms how tending a garden can help us wash away bitterness. She likens emotional cleansing to clearing out a sad, untended garden to prepare for renewed growth. "Clearing away anger, confusion, and pain, the 'trash' of the past, is a prerequisite to achieving inner peace, balance, and harmony…. [S]elf-awareness and self-control come from getting to the root of our behaviors and from 'clearing' the pain and anger of the past."

When we can't let go of bitterness, or overcome past injustices and disappointments, these sources of unhappiness may combine to become debilitating illness.

Some people believe you must consciously and constantly choose not to be bitter. Like those circling paths in the gardens of health-care facilities where Alzheimer's patients and other confused people receive treatment, bitterness always brings us back to where we started. It is an offshoot of grief or profound unhappiness, and we must avoid wandering off down that path – or we'll remain forever in that unsavoury state. No new experiences, no new growth, no broadening of our understanding or appreciation of life's journey.

Sometimes being a woman makes it harder to deal with bitterness. We've been raised to avoid confrontation, to keep the peace, placate and offer compromise. Dr. Clarissa Pinkola Estes, an analyst and storyteller, writes in *Women Who Run with the Wolves: Myths and Stories of the Wild Woman Archetype*: "There is a time in our lives, usually in midlife, when a woman has to make a decision – possibly the most important psychic decision of her future life – about whether to be bitter or not. " According to Estes, once we have given voice to all the old hurts, acknowledged the disappointments and mourned them properly, then we can return to our instinctual core and move on. Give bitterness a place in your life. Make your peace with it, after grieving over all that has made you angry or sad, just as you would mourn the death of a precious plant, a loved one, or any tragic loss. And then let it go – like a breath you've been holding too long – and feel the blessed release.

Dear Anne:

Last evening we took Bizzie for a walk along the creek. It was an all-too-brief chance to slip away from the house that Michael now calls the hospital ward. The living room coffee table, piano and bench are now shelves for all the surgical wound care paraphernalia I need daily. Poor Biz just tiptoes around for fear that that great, fluffy, German shepherd tail of hers will knock over some bottle of medicine or package of bandages. We're trying to keep an even keel; at times the weight of grief seems to tip us further than we can recover. I hope and yearn for a quiet centring, but sometimes my soul screams. Please bear with me through this heavier missive.

We walked the gardens, and I have tucked in two remembrances for you. Our apples and cedars sorely need some pruning; here's a snippet of cedar bough, just enough to scent the paper! Cedars speak of constancy and strength – fitting companions for a dispirited soul. And the rough pebble is sandstone – a piece I once discarded from my garden but stumbled upon during our stroll.

I've learned that our cedars are known as arborvitae in this part of the world, while the cedar and cypress that were biblical favourites are foreign to North America. Of the five known species of arborvitae, only two are native to this continent. Mine is – I think – *Thuja occidentalis*, Eastern white cedar. This is a sturdy, forgiving cedar found throughout our Great Lakes region. It's no wonder this shrub acquired the "cedar" moniker: the root – so to speak – of the Hebrew word for cedar actually comes from an

Arabic word meaning "firmly rooted and strong tree."

My cedars must be strong, as they grasp the sandy soil around the house and cling to the clay by the creek. They are a popular conifer because they offer a most welcome green winterscape. Eastern white cedar has a narrow, almost conical shape – much like its cones – and it almost looks pruned. However, it does need a "brush cut" now and again to keep it from looking ratty.

One of our cedars is nestled between a silver maple and a willow – an attractive trio that withstands this area's temperature extremes. Limey soil and lots of organic matter make these trees flourish.

Eastern white cedars can reach forty-five feet, but mine have topped out at about thirty. *Thuja plicata*, the Western red cedar, is the other arborvitae and is found in the Pacific Northwest. It easily reaches 150 feet, and keeps company with forest giants such as Douglas fir and Sitka spruce.

A plethora of arborvitae cultivars – from long and tall trees to short, round garden shrubs – offer hardiness, attractiveness and basic usefulness as ornamentals, hedges, screens or windbreaks. Alas, these trees face their own foes, as they are susceptible to heart rot, bagworm and spider mites. Even their diseases sound sad, don't they?

But our Canadian cedars were once used as true trees of life. Natives advised explorer Jacques Cartier to use the arborvitae to treat scurvy among his crew. Apparently, extracts of the resin could increase blood pressure and reduce fever.

Biblically, cedar references remind us of the spiritual wholeness of God's people: "So the virtuous flourish…as tall as the cedars of Lebanon" (Psalm 92:12, JB). These most famous of cedars, described as having "unrivaled distinction," were likely *Cedrus libani*, a slow-growing, picturesque, almost tropical tree. The cypress, *Cupressus sempervirens*, is renowned for its strength and was reportedly the sturdy stuff of Noah's ark. This makes sense, as cedar is a timber tree valued for its rot-resistant wood. It's also a traditional choice for canoes; we have one at our old family camp.

Today, dear friend, I need the strength of all these cedars and the endurance of the rocks of ages. I think I know why cedars grace so many graveyards; it's for those left behind! The Victorians thought cedar signified mourning, yet there's that longevity and endurance. Mary Chapin Carpenter sings of stones in the road that "leave a mark from whence they came." This piece of sandstone I tossed from my garden left a mark I easily filled with a perennial. But I'm struggling to fill the holes left in my soul by cornerstones now gone to dust. Slip this stone into a pocket and send me strength each time you touch it. Please, as it says in the Bible, be a sheltering rock for me.

Elizabeth

Dearest Elizabeth:
What do you think of silver-leaved foliage plants? I don't recall seeing any in your perennial beds when I visited, but then I've never been there at the height of the season.

Grey plants have never held any charm for me before, but I've just been immersed in them, and they're starting to look pretty interesting. One herb catalogue I get lists eighteen different kinds!

Artemisia, a bitter herb inelegantly known as Wormwood, seems the perfect symbol for this troubled time in our lives. It stands for absence and bitterness – surely part of the wave of emotion tying baby boomers in knots these days. Aren't we all grieving over the absence of something – perfect love, sublime happiness, acclaim or accolades – and bitter about past hurts and roads not taken?

Certainly you have much to grieve, and more than enough to be bitter about. Yet most days, you bear it with a grace that astounds me. And while my tribulations don't match yours, I want you to know that, on some small scale, I understand.

It's the "mommy-track" decision that eats away at me, from time to time. I don't regret for a minute leaving the working world to be home with Maggie through her formative years, but I still feel bitter about the environment that forced me to make that choice.

Why is the commercial and business world so hostile to

nurturing children and supporting families? Isn't a commitment to hearth and home critical to social stability, and to creating the next generation of decent citizens and consumers? So why do I feel so unproductive and unimportant?

Surely I don't crave celebrity or I'd have tried a lot harder in my youth to excel and make a name for myself. It's that old immortality thing, I think. Being loved by my child isn't always enough – we all want to leave our mark in some tangible way.

At least in the garden I can impose patterns that please and soothe. For the sake of contrast, texture and novelty, maybe I should plant some silver.

On the surface, *Artemisia* has little to recommend it. The plant doesn't flower enough to notice, tiny hairs give it that frosty grey look. Many types have an odd or unpleasant odour, and the common names are either ominous or depressing. Old woman, White mugwort, Wormwood, Southernwood. There are other qualities, though.

It's an undemanding perennial, and fairly easy to grow. The foliage adds a fine, lacy look to the garden without detracting from bright-blooming flowers. A mound of wormwood gives the eye somewhere to rest, I've read, and separates competing colours. A row nicely edges a border. The plant is so bitter-tasting that bugs usually leave it well alone.

Plant *Artemisia* in full sun, in well-drained soil. The various species grow to different heights, anywhere from one and one half to six feet, and they spread at least one third as wide. It is easiest to start a cutting in summer. You have to be careful what species you pick, though. *Artemisia ludoviciana* and *Artemisia pontica* are invasive and will soon want to take over. One tall, contrary type, *Artemisia lactiflora*, has green leaves and attractive clusters of creamy little flowers in late summer and early fall, according to Steven Still in *Manual of Herbaceous Ornamental Plants*.

I don't dare close before mentioning the biblical citations I've found for you. Scholars cite *Artemisia herba alba* or *Artemisia judaica* as native to the Holy Land. Although there are several references, one from Proverbs leaves little doubt as to how this plant was perceived: "Her words are smoother than oil, but their outcome is bitter as wormwood, sharp as a two-edged sword" (Proverbs 5:4, JB). Another states, "He has given me my fill of bitterness, he has made me drunk with wormwood" (Lamentations 3:15, JB). The latter could be quite accurate, as the potent French liqueur *absinthe* comes from *Artemisia absinthium* and is said to induce delirium and hallucinations.

Wormwood has been used through the ages to actually treat worms, digestive ailments and poisonous bites – even to repel insects. Both Russian and French tarragons are *Artemisia* representatives; the French variety is far tastier.

All I have to tuck in with this note is a heavenly picture, torn from the back page of a gardening magazine, of a gorgeous silver planting of sages and artemisias. Doesn't it inspire and give pause?

Anne

Dear Anne:

I've just moved some irises down to the creek, tucked in my perennials and planted more spring bulbs. Squirrels had dug up all last month's new bulbs. Those rascally rodents pilfered more than two dozen tulips! I think it's safe to replace the bulbs now, as the busiest squirrel activity – early to mid-October – is finally over.

There's a biting autumn wind off the lake today, Mom's birthday. It chilled my hands and my heart as it whistled through the bare tree branches. I'm warming up with a cup of cranberry tea as I write.

While covering Mom's lilies-of-the-valley, I accidentally turned up my one, forgotten *Gladiolus* x *hortulanus* bulb. Glads are notoriously known as funeral flowers, and I admit I have always disliked them.

Last June I had bought, I thought, an exotic iris. I planted, fed and faithfully watered it, anticipating the frilly yellow iris blooms pictured on the bag. Then it started to grow. I soon realized I had a glad, and I was not glad.

I suppose the characteristic sweet fragrance and longevity of the cut, showy spikes – they easily last a week – make glads suitable for times of public grief. Perhaps their presence as towering sentinels in floral tributes spoils their innocence for backyard gardens, reminding this gardener of her own mortality.

But short of digging up and discarding my growing *Gladiolus*, I was stuck with it. Here's what I've learned about this much-maligned member of the iris family.

First, it's also a relative of the beloved, stumpy spring crocus. *Gladiolus* comes from the Latin word *gladius*, for "sword." How appropriate, as the sight of the sword-like leaves and spiky stems can cut to one's heart! The bulbs are known as "corms" – really a bulb-like, swollen base of the long, tall stem. "Corm" comes from a Greek word that means a stripped tree trunk. Together, these "root" words fit the sorrowful role we've given these flowers, don't they?

Gladioli are forgiving, tolerating various climates and soils. But they like sunny locations best, with good drainage and slightly acidic soil. If you plant the corms at two-week intervals from just before the last frost through the end of June, you'll have blossoms through autumn. The corms should be spaced about four inches apart and four to six inches deep. A little bone meal mixed with the soil will help them along: they reach three to six feet in height and may need to be staked.

Glads range in colour from riotous orange, red and yellow to the softer lavender, cream and pale pink hues. I think a splash of showy 'Orange Chiffon' would wake up your garage wall! A Canadian hybrid, 'Anniversary', has light lavender florets. I can picture these along the southern side of your house – the cosmos and delicate sweet peas would look pretty with them.

I was disappointed about not getting the miniature iris I wanted; instead, I had stalks of screaming red trumpets. Traditionally, the glads may speak of grief, but it is a grief, I've learned, that is subdued with time, reflection and an appreciation of what the flower offers. I've enclosed a photo I snapped just before I snipped the two stems: they brightened my kitchen counter for two late September weeks.

These misunderstood flowers remind me of a verse by Adelaide Proctor: "So, you see, my life is twofold. Half a pleasure, half a grief; Thus all joy is somewhat temper'd, And all sorrow finds relief."

And yes, Anne, I've lifted the corm; it is safely stored in the coolest, darkest corner of my basement. I will plant it next spring, and maybe I'll add one or two miniature 'Little Tiger' corms to "burn bright" in my summer garden!

Elizabeth

Dear Elizabeth:

My thoughts are with you now, as I know this is approaching the season of painful anniversary dates for you.

The seeds I've tucked in here are a wee something for your spring garden. I hope they will diminish the pain, and remind you that life does, indeed, go on. They're the 'Helen Mount' type of *Viola tricolor* also known (appropriately) as heartsease. In the 1600s, the plant was used in cordials to treat complaints of the heart because its two upper petals resemble the top chambers of the human heart. There are also references to its use in an ointment for skin irritations. Some older herbals refer to sweet violet leaves being made into tea to treat coughs and throat cancer, while a syrup made from the fragrant flowers is said to calm jangled nerves. The flowers can be candied as tokens of love or to decorate cakes and pastries. I find the heartsease flower's delicate blending of yellow, purple/lavender and white always gives me pause, and the tiny, valentine face makes me feel glad – no matter what else is on my mind.

The poet Tennyson said something wonderful about this plant family, though he was probably talking about *Viola odorata*. That's the purple or white scented cousin of heartsease, of Eliza Doolittle and English country garden fame. I love it, too, for its heart-shaped leaves and those profuse spring blooms. "The smell of violets, hidden in the green, pour'd back into my empty soul and frame the times when I remembered to have been Joyful and free from blame," Tennyson wrote.

Plant these in full sun next spring if you can, but heartsease will take some shade – and flowers best when kept cool. Chill the seed for twenty-four hours first, and get it in as soon as you can work the soil. Any well-drained soil will do, and the plant rarely grows higher than six inches. Like its pansy offspring, this is an annual – but it self-seeds readily. Hence another of its many common names: "Johnny-jump-up." Kids love this little charmer, and the root system is so small that I don't mind it popping up anywhere. It's not likely to choke other garden gems.

This is an excellent edging or container plant, and shearing it halfway up the stalks in midsummer will prevent straggly plants and promote more blooms. If you pluck off dead blossoms regularly, the plants will flower throughout the summer.

In my Victorian birthday book, heartsease is for "thoughts," from the French word *pensée*. And so I've come full circle and will stop. Enjoy the dried flowers – they're samples of what yours will look like in a few months. Oh, and many thanks for the cedar and stone remembrances; they've found a special place among my touchstones.

Anne

Dearest Anne:

The news that I need either chemotherapy or more surgery has left me cold. I skipped the numbness of shock and went directly to cold. I'm warming my body with frequent soaks in anti-stress bath salts. For my soul, I'm reading all I can. I bombard the doctors with questions, and I look to my garden to express my fear. Michael and I have talked this out a dozen different ways. Whatever happens, I want to know that I did everything possible to stop this cancer. A year from now, I don't want to think, "If only I'd had the operation." I'm having the surgery.

I needed to speak with my mom, so l visited the cemetery. To paraphrase Isaiah, she too was a woman of sorrows, familiar with suffering. When I arrived at the grave there was a man standing two rows up, four plots to my right. He was stock still, cradling a bouquet. I had my coffee thermos with me and asked if he would like a cup. He nodded, and as we sipped he told me his story.

Peter's wife died twenty-seven years ago of breast cancer. He moved to Fredericton a short time after, and this was only his fourth visit to the grave. His pain was almost tactile. The bouquet of red, white and blue blooms framed with assorted silk evergreens was striking, and I told him so. When he plucked out a stem for me, I shivered – it looked like a yew branch.

The yew in Peter's bouquet was so appropriate! Long ago, the branches were used to symbolize bereavement. In fact, it was planted beside graves in Europe to keep witches and demons at bay, and to dash any hope the demons might have of turning the dead into ghosts. Perhaps the yew has summoned the angels of hope, as today the tree means life to many women stricken with breast or ovarian cancer. I just had to research this plant.

Two species of the red-seeded evergreen are native to Canada: *Taxus canadensis*, the Canada yew or ground hemlock, and *Taxus brevifolia*, the Western or Pacific yew. Other species such as *Taxus baccata*, English yew, and *Taxus cuspidata*, Japanese yew, offer hundreds of ornamental cultivars with a wide variety of growth rates and forms.

The English yew has been cultivated for more than one thousand years – no wonder there are so many cultivars! There is even one known as the Irish yew.

Legend has it that Robin Hood, that twelfth-century provocateur for the poor, used yew for his arrows. It's little surprise, then, that the word "yew" comes from an Old English term meaning "durable." What tales the trees of Sherwood Forest could tell! The yew's many properties were known even in Roman times; Caesar noted in book VI of *The Conquest of Gaul* that Catuvolcus committed suicide by taking an extract from its bark.

In our woods, *Taxus canadensis* is usually a low, spreading shrub. Despite its name, this one does not grow west of Manitoba (so says my tree book). As a tree, *Taxus brevifolia* has a conical crown and a trunk that is often twisted. It can reach heights of forty-five feet, but there's a shrub form, too. *Taxus cuspidata* cultivars are the popular ornamentals of choice for many urban gardens, as they endure dust and smoke well.

Yews are landscapers' favourites, as they are resistant to bugs and disease, offer excellent year-round colour with high-quality needles, and bear our winters well. They're practically maintenance free. *Taxus cuspidata* works especially well if the gardener ascribes to the Edward Scissorhands school of pruning.

Yews need fertile soil in areas that are moist but drain well. They are not picky about sun or shade but dislike being windswept. Do you think a yew would be a good choice for the cleared bank of our creek?

Taxus brevifolia, the Pacific yew, is the species that first brought new hope to many women suffering from breast or ovarian cancer. TAXOL®, a substance found in bark extracts of this slow grower, was pronounced one of the best anti-cancer agents in the last two decades by an American cancer centre.[2]

There was concern that it was a hollow victory, as this yew is regarded as threatened – and it takes almost thirty pounds of the thin, scaly bark to treat one patient. But now twigs and needles from this yew are also used to produce a semisynthetic version of this precious drug. The natural stands of *Taxus brevifolia* in the Pacific Northwest are the largest known tracts; that's why so much attention has focused on that area.

Indeed, some of those trees are three hundred years old. The yew's longevity is celebrated in what's called the north quadrant of a native medicine wheel, writes Loren Cruden in *Medicine Grove: A Shamanic Herbal*. "Trees in this grouping often live to be ancient giants, or emanate energies of protection and healing. North medicine is enduring and encompassing." We must find ways to sustain this giant's growth!

So, you see, my search for solace in the garden has led to what truly is a tree of life and hope. I'll close with words from Tennyson that cut close to my heart these days. "I sometimes hold it half a sin, To put in words the grief I feel; for words, like Nature, half reveal, And half conceal the soul within."

Elizabeth

---

2 Victoria Farmer, TAXOL: A Brief Insight, Internet site: http://www.ch.ic.ac.uk/local/projects/farmer/intro.htm. TAXOL® Bristol-Myers Squibb Company

Acceptance and Respite

Acceptance is like giving yourself time off from grief and guilt. It's the evening when you know your dead father's winter boots can at last be given to the Salvation Army. It's the week you get through a marker day – a birthday, death day or now meaningless wedding anniversary – without retreating to the bathtub. It's that lunch date when you suddenly notice the word "cancer" tripping off your tongue without your heart constricting in pain. As C.S. Lewis wrote in *A Grief Observed*, acceptance is "like the warming of a room or the coming of daylight. When you first notice them, they have already been going on for some time."

Clinically, acceptance is well known as the last stage in Dr. Elisabeth Kübler-Ross's stages of dying. It follows denial, anger, bargaining and then depression – stages that also apply to grief. Kübler-Ross describes this time as neither happy nor sad, one more of victory than of resignation. It is a victory because, in accepting what has come about, you are giving yourself permission to look ahead. So it is also the morning you think you had better plant some tulips and daffodils for next season's new border – and you feel a tiny twinge of excitement.

Although this chapter moves to acceptance and respite from grief and bitterness, in no way do we mean to diminish the acute anguish of the soul through the other grieving stages. Those stages crop up time and again, like the dandelions in our gardens, throughout the quest for grace and peace.

"Accepting" is one of those slippery words that can be either a noun, a thing, or a verb, an action. As a noun, it is an acknowledgment of something as real or true. But how do you acknowledge grief or guilt? Nod politely? As a verb, accepting is the action of taking what is offered. But what is it that is being offered? One thing acceptance does offer is a place to harbour all the grief work you've accomplished. You don't get around or over grief, whether it comes from disease, divorce or death, but you can get through it. It's hard work; maybe that's why grimy, gritty garden labour is so satisfying. Gradually, you find places to plant the pain, loss, sadness, guilt, anger and reminders of happier times. While your garden can be a place to put your grief, the action of gardening can also be your act of acceptance.

Recalling grief and accepting its reality are like putting things in separate rooms of a house, says Canadian author and teacher Jean Little, who as a youngster in the post–Second World War years began losing her sight to glaucoma. As Little writes in her autobiography, *Stars Come out Within,* one of Emily Dickinson's poems (No. 419) particularly helped her accept the encroaching darkness. "We grow accustomed to the Dark / When light is put away… Either the Darkness alters / Or something in the sight / Adjusts itself to Midnight / And Life steps almost straight."

Paul Tillich, a respected Protestant theologian, also wrote of the light that comes with acceptance. Tillich had been an outspoken academic critic of Hitler in pre–Second World War Germany and was barred from the country's universities. He emigrated to the United States, where he taught at the renowned Harvard and Chicago divinity schools. Tillich calls "grace" that glimmer of acceptance. "Grace strikes us when we are in great pain and restlessness…. Sometimes at that moment a wave of light breaks into our darkness, and it is as though a voice were saying: 'You are accepted.'"

Perhaps a garden of memory can be a graceful act of acceptance. Often we have tucked in our gardens plants in memory of things and people or animals we loved – simple, everyday plants that have found special places there.

A pink primrose I personally call "Lady Evelyn" graces a side border, six hyacinth bulbs are all that's left of a second cancer surgery gift planter, and a clump of tiger lilies was chopped, carted and unceremoniously dumped into a backyard plot on the day a relationship ended. In another corner, a rich peach rose named for my cousin Ruthmarie anchors a long perennial strip, a quiet reminder that someone else remembered, too.

A garden is such a satisfying, fine place to act out acceptance, and then to lean back and rest. As the Psalmist wrote, "Return to your resting place, my soul…. He has rescued my eyes from tears and my feet from stumbling" (Psalm 116:7f, JB).

* * *

Dear Elizabeth:

Don't you think there should be comfort flowers, just like the comfort foods that are in the myriad cookbooks and magazine recipe collections we're all inundated with?

It's the dead of winter, not a flower in sight, and I'm deep into post-Christmas blues. Maggie has just lit my ever-shortening fuse once again with a careless accident (nothing serious), and I'm thinking that an hour among some lilacs would comfort me and do much to chase the peevishness from my soul. What is it that makes me so impatient with my small daughter's obstinacy and rough touch – and why do I get so angry when some toy breaks, as I warned her it would? Probably it's myself I'm seeing and reacting to. Acceptance is a long, hard road, isn't it?

As you may have guessed, patience doesn't run in my family, and I have the stolen-lilac memories to prove it. Being chiefly apartment dwellers (of necessity), we were hard pressed each spring to bring nature indoors when my mom craved heady, sweet-scented lilacs for her table. Over the years, each of us had our turn fetching these bouquets, and each had a favourite spot for snitching. Too uppity for words, I wouldn't pick from a private garden, only from bushes in parks or along roadways.

Solace

This all came back to me a couple of years ago, while visiting my sister's home near Toronto. Heather and I had been out shopping – without the kids, for once – and were headed home when she suddenly veered off into an industrial park on our right. The buildings were set back behind an uncultivated field of shrubs and wildflowers including (you guessed it) several white, purple and mauve lilac bushes in full bloom. Picture two grown women with armloads of pilfered flowers standing in a field giggling and you'll know what happened. We had done our mom proud.

Some say lilacs are symbols of first love, but to me they'll always represent learning how to live with what you've got and the sense of relief that comes when a whim is finally satisfied.

One woman who knew all about accepting a plant's limitations – but never giving up on her goals – was Isabella Preston. You've probably never heard of her, but by the 1940s she was known as "the dean of hybridists" in a field that few women of her day entered professionally. She lived and worked for much of her career in Ottawa, at what is still called the Central Experimental Farm. Remember our picnic lunch there, among those gorgeous gardens?

Isabella reaped widespread recognition for her work with lilies, crabapple trees and roses – but her lilacs are especially memorable. Hers were the first Canadian-raised types, introduced in the 1920s and numbering ninety-two in all, including more than seventy *Syringa* x *prestoniae*. There's even a pearly mauve one named 'Patience'.

No less an authority than England's Vita Sackville-West paid tribute to Isabella, writing in the 1950s: "[L]et us now remember the Preston lilacs.... All the Preston hybrids are said to be strong growers, and are also entirely hardy.... Whether you prefer them to the old garden lilac, in heavy plumes hanging wet with rain, or whether you will reject their looser delicacy in favour of those fat tassels with their faint scent associated with one's childhood, is for you to say."

The sentiment-stirring lilac has been with us since at least the fifteenth century, when it was introduced to the West from Turkey.

The word "lilac," in fact, means "bluish," from the Persian *lilak*. But *Syringa* comes from the Greek *syrinx*, meaning "hollow stem" or "shepherd's pipe." While the early lilac had single blooms and a strong scent, hybridization to introduce bigger flowers and new colours was taking place by the mid-1800s, led by the French. There are now an estimated two thousand cultivars, many of them scentless. But what good is a lilac without its scent?

I have planted three types over the past eight years at the front corner of my house, an exercise in patience and humility. Two have steadfastly refused to bloom; the third, farther along the side border, sports one tiny, unscented silvery mauve bloom each May – too high for me to reach! Have I ripped these traitors out? No. I just sigh, keep them pruned to a manageable size, and accept them as nice shrubs with attractive heart-shaped leaves. (The leaves remind me of a quaint little sidewalk summer café I used to frequent years ago where flowers often dressed your order, and chilled butter came to the table on fresh lilac leaves.)

There's a good reason my lilacs don't bloom, Liz. Apparently they don't get enough sun. My sources say these shrubs or small trees need at least three to five hours of full sunlight daily, and fertile, loose, well-drained and slightly acid soil. A site with good air circulation will help avoid the powdery mildew that plagues some types, and annual pruning right after flowering will keep the plants healthy. The Preston types are especially hardy and resist pests and diseases, but these hybrids may be hard to find.

I think I'll visit a few local nurseries this weekend, and find out whether any Preston cultivars can still be purchased. There must be a sunny spot somewhere around here that I can free up for a lilac that will bloom. I'd like to plant one for Maggie, so that she can enjoy watching it grow and return in all its glory each spring. Better still, maybe I can help her plant it herself. Perhaps that patience I've been slowly learning will rub off, and the little tree will be a love token after all.

Anne

Dear Annie:

Isn't it a grand day when the first seed catalogue arrives in the winter mail? Mine did this week. Yesterday, as a January storm swirled the snow around my frozen birdbath, I made a cup of tea (green tea, this year, in deference to my cancer fight and in celebration of green plants) and curled up for an afternoon read and rest. I came across a plant I didn't know but thought I'd like to learn about. Wood betony sent me scurrying to my references.

We've been talking lately about how difficult it is to accept some things, and how hard we are on ourselves about resting. I am in a hurry-up-and-wait phase for the next surgery, and you are juggling the mommy/work/wife demands of a modern woman. We both need to slow down, take some deep breaths, and rest. The Psalmist, too, felt this need, yet he struggled with the elusiveness of it: "Oh, for the wings of a dove, to fly away and find rest" (Psalm 55:6, JB). You'd think a woman wrote that!

Now, it just happens that wood betony has been a tonic for nervous conditions of the body and soul for at least the last two millennia. According to Maud Grieve, in *A Modern Herbal* on www.botanical.com, one of the ancient scribes wrote, "It is good, whether for the man's soul or for his body." Sounds soothing!

Wood betony is known as *Stachys officinalis* in present-day botanical nomenclature, but was named *Betonica officinalis* by Linnaeus, the seventeenth-century Swedish botanist who established one of the earliest systems of plant nomenclature. In his system, the first word, in this case *Betonica*, refers to the genus, while the second, *officinalis*, refers to the species. And the word *stachys* is from the Greek word *stachus*, meaning "spike," referring to the plant's pointed stems.

Whatever official name, this perennial herb is a member of the mint family. The leaves look wrinkled, and both leaves and stems are hairy. Sounds unpleasant, but the purplish-red flowers are its crowning glory. The flowers whorl around the stem while the individual blossoms open to about one inch in length, each with two lips – one pointed up, one down. These blooms are hardy and appear in late spring, maybe even lasting through summer. That's a boon for the often-dreary August garden. The plants need to be about one foot apart, and look to be excellent for borders.

Wood betony is best grown in full sun, in well-drained, ordinary soil. Our kind of low-maintenance perennial! It is also known by a variety of common names: bishopswort, lousewort and – get these – red helmet, elephant head, walrus head, Indian warrior and beefsteak plant! In ancient times, farmers falsely feared the plant would give animals lice, hence "lousewort." The name "betony" may be Celtic in origin, from *bew*, meaning a head, and *ton*, meaning good. This refers to its reported ability to cure headaches.

The whole herb was collected in July and then dried. While a pinch of it supposedly provoked a sneezing spell, it was used to treat everything from consumption to gout to jaundice. Made into a wine, it reportedly removed blockages in the spleen and liver. But its benefits weren't just medicinal – the fresh leaves were used as a yellow dye for wool.

Annie, you will love this charming betony claim: it was said to cure sick elves! Be sure to tell Maggie that one, and would you please ask her to draw me a picture of a sick elf? I need another Maggie "original" for my wall. Enclosed is a photocopy of the catalogue photo for her to study.

As well as a physical panacea, betony was used as a mystical potion to ward off evil spirits, so it was a popular plant for church graveyards and for carrying in personal amulets.

It sure had lots of marketing possibilities, didn't it? "Sell your coat and buy betony!" advised an early Italian proverb.

Did I tell you I've taken a cue from you and sketched on paper the parameters of a new backyard garden? I'm slowly roughing in plant possibilities – and thoroughly enjoying rubbing out and replacing plants as I go! Betony belongs in our gardens, I believe. I've pencilled it in along the back edge of my paper garden.

Betony is a plant of belief: it says to me that we must face and accept our situations, muster our resources and go forward. I'll order a packet of seeds and start them indoors, then I'll tuck

Solace

a seedling or two into my carry-on for you on my next flight to
Ottawa. Tally-ho, dear friend!

Elizabeth

Liz, my patient friend:
Forgive this late-night fax; there are so many thoughts banging
around in my brain tonight that I have to let some of them out! If
I know you, you're up anyway, surfing the Net to take your mind
off leg spasms or drug side effects, So take a break, and read my
latest plant findings instead!

When you see the green or gold pinecone-like "blooms" of *Briza
media* quivering in the slightest breeze, it's easy to understand why
people in Victorian times thought this decorative grass symbolized
agitation. But the Greek root, *brizo*, comes closer to the mark for
me – it means "to nod." Just picture a few tufts dipping their heads
from a porch planter or around the foot of a garden bench, and see
if you don't start nodding too.

I think quaking grass, or trembling grass, as it is also known,
has real therapeutic potential. Sue Minter of the famous Chelsea
Physic Garden in London, England, wrote: "From the sighing and
rustling of leaves and stems in the breeze to the tinkling or rushing
of water, sounds in the garden can generate and influence many
different moods and feelings. Sounds...can trigger vivid memories
and...[t]hese can have a psychological healing effect, especially
against depression." She notes peaceful sounds can serve as an
antidote to the strains of the work world and the stress that noise
pollution induces. In a more poetic – but just as soothing – vein,
consider what Wordsworth said: "Thou hadst a voice whose sound
was like the sea."

Like most perennial ornamental grasses, this one is pretty
easy to grow – it even likes poor soil and is virtually pest free.
No fertilizer is needed, just a midsummer and late fall trim. For a
truly riveting effect, cluster several mature plants (it's slow to start
from seed or division) about one to one and one-half feet apart in
a moist, well-drained, sunny spot where you can appreciate near-
constant movement.

This *Briza* grows one to two feet tall; its narrow, slim blades are medium green, with blunt, chopped-off-looking tips. The flowering stems spread wide above the foliage, with graceful, arching "spikelets" that rustle from early summer through fall. The seed heads turn gold-beige in fall, sometimes preceded by a purplish hue, and are collected to dry and dye various colours for everlasting bouquets. Two annual types that vary in size but look much the same are *Briza maxima* and *Briza minor*.

Preserved garden catalogues prove ornamental grasses were used more than one hundred years ago to accent fresh and dried bouquets, as well as to complete garden bed designs. But *Briza* has really been cultivated for centuries, originating in Europe and Asia.

Maybe something from a lyric by Canadian balladeer Gordon Lightfoot explains what appeals to me about this humble grass. In his song "Leaves of Grass," he writes about how grass seems to be immortal – always springing back after apparent death. In contrast, he notes that the life of an individual is fragile and so easily extinguished.

Looks like I'm still wrestling with the mortality issue. We know we're all going to die sometime; it's just a question of when. But for many of us, it's a terrifying concept because we fret that we haven't seen-done-been-felt enough. And then there's always that awful fear of the unknown…

Well, three fax sheets are more than enough for one night. High time I got some rest. Sending you sweet dreams in the wee, small hours.

Anne

Dear Anne:
That late-night fax was a treat to savour with my pre-dawn coffee! I can picture a nodding clump of *Briza* near the front steps, waving an invitation to all visitors. When I read your fax I was reminded of a Confucian saying: "The grass must bend when the wind blows across it." We will keep bending, my dear friend, but we will not break.

You never saw my little house on Manitoulin Island. I think

you would have liked it, as it was on a gentle rise overlooking a small inland lake. The white clapboard house was nestled between a rock cut and old-growth woods. Each spring, white, pink and almost-rose-coloured trilliums and creamy leeks would carpet the forest floor. Two rock gardens bordered the circular driveway, and window boxes framed my modest front porch.

This morning I couldn't sleep, so I made some hot chocolate and riffled through my island albums. Annie, I have such rich memories of my time at the newspaper there. I can almost smell the darkroom chemicals and the paste-up paper from the graphics computer. We worked hard getting the weekly out on Monday nights; the goal was to have the newspaper to bed before last call at the local bar. I can almost taste that beer! Probably every weekly newspaper staffer dreams of that cool brew at the end of frenzied production nights, right?

As I scanned the pictures, I saw my glorious columbines scattered here and there throughout the rock gardens. However, I don't have columbines in this garden yet – I haven't succeeded in growing them since leaving the island. I think I mistakenly planted the seeds in an area exposed to too much sunlight. They prefer, instead, partial sun, partial shade. But I do have a watercolour painting of the dangling scarlet red and sunshine-yellow flowers, behind my reading chair. I smile every time I look at it. I can almost see those perennial blooms bobbing in the wind!

I think the columbine is a noble plant to explore, as its history is replete with time-honoured tales, curative legends and an intriguing name. It reminds me of those embellished memories older journalists trot out around a late-night table of beer and pretzels. I know you remember those newspaper days with fondness, too.

Columbine belongs to the buttercup family; its genus is *Aquilegia*. Here's a puzzle for you: the word "columbine" comes from the Latin word *columba*, meaning "pigeon" or "dove," while *Aquilegia* comes from the Latin *aquila,* meaning "eagle." The spur-like petals are said to resemble an eagle's beak. I picture eagles cutting into the wind, soaring heavenward, while doves glide with the wind, descending from above. The flowers do reflect this dichotomy, as the brilliant red petals look downward, as if descending to the ground, while the bright yellow spurs gaze skyward.

Isaiah's famous verse about eagles is so visual: "But those who hope in [the Lord] renew their strength, they put out wings like eagles. They run and do not grow weary, walk and never tire" (Isaiah 40:31, JB). And Matthew, that faithful New Testament scribe, attributes to Jesus this reference: "Remember, I am sending you out like sheep among wolves; so be cunning as serpents and yet as harmless as doves" (Matthew 10:16, JB). New Testament authors also reverently refer to the Holy Spirit – the third member of the Trinity – as a dove. Matthew chronicles Jesus' baptism in the River Jordan by John as the time when the Holy Spirit descended "like a dove" from God the Father, anointing the carpenter's son (Matthew 3:16, JB).

I'm amused at the significance that has been attached to columbine over the years! It's a favourite with folklorists, as references abound with various meanings. To some, columbine was a symbol of unfaithfulness or of a deserted lover. In Queen Victoria's time, messages were often secreted in flowers sent, and columbine certainly was popular. A red one meant anxious or trembling, a purple-blue nosegay meant resolved to win, a woman was insulted when she received a columbine, and it meant bad luck for a man to be given the flower. Imagine a woman in the waning years of the nineteenth century receiving a columbine – what would she have thought? Her anxious, unfaithful (and now deserted) lover had sent her the ultimate insult!

Columbine was also a favourite posy with ancient herbalists. The juice was used to treat jaundice or abdominal pains, and the plant was a supposed remedy for measles and smallpox. One legend even purports that lions consumed columbine to boost their strength.

Aquilegia canadensis, the Canadian or wild columbine, is native to North America and easily reaches two feet in height. This is the one with the nodding red and yellow heads. This plant just seems to be waving hello! Although columbine self-seeds and reportedly grows easily, given my luck I think I'll start some indoors this spring. With their height, they'd be pretty at the back of the house where they'd get morning light and afternoon shade, and where the soil is well drained. And this plant does well as a cut flower. *Aquilegia alpina*, the alpine columbine with its almost-solid-blue flowers, hails from Switzerland and is a hearty choice for rock gardens.

As horticulturist Trevor Cole writes, "No spring garden is complete without columbines. These colourful flowers dance and sway in the slightest breeze and fully justify one of their common names, dancing fairies."

Alas, irksome leaf miners – insect larvae – can burrow into *Aquilegia* leaves. The tunnel-tracked, discoloured leaves need to be plucked immediately, and the entire plant may need early spring disinfecting to fight off the pesky pests.

In this round with cancer, I'm partial to columbine's "resolved to win" attitude. Although I accept that I have cancer, as I've accepted the multiple sclerosis, I cannot give up. I do need to rest for a while, finalize my fight strategy, and then get back into the game. What a comfort you have been! How will I ever thank you for listening through all the long-distance telephone hours and these soul-searching letters? Michael has had to live the pain and fear with me; he doesn't need to hear every panicked thought as I stumble through the valley of life.

On the wings of a dove I'll send this letter, enclosing an origami dove for Maggie. Hold the base of the neck securely, tug gently at the tail and watch the wings – just pretend I'm waving hello.

Elizabeth

Dear Elizabeth:

Many thanks for your columbine letter and growing tips. You've strengthened my resolve to have those jesters' caps dancing in my garden. Earlier attempts have not been successful. According to my dictionary, "Columbine" is the name of Harlequin's sweetheart in traditional Italian comedy and pantomime. How appropriate, as she's laughing!

As soon as I read about the history of this precious little plant (sketch enclosed), I knew it was for you. It's lady's bedstraw, *Galium verum*, which I picked up at the plant sale Maggie's school had this week. I'll get it going, then root a slip for you to take home from your next visit.

It is said this perennial herb got its name from being present at the nativity: the baby Jesus was supposedly laid on a bed of bracken and bedstraw, and the charmed bedstraw burst into bloom at the honour. Its whitish flowers have been gold-tinted ever since. Thus it was called Our Lady's bedstraw (or sometimes Mary's bedstraw) after the Virgin Mary, and shortened in common usage. It is honey-scented, and was once widely used to cure hysteria. That's a handy plant to have around as we work our way through various ills, don't you think? The dried stems were used to stuff mattresses in the Middle Ages, and bedstraw in a pillow was said to promote sound sleep. What sweet respite!

The sweet woodruff under my old spruce tree is a close relative, *Galium odoratum*, but lady's bedstraw is finer in appearance. It has wispy, narrow leaves growing in whorls up the stem, and the panicles of tiny flower clusters bloom throughout the summer. The plant likes dry soil and some shade, and stretches anywhere from under a foot to about three feet in height. It makes a great edger because it increases outward, in a tidy clump. Place new plants at least twelve inches apart, and clear away all old foliage in spring. In midsummer, it helps to clip off the top couple of inches to prevent weak, sprawling stems. You can divide oversized patches in spring. That's all the maintenance bedstraw needs!

This plant's stems and leaves make a rich yellow dye for fabrics or cheese, but the roots produce red hues. Another common name, cheese rennet, comes from the milk-curdling qualities of its acidic juice. Other uses are to stop internal or external bleeding and to aid in treating urinary and kidney diseases. The word *Galium* comes from the Greek word *galion*, a plant Dioscorides – the ancient Greek army physician – was believed to have used for curdling milk. The Greek *gala* means "milk."

Solace

In closing, let's take heart from what the late Canadian poet Bronwen Wallace said to a friend about her wild passion, one we share: "'I'm planting perennials this year,' you tell me, 'because I'm scared and it's the only way I know to tell myself I'm going to be here, years from now, watching them come up.' Maybe it's a phase we're going through, since I'm at it too..."

Anne

Courage and Determination

" **N**o, I shall not die, I shall live" (Psalm 118:17, JB). Now that's courage speaking.

Sometimes courage involves big questions, like whether to live or to die, but often it is about the day-to-day details. When your mind is chock full of memories of times or things past, sometimes it takes courage to look ahead and plan for a future without those people or places. Decisions we make this year as wives, fathers, sisters, brothers or simply as citizens and people at work have a quirky habit of finding paths back to us. It takes guts to revisit them.

It seems courage is about choices: how we make those choices and how we live with them. "Everyday courage is all I ask," pleads one woman's journal entry. It truly is a heartfelt plea as courage comes from the Latin word *cor*, meaning "heart." In ancient times, the heart was believed to be the seat of thought and judgment, so courage was an action of the mind, not necessarily an emotion.

But it can't help but be enfolded in our emotions, in all our senses. It takes something more than a little courage to phone your family and tell them about a confirmed cancer, following that dreaded after-hours telephone call from the surgeon. Courage is the absolute terror that chills a body despite the warmth of a dusky orange October day, alive with the scent of burning autumn leaves. It's the one time to be almost grateful a doting parent is dead, and won't have to deal with this one.

Solace

Sometimes it takes immense courage to close your eyes and go to sleep, for fear of waking in the morning, knowing this is all real and your life is changed forever. God knows what other tales your morning tests will tell. But you don't think about it – you think about everything from your husband weeping to the mess in your closets to feeling betrayed by your body. Nothing seems logical because nothing is, right then.

"Courage is fear holding on…a minute longer," wrote the American General George S. Patton. Those minutes can stretch into hours as night falls on a battlefield frozen with fear and the blood of fallen comrades. More courage is needed. Often, ordinary men do the extraordinary under such conditions, dashing across open ground under fire to pull a buddy to safety. "Stay with me, God. The night is dark / The night is cold: my little spark / Of courage dies. The night is long; / Be with me God, and make me strong," prays an anonymous soldier.[3] Too often, and so sadly, we have to find an even tougher endurance as the days dwindle.

"She was so brave," whisper friends huddled around the fifty-cup coffee pot at the back of a funeral home. They murmur that their friend flaunted life in the face of death – like a matador's crimson cape – by wrapping those near her in love. "Because of deep love, one is courageous," wrote Lao-tzu five centuries before Christ.

"Be of good courage," Isaiah wrote (Isaiah 41:6, JB). But what is good courage? Is there bad courage? Good courage just might mean making decisions or choices that are true and right for you, however frightening they are.

Take reassurance from the certainty and serenity that the late Ottawa singer-songwriter Beth Ferguson expressed in "What Is Mine," a song she penned less than two years after she was diagnosed with breast cancer. "[W]hat is mine will come to me / Can't push the river, still I choose to believe / What is mine, with patience and time / Will come to me."

---

3 John Bartlett, *Bartlett's Familiar Quotations*, 16th ed. (Toronto: Little, Brown, 1992), p. 783. This poem was found on a scrap of paper in a slit trench in Tunisia during the Battle of El Agheila, later printed in *Poems from the Desert*, by members of the British Eighth Army 1944.

Determination is not confined to man alone – or to woman, youth or child. Watch any dog with its bone, any butterfly emerging from its chrysalis or any salmon forcing itself upstream, and you'll know the single-minded intensity required when a living creature has an objective that must be met.

Closer to home, we might marvel at the way a toddler is utterly absorbed in the task of fitting bafflingly different shapes into the various holes of a shape-sorter toy. Adults need that same unswerving focus when there are important decisions to be made, or big things to accomplish. But in the din of daily life, concentration is often lost – or we're too sapped to summon it.

The hard physical work required in the garden can give us back that childlike simplicity and strength of purpose. The plants themselves can be the perfect role models. Is there anything more determined than a spring bulb working its way through rock-hard ground and crusty snow to unfurl new leaves in the fleeting spring sun?

Mary Kenady, a former journalist who turned later in life to full-time gardening, has written: "I was gardening, in part, to maintain my mental health.... I suppose I still garden for [that], but I am in remission.... I have a more urgent sense of creation, of making something, of working with nature to achieve a compromise between us which will satisfy both. I am more purposeful."

Quite apart from the firmness of purpose that is involved, another facet of determination is equally relevant – the weighing and fixing of what is to be done. Legally, we speak of coming to a "determination" about how a property will be divided or about the value of an asset. The decision, it seems, is just as important as what it will take to get us there.

In personal terms, it could be no less than deciding the standards you'll live by, or choosing the people in whose company you will spend your precious time. There's careful calculation involved, digging and sifting and assessing. What's left may be radically different from what there was in the beginning. There is also a ruthlessness about it. Setting the scene or atmosphere that feels right means deciding what is most important – and cutting loose from the rest. That gives you true focus.

"[Y]our worn-out idea or endeavor can shine more brightly if you will take some of it and throw it away. It is [like] the sculptor removing more marble in order to reveal more of the hidden form.... If you've lost focus, just sit down and be still. Take the idea and rock it to and fro," advises Clarissa Pinkola Estes. In its own time, she says, the good and the strong will re-emerge.

The late Stan Rogers, a loved and respected Canadian troubadour, wrote heartening words about how we can "rise again" from all manner of life's troubles and tragedies in his ballad "The Mary Ellen Carter," about an imaginary East Coast working vessel. "It is as close as I'll ever come to a 'song of inspiration,'" Rogers wrote in a 1982 songbook of his words and music. "And you, to whom adversity has dealt the final blow, / With smiling bastards lying to you everywhere you go; / Turn to, and put out all your strength of arm and heart and brain / And, like the Mary Ellen Carter, rise again!"

There is a place for every shape; we just need to work with the puzzle a while and concentrate fiercely, like the toddler, until we can find it.

* * *

Dearest Anne:

What a delight to go out this morning – yes, it was early – and find your lady's bedstraw sketch in my mailbox.

Michael and I spent the weekend at the cottage, readying it for winter. Stowing the boats (after one last canoe ride) and gear, wrapping the bedding in plastic and emptying cupboards – all those sad signals that the season is over. Actually, Michael did the work while I sat on the veranda, read Anne Tyler's Ladder of Years and watched the cat's-paws on the bay. Finally, I decided to check our old hazel bushes tucked behind the boathouse. Did you know hazel is a magical and powerful branch to grasp when calling for courage? Ah, more about that later!

Back behind the boathouse, I was in luck! There were still a few nuts hanging from the slender, tender-looking branches. As a child, I was sent out September weekends to pluck the round, brownish-green nuts for Mom to make her annual Hazelnut Crumble Muffins. Sheer delight! There's something so satisfying about gathering food from the forest.

The deciduous twelve-foot shrubs enjoy our cool, moist summers, but the winters are often too harsh for them. Our hazel at camp is likely *Corylus avellana*, one that was introduced from Europe. Hazel bushes are also called filberts, especially the nuts that are used in recipes. Medieval Normans honoured the seventh-century Benedictine monk St. Philbert, originally a nut-grower by trade, by naming this nut after him.

Hazels, or filberts, are members of the birch family. They enjoy shady, sheltered spots with good drainage. I guess that's why the ones I know do so well near the boathouse in the sandy soil. Once the young plants have been pruned – in early winter, no less – to encourage bushy growth, they are almost trouble-free. In a particularly dry spell, they do need watering. Although 'Rush' and 'Winkler' are the hardiest cultivars, we can grow others such as 'Daviana' or 'Du Chilly'!

Hazel's lore and legends are as rich and sweet as the nuts themselves. Hazel was the stuff of staffs, royal sceptres and magic wands: the rods of Moses and Aaron were said to be made from it. Apollo gave Mercury a hazel rod that he used to assuage human passion, and the Scandinavian god of thunder, Thor, used hazel as protection against lightning. St. Patrick supposedly drove the poisonous snakes out of Ireland with a hazel rod. Essentially, a hazel rod was deemed effective in warding off witches, fairies and all sorts of evil!

In Hebrew legend, Moses's hazel staff is traced back to one that Adam cut in the Garden of Eden; it was later taken by Noah into the ark for safekeeping. Interestingly, there's only one reference to hazel in the Bible, Genesis 30:37, and then only in some translations. In the King James Version, Jacob feeds poplar, hazel and chestnut wood to flocks of goats and sheep to strengthen them.

Many translations change "hazel" to "almond," but I appreciate what hazel offers that verse.

My favourite hazel legend involves the head of John the Baptist. An ancient Germanic tale tells of Herod's wife, Herodia, attempting to kiss John's head when it was brought to her on the famous platter. The head despised the action and blew Herodia to the top of a hazel tree where she was doomed to spend eternity, never able to climb down. Ooh, what sweet revenge that is!

And the hazelnuts were handy, too. Scots would keep doubles close by to throw at witches. In Irish lore, the salmon of Conla's well nibbled nine hazelnuts and became the wisest living creature. I doubt my red squirrels acquired much wisdom from the few hazelnuts I let them have! But they chattered, scrapped and scurried to steal the stale peanuts we put out by the cottage. Do you think they ever find the nuts they bury?

Hazel still holds mystical associations today. It is commonly used for water-witching or divining: the trick of finding water with a forked stick. Thirty years ago, a hazel branch was used at our camp to find new water. I can still see the branch quivering in the diviner's hand, suddenly shooting downward like a dart finding its mark. Our pump still draws sparkling chilled water from that well.

In the language of trees, hazel symbolizes reconciliation. When my hazel-coloured eyes are blazing I doubt anyone sees reconciliation – rather, a dogged determination to keep on keeping on!

I'll close with Mom's recipe, one I'm sure you'll enjoy even if you, my urban friend, must buy the delectable nuts!

Hazelnut Crumble Muffins
1/2 cup sour cream
1/4 cup oil
1 egg
1 1/3 cups flour
1 1/2 tsp. baking soda
1/4 tsp. salt

2/3 cup brown sugar
1 cup diced pineapple

Topping
1/4 cup brown sugar
2 tsp. melted butter
1/2 tsp. cinnamon
1/3 cup chopped hazelnuts

Blend first three ingredients; set aside. Mix next four ingredients; stir into first mixture. Blend in diced pineapple. Put in greased muffin tins, filling two thirds of the way up. Mix topping ingredients together; sprinkle a little on each muffin. Bake at 350°F for 20 to 25 minutes. These freeze well. (Microwave frozen for 20 seconds on high for a taste of September in January!)

Elizabeth

Dear Elizabeth:
"You must plant lilies in your garden!" said my horticulture teacher. To her, it's a given. She feels no perennial garden is complete without the sweet scent, eye-catching colour and regal bearing that the lily can offer.

Well, sure, I have lilies too. But mine are the common, rusty orange day lilies you see everywhere, and they're confined to two discreet oval beds along our property line. There's no attractive fragrance, and they're so self-sufficient they've become, well, boring. I want to spice things up a bit, but with literally thousands to choose from I'm becoming quite lily-livered about the whole thing!

Actually, I think anyone who grows true lilies – *Lilium* as opposed to *Hemerocallis*, the day lily – is very brave. They require "perfect drainage," one gardener asserts, or the bulbs will rot. Aphids can transmit lily mosaic, a viral disease that mottles the leaves, and there's a dreaded orange-red lily beetle that can only be thwarted by hand-picking and personally destroying it. Worse, lily bulbs can get very expensive, so you don't want to lose too many.

Solace

The grocery stores got me started on this kick. While we're still wrapped in snow, they've been displaying saucy daffodils, tulips and crocuses. (I've only succumbed to one buttery primula so far; long-suffering Brian just rolls his eyes.) The Easter lilies will be next, though that's still several weeks away. The traditional white Easter lily is *Lilium longiflorum*, a close relative of the Madonna lily, *Lilium candidum*. Both stand for purity and innocence.

Insisting on a fragrant lily reduced the number of candidates for me, but only a little. Finally, in deference to you and all the spiritual explorations we've been doing, I've settled on the elegant and eloquent Madonna lily. And now I find the white lilies sprouting on my bathroom tiles look suspiciously like the kind I've chosen to plant. Perhaps the designer was thinking of Virgil's quote, "Give me handfuls of lilies to scatter!"

I know I'll have to improve the soil in my lily beds. The experts say these plants like humus-rich loam with a bit of grit. There's a garden maxim that applies: heads in the sun, roots in the shade. That means a mulch of one type or another, an organic layer over the soil or a living cover of short, shallow-rooted plants to keep the ground moist and the roots cool. I think I'll also build the beds up a bit, to be sure excess water always drains off. Then I can plant a couple of triads of bulbs in August, leaving about ten inches between each and placing them no more than two inches deep, as prescribed. The triads will eventually join and I should have a delicate cluster in a few years.

Fortunately, my lily beds are already in near-full sun; I'll just have to be careful not to let them dry out during hot spells. These flowers reach three to four feet, so staking probably won't be necessary. I may need to dig up some of the new bulblets that will be produced in a few years, but happy lilies can last for decades in a garden.

I hope this verse by Mary Tighe is an accurate description of what I'll have to look forward to: "The careless eye can find no grace, / No beauty in the scaly folds, / Nor see within the dark embrace / What latent loveliness it holds. / Yet in that bulb, those sapless scales, / The lily wraps her silver vest."

Despite its name, I hadn't realized the Madonna lily is so completely associated with the Virgin Mary. It is also known as the Annunciation lily and has been painted and depicted on pottery and mosaics since earliest civilization. Many scholars believe this species is the lily referred to in the Song of Solomon; later, the doubting apostle Thomas apparently found Mary's tomb filled with roses and beautiful white lilies. Unfortunately, it's not what the Book of Matthew referred to in that memorable phrase, "Consider the lilies" (Matthew 6:28, KJB). Those were likely anemones.

A healing ointment was once made of the root of white lily mixed with rosewater or honey to treat dropsy, hearing problems, bile and faint-heartedness. And the Madonna lily was the first official floral symbol of Quebec, chosen in 1963 because it resembled the fleur-de-lis symbol of France, one of that province's founding nations. (A native iris replaced it as the provincial flower in 1999.)

You can take your pick among creation myths for this distinguished plant. One says the flower was created from drops of Hera's milk as the Greek goddess breastfed the infant Hercules. Another holds that lilies were created by Eve's tears as she left the garden of Eden. And we green-thumbers have been trying to get back there ever since!

Anne

Dear Annie:

Your package with the rose mineral salts and energy soap has just arrived. How clever of you to send soap with ylang-ylang oil, which according to the package "gives courage and self-confidence and stimulates life energy." Let's get a franchise on that product!

I often wonder what my mail carrier thinks as he delivers everything from lingerie to lawn mower catalogues (I guess I'm the jackpot on someone's direct mail list), from cancer updates to MS updates, and from fat, newsy letters to these chunky mystery packages from Anne of Afar!

The lack of colour these dim winter days has left my soul rather lacklustre, too. I've dragged out my dog-eared landscape books with an eye to planning the windbreak we need across the hill above the drainage ditch. I'm tired of biding my time as I heal, so I'm not in the mood for waiting decades for trees to mature. Am I that impatient or just feeling cabin fever? I would like to be able to say, as Gandhi did, "I shall be content to be restless." That would be a fine achievement.

Since Michael and I – and, of course, you when you visit – enjoy using the deck overlooking the hill, I'm hunting for a tree that will be pleasing to both our eyes and our ears. I love the sound of leaves trading whispers with the wind. Even the scratch of bare branches in autumn storms tempts my senses. (These cloud-coloured January days seem to mute even the tree sounds.)

I think I'll call you "Anne of Windy Poplars" (after the L.M. Montgomery book) today, as that's what I'm aiming to plant. The poplar is amazingly fast growing, and is known in folklore as the talking or singing tree. I can just hear those heart-shaped leaves whispering now! There is an ancient legend of the Speaking Tree in India, a tree that "could answer questions in the language of any man who addressed it." This tree warned Alexander the Great against trying to conquer India. That would be a great tree to have around, wouldn't it?

The common poplar will have to suffice, and it is indeed popular, as it grows in every province. There are at least thirty species of *Populus*, from the family *Salicaceae*, with maybe half a dozen native to Canada. Their speedy rate of growth is one reason poplars appeal to me – but sadly, they're short-lived. *Populus alba*, also known as the white poplar or silver-leaved poplar, has white leaves that are fuzzy to touch. This species is perhaps the most disease-resistant. The Japanese poplar, *Populus maximowiczii*, also stands pretty tough against disease. By contrast, the once-favoured Lombardy black poplar has been laid low by a deadly canker disease.

Aspens are among the poplars that dot our countryside. The best known is probably quaking or trembling aspen. Like your quaking grass, "quaking aspen has leaves that wave in the lightest breeze." In some Native Canadian languages, trembling aspen translates as "noisy leaf"! Alas, several translations call this dear tree "woman's tongue."

My grandmother used to say the upturned leaves of the poplars at Batchawana meant rain was on the way. It always does seem to rain, but I think it is because the wind is blowing ill from the east – more weather trivia!

Hercules supposedly wore a crown of poplar leaves on his visit to the underworld. There, the tops of the leaves were blackened by the heat, while the undersides took on a silvery sheen from the hero's sweat. He was triumphant in returning from that world and poplar came to represent life after death. I do like that imagery! I'm sorry to say the trembling aspen has a far sadder tale in Christian lore, according to Alison Jones in *The Larousse Dictionary of World Folklore*. "This trembling is attributed to the aspen's arrogance at Christ's crucifixion; while he suffered all trees bowed their heads and trembled except for the aspen, which is now condemned to do so until Judgment Day." Variations of this myth say the aspen would not bow before the Christ child as the Holy Family escaped Herod's rule by fleeing into Egypt. The tree was then cursed; it is said this aspen trembles with guilt, as its wood was used for Jesus' cross.

Annie, I know we plant so many of our hopes and fears in our gardens. I think, though, by exploring the history and the culture of what we plant we somehow honour the plants. What rich ancestries they have; I like to think we're helping ensure their legacies.

I've learned that poplars prefer deep, well-drained and moist soil but they aren't really too fussy. The one warning I will heed is to keep the trees away from pipes, as the roots wander far and wide. The hill is safe, I think. These trees reach heights between forty and one hundred feet, and fortunately tolerate air pollution.

This species certainly has been valued across the country. The roots of the eastern cottonwood, *Populus deltoides*, were used by some Native peoples to make fire by friction. This poplar is found in southwestern Ontario and southern Quebec, as well as in some parts of the southeastern United States. The light, soft wood of the black cottonwood, *Populus trichocarpa*, found in Alberta and British Columbia, is used for furniture making. And a fishing boat can be crafted from the bark of the balsam poplar, *Populus balsamifera*, which grows throughout Canada.

The Balm-of-Gilead poplar, *Populus candicans*, is occasionally found as an ornamental tree. The biblical prophet Jeremiah laments, "Is there not balm in Gilead anymore?" (Jeremiah 8:22, JB). That balm is actually a fragrant ointment made from the resin of a small evergreen found in Asia and Africa. But balm of Gilead can also mean anything that has a calming or soothing effect. So I guess this letter has been a balm today, as my body and spirit have settled down. I am determined not only to plant those poplars, but to watch them grow to grand and glorious heights.

So what if they don't last a hundred years? They will last my lifetime! Do I hear you humming the chorus "Just like a tree that's planted by the water / We shall not be moved"?

Elizabeth

Hope and Faith

Where there is life there is hope. In a garden, as indeed anywhere on the planet, the miracle of continuing life is cause for the most profound optimism. It's that simple – or is it?

"You ask me why I dwell in the green mountain; / I smile and make no reply for my heart is free of care," wrote the Chinese poet Li Po. "As the peach blossom which flows downstream and is gone into the unknown, / I have a world apart that is not among men."

Who among us can look upon a newborn's innocent face and not see some form of eternity, something far bigger and better than all we are or could ever perceive our world to be? Sometimes we need only look around. "Gardens are our link with the divine," said William Howard Adams, and poet W. Bliss Carman wrote, as if in reply: "What is heaven? Is it not just a friendly garden plot?"

Yet we puzzle about the meaning of hope on a personal level, and sometimes it seems far, far from our grasp. Where is the hope when a loved one succumbs suddenly to a terrible disease or an awful fate, or when we fail once again to meet our own expectations? What is there to sustain us when something precious is taken away through senseless violence or an act of vandalism? Where is hope when the forces of nature lay low our surroundings and cut away all that we thought was ours to keep?

As life is slowly ebbing from a dear one's face, where is the hope? That, theologians will tell you, is when faith steps in. And maybe that's when we draw from the love and strength of others, or when caring about someone or something else draws us out of that lonely, dark, small space we've been inhabiting.

Dictionary definitions tell us that hopes are wishes and expectations, our desires expressed. They are also, in a sense, a measure of our optimism and confidence in the future. Canadian astronaut Roberta Bondar, who has viewed the earth from a perspective few others can ever know, experienced a renewal of personal optimism after her January 1992 voyage aboard the space shuttle *Discovery*. She felt exhilaration, she writes in *Touching the Earth*, upon seeing Earth from afar: "I am absorbed by the planet and the soft strength of its shimmering blue atmosphere.... From out here, I don't attach the same importance to what now appears to be a remote event on a tiny part of the earth's crust. In space, I feel like a pretty small, fragile life form. The huge physical presence that I see below will endure long after I and my kind are gone." She later delights in reflecting that Earth will remain beautiful, whether or not there are human eyes to view it.

However, hope can't thrive in a vacuum – it requires courage. An act of hope almost always involves taking a step into the unknown, and that is at least daunting, perhaps paralyzing. If this happens to you, it is time to take strength from the beauty, compassion and caring that are available. Seek out those qualities, and don't be afraid to use them as pillars of strength.

One who learned how to do that is Rick Hansen, the Canadian athlete who took the world by storm with his unprecedented 1985–87 "Man in Motion" tour around the world. Paraplegic as the result of a car accident at age fifteen, Hansen refused to give up. He worked his way painfully through rehabilitation, university, success in wheelchair sports, and then the 24,902-mile international tour that raised millions of dollars and improved awareness and prospects for disabled people everywhere. He consistently told people they should never be afraid to dream, and once summed up his philosophy this way: "When the hope dies, a terrible thing happens to a disabled person. You get it into your head that you can't do things.... I had to realize that there weren't too many things I used to do that I couldn't do again, but that some of it wouldn't be the same. All I really had to do was adapt."

Just as it takes courage to find hope, a willingness to change is also necessary. This is when we must be flexible in our approach to life, and in how we think things should unfold. We can learn from that much-loved childhood hero, Winnie-the-Pooh. He tells us in a poem, courtesy of author A.A. Milne, "Then Piglet (PIGLET) thought a thing: / 'Courage!' he said. 'There's always hope. / I want a thinnish piece of rope. / Or, if there isn't any bring / A thickish piece of string.'"

If there's any need for further testament to our indomitable capacity for hope, let it come from the immortal Anne Frank. This Jewish teenager died in a Nazi concentration camp during the Second World War, and left us testament in the form of her diary. In July 1944, while still in hiding, she wrote: "In spite of everything I still believe that people are really good at heart."

Some say faith is the absence of reason. If something can be figured out, faith isn't needed. This works well if one is explaining fertilizer. Most of us have faith, which seems to be trust or confidence, that adding fertilizer will enhance our garden's growth. If the chemical and biological interaction of the fertilizer is explained, we reasonably understand why fertilizer works. Then our experience with the fertilized ground and the growing plants gives rise to our experience of a healthy garden. That is a testament to what was originally considered faith. We can see the fruits of our labour.

But faith gets called on the carpet when real-life issues are involved. A newly retired man whose loyal wife is fading into the shadows with Alzheimer's must trust she's not feeling pain. A young mother lying on a hospital gurney musters confidence in her doctor as she's about to undergo cancer surgery. Despite everything being reasonably explained to us, we fear. In *For Christ's Sake*, Tom Harpur, a prominent Canadian writer, teacher and Anglican priest, tells us that Jesus took issue with the disciples' fear and anxiousness, not their various sins. Jesus "uses 'faith' or 'confidence' in a general sense to describe a basic emotional and mental outlook."

We seem to be either offering reassurance or seeking it. "I love you," we repeat over and over to our mates. "I promise I'll never leave you," we tell our children. Somehow our fear and anxiety strike the heart of where we live, at home. "Jesus knew that ultimately life comes down to personal relations, to community and friendship. But these depend on trust, and their greatest enemy is fear," writes Harpur.

Faith acknowledges fear but takes a big leap outside that vicious circle to a place where hope resides. Here faith can call for help.

"Come now and succor me in the hour of my calamity. Support my broken life, and give me rest and peace," wrote the second-century Roman author Lucius Apuleius.

Jesus' answer to fear was love. "I give you a new commandment: love one another; just as I have loved you, you must also love one another," as the Gospel of John almost sings (John 13:34, JB). Jesus then urges his disciples to call upon God, but in an expectation of being answered. "Ask and you will receive" (John 16:24, JB).

Oh, and how we have asked! "Be near me when my light is low... Be near me when my faith is dry... Be near me when I fade away," wrote Tennyson, in a lengthy obituary for a dear friend.

And faith surely must be the simple inscription "Help me," found scribbled in a hospital bedside Bible. The apostle Paul says it so smoothly: "Now faith is the substance of things hoped for, the evidence of things not seen" (Hebrews 11:1, KJB).

With faith we tremble to touch the unattainable. In our gardens we can dig as deep as we want for the divine. And sometimes we really do find answers at our fingertips. As Dorothy France Gurney put it, "This kiss of the sun for pardon, / The song of the birds for mirth, / One is nearer God's heart in a garden / Than anywhere else on earth."

* * *

Dear Anne:

I could not believe the magic in my garden this morning – I found snowdrops peeking through what I thought was still frost-encrusted soil. I shudder to say this for fear of tempting the snow gods, but we have had such an easy winter for being in a snowbelt.

Let's keep this a secret: I tiptoed around the edge of the garden and was thrilled to see crocus tips. Then, I grinned like your Jasper-cat when I saw the snowdrops! And all this life despite significant patches of snow under the trees in our woods.

"Grief melts away / Like snow in May / As if there were no such cold thing," wrote George Herbert, a sixteenth-century English clergyman and member of Parliament. Oh, Annie, I felt like that this morning! I have made it through the winter, and another MS attack. Perhaps I'm a little worse for wear – but I'm here! But I'm sorry to tell you my eyes have worsened.

The enchanting snowdrops are *Galanthus*, a small woodland perennial. Mine are in the thicket across the brook, but I have a few edging a garden area that gets good shade throughout the spring when the sun's angle is still low. I hope I can coax Michael into transplanting a few more from the woods for me. I also found at least a dozen of the wee plants interspersed with the scattering of crocuses on the hill down to the creek. Here's a quote I found that you, lucky Ottawa-dweller, will appreciate about the springtime blooms that tease our eyes, noses and hearts. "You can hardly move through the [Ottawa] parks for the numbers of winter-weary Canadians drifting, dreamy little smiles on their faces, from one swath of color to another," comment Dinah Shields and Edwinna von Baeyer in *The Reluctant Gardener*.

My durable-yet-delicate snowdrop belongs to the amaryllis family (that ever-popular Christmas gift I resort to when I haven't a clue what to give). The snowdrop's dangling, almost translucent white flowers look like miniature, mouse-sized underwear hanging out to dry. Louise Beebe Wilder pens a much prettier picture: "They never seem to sleep, taking advantage of every relenting moment to edge upwards, the green spears often sticking through snow and ice for weeks at a time, waiting for a soft day when they will quite suddenly hang out the little frosty bells."

While a few of my snowdrops have opened, most still have their tough, beak-like tip showing between paired leaves. If winter does return – which I am sure it will, as we are never safe from snow until June – the buds will remain visible but closed in a protective embrace. It reminds me of a verse my Grade 5 teacher quoted: "They looked like rosebuds filled with snow." These sweethearts seem to withstand anything this northern clime can offer, from sleet to slushy snow – and often mud, when Bizzie is out kicking up her heels in celebration of the season.

Apparently it is best to plant the bulbs as soon as possible after buying them, as they dry out quickly. "Not to do this," warns an expert, "is to court loss and a poor showing for many years."

Snowdrops are originally from the deciduous woods of Europe and Asia Minor. There has been considerable concern in the last decade that snowdrop bulbs sold in North America may have come from Turkey. This depletes the Turkish wild stocks so much that some botanists fear various species, such as *Galanthus elwesii*, are endangered. This is the giant snowdrop that grows six to twelve inches tall, with inch-long (or better) flowers. This behemoth of the snowdrop world prefers warmer temperatures than ours. Apparently, the collected wild bulbs are cheaper than the cultivated stocks. This is one thing I don't feel guilty about because my *Galanthus* came with the house purchase!

The bulbs should be planted in the fall, three to four inches deep and two to three inches apart. Once nestled into the ground, they resent any meddling. If you want to transplant some, do so when they are flowering or right after. Gently lift a small cluster (no more than five or six) with roots and soil attached and immediately plant in the new, shady location. "How beautiful are the snowdrops," said Mary Pamela Milne Holm in *Notes from a Border Garden*, "a perfect sheet of white, nodding their heads and literally scenting the air."

Well, Annie, I've babbled like my brook today, so I'll close for now. I hope you can sense that my soul feels free with that tried-and-true old adage that "hope springs eternal in the human breast." I've enclosed a new photo of Bizzie for you to give Maggie, with lots of dog kisses (yuck)!

Elizabeth

Dear Elizabeth:

Now you'll know I'm certifiably crazy – the little clay figurine I've enclosed in this package is St. Patrick, soon to be the patron saint of my back lawn. I picked him up at a post–St. Paddy's Day remainder table in a card shop. Isn't he cute, brandishing his shamrock?

I know you have no Irish heritage to speak of – neither do I – but there is method to my madness. I've been pacing through the lawn section of various garden catalogues, wondering what to do about my ratty backyard this spring. It has thin, rocky, terrible topsoil and the grass is struggling – but the clover is taking over nicely! Neither Brian nor Maggie is ready to give up an open, grassy area where they can play, so I'm thinking of giving in to the clover. It nourishes the soil, it's a fast-spreading, low ground cover, and the little flowers smell heavenly in early summer.

Any self-respecting gardener would recoil in horror, but why shouldn't I try it? Of course, I know I'll have to edge the garden beds now and be vigilant about clover invading my flowers and vegetables. But I don't think it's that onerous a task. In fact, the landscaping book you loaned me ages ago advises people to roll in the clover, so to speak! As the author points out, clover smells good when it's cut, stays green even through dry summers, and provides lazy-day entertainment for kids. "Send them searching for a four-leaf clover," chortles Marianne Binetti, "and wish them luck."

That brings me to the folk history attached to this plant. Almost everyone has heard that a four-leaf clover is lucky for its finder, but did you know that it loses its potency when given away? And let's not ever seek the elusive five-leaf specimen; it is said to bring bad luck or foretell sickness. You've had enough of both, I think.

The Christian beliefs about clover have to do with St. Patrick of fifth-century Ireland. He apparently used this common plant's trademark tripartite leaves to explain the Holy Trinity to King Laoghaire. Three leaflets make up one leaf of a clover plant, he explained, just as three personages (Father, Son and Holy Ghost) make one God. Therefore, the clover was regarded as a kind of protective charm against witchcraft and evil. The Druids had similar ideas, but their clover could symbolize good or evil. It seems this humble plant inspired faith in many people.

In Victorian England, clover represented fertility, and that has some basis in fact because the plant actually improves the land where it grows. One gardening book I consulted mentioned clover in the "Lawn Weeds" section, where it declared that this unwelcome guest can be controlled by lifting and severing its creeping runners before mowing the lawn. The book acknowledges, though, that clover is sometimes used as a green (living) manure that puts nitrogen back into soil. It drains the element from air pockets in surrounding soil and fixes it via the bacteria in nodules on its roots. Sounds like quite a process, doesn't it?

For me, clover will forever conjure up wonderful memories of the summer Brian and I went cycling in Prince Edward Island during a too-short holiday. In places where farmers were giving the land a break from intensive potato production, there were whole fields of purple clover in bloom, and the fragrance was intoxicating as we pedalled by! Ours is white clover, I'm pretty sure, another fragrant type sometimes used as a pasture crop. Also called *Trifolium repens*, it is one of the most important types for honey-making. I don't think we'll have enough to set up our own apiary, but I don't mind attracting more bees and giving them sweet nectar to encourage them in their pollinating rounds throughout my garden. My herbal book says I can use the plant in wines, tea mixtures, bath concoctions, or pickled in salads – though I can't imagine getting that ambitious.

Originally from Europe, clover became naturalized on this continent long ago, and there are now about ninety species of almost three hundred known to exist. You see it everywhere in

grassy expanses and along roadsides. A white, rounded band near
the base of each leaflet identifies the type we have. The flowers are
round balls of white or pale pink that I remember pulling apart, as
a child, to suck the nectar from individual, tube-like petals. My
neighbour's kids would certainly approve of a wild clover lawn
where they could play with Maggie – their pet guinea pig came
often for visits last summer to feast on the stuff.

Maybe I'll share with them this bit of verse I found in an Emily
Dickinson collection: "The pedigree of honey / Does not concern
the bee; / A clover, any time, to him / Is aristocracy."

Anne

Dear Anne:

Please excuse this handwritten scrawl, but the computer is
down and I wanted to dash off a letter to enclose with this mystery
packet. Let your gourmet sense of scent guess the contents! I'm
also wondering if you've seen any sign of the Dutch crocuses I sent
you last autumn. Don't crocuses just lift the weight of winter off
your soul? They do mine.

Late last September I thought of enhancing my "naturalized"
garden by sprinkling them around the bases of the red oak and rock
elm, then strewing them across the lowland above the creek. A
few lonely stragglers were in need of new companions. Scattering
corms is like colouring the fabric of a property; six yellow here,
a few violet here, a smidgen of white back there. Louise Beebe
Wilder said it best: "In his garden every man may be his own artist
without apology or explanation. Here is one spot where each may
experience the 'romance of possibility.'"

Planting corms or bulbs in autumn seems to me a gardener's
expression of faith in another year, and hope for the rich, vibrant
colours that will shout, "This tiny plant is alive!" Of course,
anything is possible when you plant – remember my exotic iris
experience and the *Gladiolus* I got instead? Served me right for
being so coy about that iris. At least I recognize this favourite
member of the iris family!

What I sent you were *Crocus vernus*, the common Dutch crocus. You needed no introduction, as I remember a patch of these harbingers of spring in your side garden. It faces south, doesn't it? I often mistake the leaves of these babies as some kind of grass, and have been known to pluck an innocent bulb from its snug ground home. The plant's crisp colours range from white to purple, with three inner and three outer petals. I love how the flowers close at night and stay shut on cloudy days. Just like us, some days: draw the drapes and soak in some suds!

Crocuses like to be tucked into well-drained – even sandy, if possible – soil with good steady sun. Did you plant the corms three inches deep and four inches apart? Don't forget that the leaves must remain tall a good four weeks after flowering, to ensure the corm is nourished, for next year's encore.

Crocus ancyrensis offers the sunny six-petalled orange favourite. "A single mild afternoon coaxes buds into...stars," writes Patrick Lima in *The Harrowsmith Perennial Garden: Flowers for Three Seasons*. "They are among spring's best gifts to gardeners."

There is a host of cultivars from the pure white flowers of the *Crocus vernus* cultivar 'Jeanne d'Arc' to 'Lady Killer', of purple violet petals, from the *Crocus chrysanthus* species.

The *Crocus sativus* species is especially interesting for you, I think. I remember the delicious saffron rice you made for me two hospital trips ago, but I had no idea that herb comes from the tiny Old World crocus! The saffron yellow we all know refers to the plant's yellowy-orange stigmas.

I will look at the saffron in my cupboard with new respect after researching this species. It takes about 35,000 flowers to produce one pound of the saffron we sparingly pinch into rice or onto fish or poultry. That one pound is valued at about $4,500! And in earlier times this precious extract was used as a dye – hence the term "saffron yellow." Greeks, the Chinese, as well as the Tibetan Dalai Lama, have used this dye for royal robes, and the mythical Greek divinities were also fond of saffron-coloured attire. Later, wealthy Romans used saffron to scent their homes, notes *Rodale's Illustrated Encyclopedia of Herbs*. "The scent was valued as much as the dye," writes Maude Grieve in *A Modern Herbal*. "Saffron water was sprinkled on the benches of the theatre, the floors of banqueting-halls were strewn with crocus leaves, and cushions were stuffed with it."

Five hundred years ago, European spice dealers were known as "saffron grocers" because this spice was so valued for its medicinal and flavouring uses. Medicinally, saffron was used to combat everything from colds to cancer, and as appetite or aphrodisiac aids.

Crocus sativus blooms for about a week to ten days between late October and early November. Its leaves reach one to one and one-half feet, and its lavender, white or reddish-purple petals are up to two inches long. The stigmas must be harvested during that brief season. Some say the best saffron comes from Spain, where *mondadoras*, or peelers – most of whom are women – strip off the petals to pluck out the stigmas. An experienced peeler can work ten to twelve thousand flowers a day! The stigmas are placed under a heavy weight to dry. Be sure to store your saffron in a cool, dry place to keep it fresh and potent.

The word "crocus" comes from the Greek *krokos*, and a sad Greek legend is attached to the word. Apparently, Krokos was an attractive mortal who fell head over heels for Smilax, a nature spirit. She was a nymph, one of the lesser divinities who lived in forests, meadows and even streams or the sea. Nymphs were always beautiful and young ('tis ever thus, eh?) and they enjoyed toying with mere mortals. Anyway, Smilax wasn't smitten with Krokos so, in one magic moment, he was reduced to the lowly flower. I guess she showed him! Next time Brian gives you grief, just tell him he's lucky he's not a crocus – especially a saffron one! As always, love to you all.

Elizabeth

Elizabeth, my frisky friend:

So spring has you feeling euphoric, does it? Well, I envy you. We won't be seeing soft ground for a while yet. But when the tips of my Egyptian self-seeding onions start to show, I'll know it's truly spring planting time; they're so dependable.

Did the ones I gave you make it through the winter? If not, there are always more of the bulblets lying around that I can share. I've found yet another use for the little darlings, one I'll introduce you to when you visit again. It's a delicious, aromatic, savoury onion bread that I adapted to make the Italian-style, round flatbread "foccacia." You just pulverize a couple of these onions (I only use the white bulbs) in the blender, then stir the puree into basic bread dough before enough flour has been added to make it stiff and kneadable.

You know how I love to pound and knead bread dough from time to time, to work out the various frustrations of a tough day. Well, this recipe is especially cathartic because you get to cry, too! Kind of a comic sight, but I highly recommend it. "All griefs with bread are less," as my book of garden proverbs proclaims.

Forgive my getting tutorial again, but I've learned the most interesting things from my onion research. In ancient Egypt, the onion bulb was said to represent the cosmos. (I take great comfort in finding my own small cosmic emblems reappearing each year in the vegetable patch.) An even better reason to revere the onion is found in its common name, from the Latin *unionis* – meaning "union," a whole and perfect entity. My grandmother would certainly have thought so; I can picture her yet, closing her eyes in rapture as she bit into a bread-butter-Bermuda onion sandwich. It was her idea of the ultimate snack.

The Egyptians worshipped the onion, and the plant was depicted more often than any other in tomb paintings. Pyramid builders ate huge quantities of onion, garlic and radish, apparently. In the Bible, the people of Moses complained during their long wanderings in the desert about leaving behind the good food of Egypt, including "the cucumbers, melons, leeks, onions and garlic" (Numbers 11:5, JB). Onion remains a staple in the Middle East, while elsewhere in the world it is more often used as a flavouring, accent or salad vegetable.

The onions of the Bible are presumed to be *Allium cepa*, a mild and sweet-tasting variety with narrow, small bulbs and tall, cylindrical leaves. Mine are similar, but my herb catalogue calls them *Allium x proliferum* – presumably because they proliferate by way of tiny bulbs produced late in the growing season at the top of long stalks above ground. Members of the lily family, these Egyptian onions are called *Allium cepa* var. *viviparum* by some sources. Whatever the name, I couldn't ask for a more agreeable, easy-growing vegetable.

You mentioned that you gave some to your sister-in-law last fall and she wants to know how to care for them. Mine flourish with virtually no attention at all, but I'll pass along what the books say. Any soil will suffice, but adding organic matter will improve the yield. Mulching can also help retain moisture during the hotter, drier days; that's useful because onions generally prefer cool weather. Egyptian onions are planted in late summer, when new bulblets are perched atop the plant stalks or lying on the ground where the stalk has fallen due to their weight. Plant shallowly, keep them well-watered, and enjoy next year's harvest! I use the slender, immature green parts diced in salads or potato-and-Parmesan-cheese barbecue packets, but later the leaf tubes are too tough and juice-filled to be palatable. The underground bulb, though, can be pulled up and chopped anytime for use in soups, stews or stir-fries, cooked on their own or pickled. The plants are hardy, but a winter covering such as evergreen boughs or leaves is recommended to prevent drying or frost-burning where there isn't good snow cover.

I like what you said about my sharing the onions from my garden with other gardeners – that it's kind of an act of faith. You hope others will give your plant youngsters good homes, that in the future they find the same pleasure with the plants that you do. Maybe you're right when you say sharing plants is sharing a bit of yourself with others. Giving away my plants is a joy, but giving away a part of my soul is not something I have ever done easily. Perhaps the plants are now helping me to do that.

Solace

"It's the one who won't be taken / Who cannot seem to give /
And the soul afraid of dying / That never learns to live."

Anne

Dear Anne:

Aaah! These hot flashes still drive me crazy! One minute I'm
sweating buckets, the next I feel flu-like chills. Which is worse,
I dare not say. The doctor wasn't kidding when he said I'd go
into immediate menopause after the second surgery – I did, like
hitting a brick wall at full steam. Besides the extreme temperature
fluctuations, I am bothered by crabby moods and odd sleep patterns.
Instead of ditzing around the house at 3 a.m., I thought I'd fire off
this e-mail to greet your morning.

You've mentioned you're experiencing some menopausal
symptoms, so I'll share what's helped me. I hope you enter this
period of your life with more grace and good humour than I've
mustered. Of course, I also hope time is gentler with you, letting
you slide gradually through what author Gail Sheehy calls the
"silent passage."

I have not been so "short" (read: snarky), Michael attests, since
taking evening primrose oil capsules daily for the last year. I admit
to feeling more even-tempered, despite these annoying flashes.
The oil is from the common evening primrose, *Oenothera biennis*,
a biennial with large, showy yellow flowers found throughout our
temperate zones. It blooms from June through September. Not
surprisingly, given its name, the flowers open at night. (Does
this nighttime activity remind you of anyone?) The plant, which
prefers dry, open spaces, can spike to over five feet in height by
its second year of growth, with lance-shaped leaves that are about
eight inches long. This plant also favours sandy soil and tolerates
the wind. When it is open at dusk, the scent is obviously stronger,
in the hope of attracting some nocturnal moth or insect. If the
plant doesn't get pollinated during the night, it will stay open
for a few hours in the early morning to chance a daylight insect
rendezvous. "If you see an evening primrose that is still open in

the morning, you can be sure that this particular blossom was a real wallflower in the previous night's festivities," writes Laura C. Martin in *Wildflower Folklore*.

This brings me to the oil's reputed benefits. Seed capsules contain the oil, which is rich in gamma linoleic acid (GLA). This helps "mediate hormonal activity." What a professional way of saying it takes a bite out of bitchiness! According to one of my favourite plant catalogues, GLA is a precursor of prostaglandin E1, which helps regulate our immune systems. Consuming GLA supposedly helps us offset a poor diet, as well as our female aging woes.

Evening primrose is a true New World plant, with about eighty species native to North and South America. In fact, it must have hitched a ride back to Europe very early on, as it was described there by writers in 1600.

It is an edible plant, with the roots used in soups and stews and the leaves chopped for salads. It is also a food favourite among the woodland animal set. The leaves are said to be tasty while nourishing.

Annie, I simply can't end this message without saying something positive about this stage in my life. Despite my body's hormonal upheaval, or maybe because of it, there is some good news. Perhaps it is the cancer experience, perhaps my age, perhaps the loss of hormones (likely a combination of all three), but I'm really learning to focus. A lot of garbage in my life, stuff I thought still mattered, is slipping away. The image of who I am is not nearly as important as knowing who I am. Twice I tried to read *The Silent Passage*. That was when I still had ovaries. I couldn't finish it. Now, as I reread Gail Sheehy's words, I recognize the woman she's describing. "I am not the same me anymore. I am an older woman.... The outlines of my future self are coming into focus – and I like her. She is focused but not so driven. She dares me to follow my purest instincts in what I think and read and write, rather than what is expected...." Now, that fits!

I'll sign off with a verse I'd like to call my own: "She is clothed

Solace

in strength and dignity, / she can laugh at the days to come"
(Proverbs 31:25, JB).

Elizabeth

Dear Elizabeth:

Your letter has me itching to see my newest crocuses in full
bloom – any time now. What a great history the little spring
heralds share!

I can't help agreeing with Canadian garden writer Patrick Lima
when he writes: "I welcome spring more than ever, for while my
nose sniffs out the best scent of the year, my eyes quest for color....
When we touch the earth and involve ourselves cooperatively
with nature's cycles, we reaffirm our link with the living planet
that sustains us."

Fetch yourself a glass of wine (dealcoholized, of course), and
settle back for this next bit, Liz. It's a rant. I'm upset with my
neighbour about his plan to rip out the wonderful old grapevine
that grows along the fence between our properties. Granted, the
vine is pretty tired-looking and overgrown, and it hasn't produced
many grapes in recent years, but it's a great privacy screen. It just
needs pruning – and some tender, loving care.

I hate it when people show such disrespect for living things! If
they can't be bothered to maintain a plant properly (or won't admit
their own horticultural ignorance), they should bow out gracefully
and offer the greenery to someone who can. My neighbour's yard
and garden are none of my business, I know, but it would be nice if
he'd ask my opinion or advice before destroying something that so
affects both yards. I love the leafy shade that living fence throws,
and the heady smell of ripening grapes in late summer and early
fall. That leafy vine lets me try new shade plants beneath it, too.

Not that I'm any authority – I wouldn't even know where to
start cutting the gnarled old thing. But I'd certainly be willing to
take a stab at researching it, and to offer whatever help I could
find. He is stand-offish and wouldn't be too receptive, I'm sure,
but maybe I can get his wife's ear before it's too late. She's a young
and eager novice gardener with lots of enthusiasm, and clearly the
decision-maker regarding plants. Perhaps she can be persuaded.

What they really need is an old Italian gardener who knows his grapes!

We had just such a gift a decade or so ago, when we first moved to Ottawa. We were renting a townhouse from a kindly old Italian couple who kept asking hopefully if there would soon be *bambini* to fill up the extra bedrooms. The place came with a smallish fenced backyard where I could indulge my sporadic gardening tendencies, and – glory be! – there was a young grapevine. That spindly-looking vine covered the tiny patio-stoned terrace by June, and in fall the fragrant blue-violet grapes hung heavy on the metal frame extending over our heads. The grapes weren't edible, I was warned, but "good for the jam, jelly, eh?" (They were, too – I tried it one season, but never again felt moved to spend all that time stirring and straining over a hot stove on a fine autumn day.)

Just in case my young neighbour will listen to reason, I've started looking into the history and culture of the genus *Vitis*. As you know, grapes pop up repeatedly in the Bible. One author states there are approximately two hundred references to the noble vine, spanning Noah's and Jesus' times. Just like the Egyptian onion, the fruits of the vine were a life-sustaining crop for people of the Holy Land, and remain important today in many parts of the world. I'm sure their role in winemaking has something to do with that! Let us not forget Bacchus, the lusty Roman god of wine.

"They sow the fields and plant their vines, there, they show a profitable harvest," said the Psalmist (Psalm 107:37, JB). And Jesus explained, "I am the vine, you are the branches" (John 15:5, JB). Subtle, huh?

Egypt's Fourth Dynasty dates viniculture to as early as 2400 B.C. Roman Legionnaires are thought to have brought cuttings back to Rome, then later introduced the grapevine to England.

Although the earliest settlers toted grapevines with them to North America, a native insect called *phylloxera* wiped out almost all the vineyards. Only by crossing the Old World's *Vitis vinifera* with various wild native grapes were hybrid species developed that could resist the pest and be hardy enough to prosper. *Phylloxera* eventually made its way to Europe and wreaked the same kind of havoc there, until resistant rootstocks from North America were shipped in to restore good grape health in the homeland.

Grapes are classified according to end use: there are table grapes, wine grapes, grapes for preserving and raisin grapes. I'm not sure what kind my neighbours have; the vines have been strictly ornamental for as long as I can remember. The fruits are green, though, even when ripe. They love the full-sun site, where they cling to a sturdy chain-link fence in fairly fertile and very well-drained soil. Because their tomatoes and my roses live nearby, there is pretty regular watering during dry weather.

References tell me some shelter and a long, hot summer are advisable for good yield. In commercial vineyards, a plant isn't even allowed to bear fruit until its third summer – after careful pruning has produced a tough, self-supporting main stem. My neighbours would need an excellent reference book or a pruning expert to lead them through the intricacies of grape pruning systems. It looks like they should start, though, by cutting the whole thing back to a single main stem with only a few buds left, close to the ground, after ruthless fall pruning. Then in spring, a couple of lateral shoots could be trained along the fence and cut back to five or six leaves, while the main leader is trained along the fence top.

Annual cutting-back would be required from then on, and thinning to one cluster of fruit per foot to get good fruiting. They would then need to trim individual fruit clusters to ensure that every grape gets good air circulation and maximum sun, and that the cluster itself is well formed.

At harvest time, you are supposed to cut the vine a couple of inches on either side of where the fruit cluster hangs, making a convenient handle. You're not supposed to touch the fruit or you'll ruin the "bloom." Do the grapes creeping over your woodshed get many diseases, by the way? My sources name several possible problems, including black vine weevils, spider mites, blight, downy mildew, wasps, whiteflies and a number of underground pests and ailments. I don't remember ever hearing of sick grapevines before.

Just in case the neighbours aren't cooperative, how about we take a cutting from your grapevine next fall? Apparently, a two-bud cutting taken in the fall and put into a peat-soil-sand mixture to root can then be potted and kept in a greenhouse to plant the following spring. I'd just have to find someone (maybe at the college?) with a greenhouse who wouldn't mind a stowaway; then I could plant the vine where I want and enjoy grapes of my own a few years from now. Can't you just see Brian's face when he hears that one?

All I'd need is one cutting to survive, as a single vine can grow enough in one season to cover an arbor, trellis, pagoda or deck/terrace area. Strong, well-tended grapevines are said to last hundreds of years, too. Now that's enough to inspire faith in the natural world, isn't it? Cheers!

Anne

Dear Anne:

What an education about grapes! I'm encouraging Michael, resident apple tree pruner, to branch out and tackle grapes this season. I read him your letter and he actually hustled up the trellis to check out our old vines for any obvious trouble. "Tell her she can have the whole damn thing," he muttered at me, after catching his foot in the knotted vines climbing down. "At least it's healthy." Annie, you heard it from my tree guy: no apparent disease, and you are quite welcome to cuttings.

Your letter arrived the day I was cleaning out old boxes from Manitoulin Island. Did you know I was made an "honourary Haweater" while I was at the newspaper? True islanders carry that moniker with no small degree of pride, and some off-islanders are bestowed the honorific – I have the scroll to prove it. I've never been too clear on the criteria, so God knows what I did to get it (those halcyon twenty-something days)! Anyway, the "haw" refers to a berry, from a bush found across the island. We have two hawthorn shrubs here that bear fruit suspiciously like the hawberries I remember. (If you ever see Manitoulin hawberry jam for sale, buy it! It is delicious on a toasted English muffin or a crumpet.) Only a few birds enjoy the fruit, so it is usually around for a while.

Michael has threatened to chop out one bush, but the white flowers have such a heavenly scent I know he won't do it – though the slender thorns nailed him several times last year when he was aboard the lawnmower. The low, wide branches do make it difficult to grow grass under the tree. That said, I wish you lived closer so we could take a fragrant stroll when the hawthorns, apples and chokecherries are in bloom. The scent of one hawthorn species has been described as "the sweetest of open-air perfumes." Biz is having a ball, as the bees she is so fond of chasing are zooming in zigzag patterns across the yard. She makes me smile just watching her.

Hawthorns seem such natural symbols of the twin forces of death and life, with their sharp thorns and dainty blossoms. But the shrub means hope in one book I have. Just like life, eh? There's pain, but as sure as there's spring there's pleasure.

There are more than one thousand species of hawthorn, *Crataegus*, with over thirty in Canada. "This is a very large genus of small trees," notes my *Native Trees of Canada* text. I think we have one that's found everywhere, *Crataegus chrysocarpa*; it ranges from Nova Scotia to Alberta. Black hawthorn, *Crataegus douglasii*, and Columbia hawthorn, *Crataegus columbiana*, are native to British Columbia. Hawthorns like to stretch their branches, but the trees rarely top twenty-five feet. Branchlets develop from two buds: one becomes the new twig that will bear leaves, flowers or both; the other forms that telltale shiny, pointed thorn. Is it any surprise hawthorns come from the rose family?

The wood is apple-like, hard and heavy. Supposedly, the hawthorn provides the hottest wood fire known. It's a bit like sharing these garden descriptions and dreams, Annie. They've helped fan my hope to keep it burning strong.

Trees have long been symbols of life, hope and even death. There's the wood Noah crafted into an ark, the cross on Calvary, and the Banyan tree under which the deity Vishnu was born.

Greeks looked at the hawthorn and saw fertility, so its flowers were used for wedding crowns and its wood was used for marriage torches. What passion they lavished on their occasions! In Rome, hawthorn leaves edged the cradles of new babies as a protective charm. But in Teutonic legends, hawthorn represented life's twin – death. It was often used for funeral pyres and was believed to have sprung from lightning.

You've been waiting for this, haven't you? Yes, some believe Christ's crown was made of hawthorns. Joseph of Arimathea, the wealthy Samaritan councillor who asked Pontius Pilate for Jesus' body to bury in his own rock tomb, supposedly visited England with the Holy Grail in the years after the crucifixion. According to legend, he built a church at Glastonbury, and his flowering staff – known as the Glastonbury thorn – is said to have been a hawthorn branch.

Medieval Christians held that the shrub's purity could protect against all manner of evil, from disastrous storms to wandering ghosts. In 1485, England's Henry Tudor was ceremoniously adorned with a crown, found perched atop a hawthorn bush! Tudor's forces had defeated those of Richard III at the Battle of Bosworth, ending the long, bloody War of the Roses. Richard was killed in the fighting; the new king was Henry VII.

Ireland looks quite fondly on the hawthorn, too. There it is regarded as a fairy bush, and to cut one down is grievous – I guess you could say you lose the luck of the Irish! On that note, I'll close with this rhyme from Cicely Mary Barker, for Maggie: "My buds, they cluster small and green; / The sunshine gaineth heat; / Soon shall the hawthorn tree be clothed / As with a snowy sheet."

Elizabeth

Dear Elizabeth:

Here I go again, yammering on about yet another spring plant, but it's the last one this season, I promise! I had to fax you right away, though, because this enchanting spring bulb has done the impossible. It has interested my little tomboy in growing things – for now, at least.

Solace

Do you remember last year when I was so disgusted that Maggie wouldn't take to gardening? No matter how many sunflowers, radishes, marigolds or other "Mystery Garden" packets we tried, she could not be convinced. Oh, sure, she took a passing interest in the new shoots and would glance now and then at "her" sunflowers – but she flatly refused to have any part in their care. "You'll be out here all day anyway; you do it," she'd huff, tossing her curls and throwing dark looks at the garden as she marched off to play with the boys across the street. When I wasn't furious with her, I was deeply disappointed this wasn't going to be a passion we could share.

Well, yesterday's visit to a restored turn-of-the-century garden may have changed all that. I dragged Maggie along while I went to see how the old walled garden had fared this awful winter, and she spied a whole carpet of dancing bluebells over in one shady corner. "Mommy, why don't we have some of these?" she demanded, sniffing the delicate scent in delight. Why not, indeed? It was all I could do to keep her from picking an armful to take home for bouquets. (I couldn't let her see the smile on my face.)

So I'm back to the plant books and seed catalogues – but it's more confusing than ever. My plant of the day is *Scilla nutans*, also known as *Endymion nonscriptus*, easier to think of as English bluebell. A few older texts refer to this plant as a type of *Hyacinthoides*, and it looks so much like the well-named grape hyacinth, *Muscari*, that some nurseries aren't too careful how they label it. At least they all agree it's a member of the lily family, and a self-reliant woodland plant.

Apparently, another common name is "Ring-o'-bells." That could be a reference to its status as a fairy flower. I can pass along to Maggie this snippet from "The Song of the Bluebell Fairy" from the book you sent her: "My stems are tall and straight and strong; / From ugly streets the children throng, / They gather armfuls, great and long, / Then home they troop in pride – / Ah yes, / With laughter and with pride!"

We could easily pick up some bulblets that have been divided and have already sprouted from the horticultural society sales or plant exchanges, I think, since it's too late to buy bulbs that will flower if planted this year. And my impatient daughter certainly won't be able (or willing) to sustain any interest until the proper fall planting time. They like shade, so I could tuck some in under my non-flowering lilacs and leave them to naturalize in years to come. These lovely bells need organic, well-drained soil that is fairly acidic, and I think those conditions exist at the spot I have in mind. I'll just have to watch for them spreading too far. One reference book warns that "all this blue enthusiasm" will go on forever, eventually spreading into the rest of the garden and nearby lawn to the point that "[t]his could give a meticulous gardener a depressing case of the blues."

But if Maggie likes them, they stay. Besides, can there ever be too much of a lilting May expanse of violet-blue that has a "pleasant honey-like sweetness"? Maybe we'll try planting bulbs in the fall, too, placing them the recommended three to four inches apart and surrounding them with other perennials to hide the dying foliage. You have to leave the ugly yellow leaves as they die down, to replenish the bulb for next season. One author says an early type of hosta would work well as a screen, so that's an idea.

Maggie won't care that this plant has some biblical connections. Its cousin, the Oriental hyacinth of the grocery stores, is considered by many authorities to be the "lilies" of the Song of Solomon. (I guess those are the scholars who haven't assigned that honour to the Madonna lilies.) *Hyacinthus orientalis* grows throughout many northern parts of the Middle East, carpeting the old hills of Galilee in spring with vivid blue. Maggie's bloodthirsty enough to like the myths about Hyacinthus, though. I won't tell her that the god Apollo had a penchant for boys and loved Hyacinthus best of all; I'll just pass along the part about how the flower sprang up when the handsome youth was accidentally killed in a discus-throwing competition. She'll be thrilled by the idea that the purplish hue is from his spilled blood! That's why one floral directory says the Oriental hyacinth stands for sport, I suppose.

Personally, I am happier with the image conveyed by the birthday book you and I both love; it says the English bluebell represents constancy. If I ever succeed in teaching Maggie a love of growing things, that will be a most satisfying accomplishment and might ensure a constancy of sorts for my garden treasures. One can always hope. Now, back to your digging, digging, digging!

Anne

Dear Anne:

It's a soft Sunday afternoon and I'm feeling quiet – please excuse this pensive mood. I attended church today – the first time in quite a while – and we sang "Holy, Holy, Holy." I love that hymn so much that this off-key alto even sang! "Early in the morning our song shall rise to Thee: / Holy, Holy, Holy! / Merciful and Mighty! / God in Three Persons, Blessed Trinity."

I was raised with the concept of the triune God, but it's one I puzzle about daily. As I sat in the back pew (Baptist churches should be built with only back pews, as we all seem to sit there), I remembered you telling me about St. Patrick glimpsing something of the Trinity when he looked at a shamrock. After lunch, I had Michael help me over the bridge to our "other" garden, the wild one. I wanted to see where the trilliums will be. Their name isn't the only resemblance to the Trinity. In early spring, a single, stiff stem emerges with a whorl of three leaves, topped by a lone three-petalled flower. This triangular form is the root of the nickname "trinity flower."

It seems you and I are forever seeking the transcendent in or through our gardens. Blake captured that for me: "To see a world in a grain of sand, / And a heaven in a wild flower; / Hold infinity in the palm of your hand, / And eternity in an hour."

Like you, no doubt, I grew up in awe of the trillium, Ontario's provincial flower. My public school teachers drilled into us the message "Don't pick the trilliums!" Trouble was, they never told us why not! There are a couple of reasons. First, it takes the plant a good four to five years to produce its first bloom – and seeds. Second, the trillium doesn't transplant well. Over the years, the flowers of this member of the lily family have been picked a few times too many, and the plant hasn't had the time to regenerate. One gardening book pleads, "Never dig up wild ones, please...."

Trillium grandiflorum is known as the great white trillium, the snow trillium or the white wake-robin. Isn't that delightful? No doubt about the colour or the season! *Trillium stylosum* is pink, although white wake-robins also blush a light pink as they age. Trilliums are native to both North America and Asia, with more than twenty species on our continent.

Trillium erectum is described as "a handsome, native species remarkable for its nasty smelling reddish flowers," notes Louise Beebe Wilder in *The Fragrant Path*, in a chapter called "Plants of Evil Odor." This brownish-purple plant is also known as birthroot; in Indian herbal medicine it was a remedy to stop bleeding after childbirth. *Trillium sessile* is known as toadshade or red trillium for its colour. It was used as a herbal eyewash. The term "Stinking Benjamin" tells you about its scent!

One Indian story tells of a beautiful young girl boiling a trillium root as a love potion to slip into the food of a man she desired. In the process, she tripped, the root spilled onto the food of an ugly old geezer and he gobbled it up. You got it – he fell for her and she was stuck with his attentions for months. Will we never learn?

The seventeen trilliums I had last spring were quite striking as they stood above the hundreds of mottled yellow dogtooth violets. When we moved here we had fifteen trilliums, so we're going in the right direction. "Patience is essential," advises one garden textbook.

These are such perfect woodland plants, I can't picture them in a formal garden. It's difficult to reproduce the natural conditions, as trilliums like moist soil with dappled shade from a small-leaf tree, such as birch. Warnings abound about trying to grow trilliums in unlikely settings. "Wildflowers generally must be planted where they will grow, not just where we would like them to grow," cautions one guide.

You had asked about sharing a root. Annie, I hope you don't think it presumptuous (it is, I know!), but I don't think trilliums would be right for your yard. They are individual plants and need a lot of ground to show their glory. In fact, one landscaping book suggests a gardener needs a quarter-acre to create a woodland setting. I am so grateful to have a full acre.

Suffice to say, Biz is not allowed on the hill where the trilliums live – at least in the spring. Let's plan for you to visit next spring – maybe we'll top twenty trilliums. I can hope!

The enclosed ceramic sundial is for your stalwart Brian. We picked up the cherubic disk at a garage sale. Tell him it will soon be time for gin and tonics and barbecues on the patio!

Elizabeth

Patience and Compassion

"To everything there is a season, and a time to every purpose under the heaven," says the preacher in the Book of Ecclesiastes (Ecclesiastes 3:1, KJB). That means being able to wait, to contain oneself long enough to know the right time and place for all things to unfold as they should – and to be able to understand what is taking place. Elsewhere, especially in the New Testament, references repeatedly describe a beneficent God or Christ, the epitome of undying patience and love.

And so we struggle to meet those lofty ideals. A New England gardener who works with an ever-changing woodland garden ruefully admits that despite time and considerable effort, she may not always know better or have the final say. "For more than 30 years, I've been editing a woodland in Zone 6A of New England, between granite ledges left behind by the last trans-Atlantic collision of tectonic plates," writes Susan Dumaine in an essay in the Brooklyn Botanic Garden booklet *Woodland Gardens: Shade Gets Chic*. "Over the years, nature has not entirely respected my philosophy, and remains the senior editor."

Renowned Canadian garden writer and horticulturist Marjorie Harris also discusses the garden's role as teacher in her book *The Healing Garden*. "Handling plants brings a person back into touch with the changing cycles of life and death. It also adds another dimension to time – patience – in waiting for a blossom to open up or a shoot to appear from a seed."

Solace

Garden proverbs advise us to "plant patience" or "let patience grow in your garden." But never assume that it's easy! One writer huffily declared in a *Reader's Digest* issue that "nature thrives on patience; man on impatience." And an English naturalist of the seventeenth century noted that patience is a flower not everyone can grow. Wrote U.S. journalist Ambrose Bierce at the turn of the century, "Patience, n. A minor form of despair, disguised as a virtue."

The new parent learns very quickly what patience is all about – there's no reasoning with an infant to postpone crying until later. People who do creative work also acquire this trait as they labour, often repeatedly, to get precisely the effect they want, to convey just the right message.

The French realist painter Edgar Dégas remained doggedly true to his vision between 1879 and 1881, when he cast in wax a work that would earn him considerable scorn and disapproval. Though the sculpture *The Little Fourteen-Year-Old Dancer* was so lifelike and stirring that it could not be ignored or forgotten, critics railed against the work when it was first unveiled. It wasn't pretty enough by the standards of the day; the young dancer should have been beautiful, perhaps ephemeral, even noble. But under Dégas's hands she emerged after close to three years of work as thin, sullen and perhaps pouting. She was unlovely – but she made crystal clear the painter's feelings about lines of the body, honest depiction of emotion, and the need for true, natural expression in art. She was presented in realistic, flesh-coloured wax and wearing a puppet's wig, with real fabric ribbons, stockings, ballet shoes, bodice and crinolined skirt. At close to life size, she sent shock waves through the art world. People loved or hated her, but many were soon clamouring for the work to be cast in bronze and copied so that they might possess her. Until his death in 1917, Dégas presided carefully over the plans that would see the sculpture cast in bronze for posterity.

Perhaps Degas had all too accurately reflected the mood and expression of his model. Just think how patient she had been, first in achieving enough success as a ballet dancer to be a student at the Paris Opéra, and then in sitting often as an artist's model. She was proud, yes, but also probably supremely bored.

Dictionaries have many illuminating descriptions of patience that can help us in our quest. Patience is anything requiring long, hard work or steady effort – but it's also the ability to accept those conditions. It means stepping back to look at the big picture and deciding that the end result will be worth it. Years of devotion and effort will pay off when the child becomes a fine, strong, lovable personality of his or her own. A personal sense of nurturing and accomplishment will be replenished every time a plant reaches healthy, glowing maturity in the garden. Peace of mind and spirit will be attained when we can overcome petty irritations and jealousies and learn to love ourselves and each other for all our foibles and differences.

"Patience suggests calmness and self-control in enduring suffering or trouble, in waiting, or in doing something requiring steady effort," one definition states. There are different levels of patience, too. There is forbearance, where self-denial or self-control in the face of temptation is exercised, and fortitude, where inner strength and courage are called upon to meet some danger or enduring hardship with calm ability.

Coupled with patience in our quest for spiritual enlightenment is compassion, our ability to reach out and feel what others feel. An elementary school classroom poster about compassion explains it this way: "I held my brother's hand when he was scared." And then there's the comforting simplicity of that wise old 1934 prayer, "The Serenity Prayer" by Reinhold Neibuhr: "God, give us grace to accept with serenity the things that cannot be changed, courage to change the things which should be changed, and the wisdom to distinguish the one from the other."

In a very quiet way, the garden is a living example of compassion. A garden doesn't know or judge the character of the hands that loosen the soil, hold the watering can or sprinkle the fertilizer – they could be any hands. Instead, the garden reaches out and rewards, without stopping to assess the worthiness of the gardener. It simply shares itself with the gardener. "If I can stop one heart from breaking, / I shall not live in vain; / If I can ease one life the aching, / Or cool one pain, / Or help one fainting robin / Unto his nest again, / I shall not live in vain," mused Emily Dickinson.

Sharing seems to be the very essence of compassion, a word that comes from two Latin ones meaning "with" and "suffer." It is much more than pity, or tenderness, or consolation, although all those may be part of compassion. The word can also mean "feeling." As Milan Kundera wrote, "to have compassion (co-feeling) means not only to be able to live with the other's misfortune but also to feel with him any emotion – joy, anxiety, happiness, pain."

The Lotus Scripture, written around 250 A.D., has been described as the most important scripture of East Asia. Used in most Buddhist schools, it has been a tremendous source of inspiration for much art and literature – it speaks of universal compassion. "So long as a person has the slightest devotion or faith, the Buddha's great compassion, personified in the *bodhisattva*, will deliver him from suffering," note the authors of *The Great Asian Religions*. The *bodhisattva* is one who has attained enlightenment but has stayed in this world to help others. "Among the most adored of all *bodhisattvas* is Kuan-yin.... He is the most complete embodiment of the Buddha's mercy and compassion. He has four, eight, eighteen, or a thousand hands, to save beings, in all possible ways with all possible weapons and under all possible circumstances."

Reaching out to share with others inspired Jean Vanier, the son of a former governor general of Canada, to pen this poetic expression of compassion: "compassion / is a meaningful word... / sharing the same passion / the same suffering / the same agony / accepting in my heart / the misery in yours, o, my brother / and you, accepting me." In 1964 Vanier founded a village for mentally challenged adults near Paris, France. He then established similar centres in countries worldwide, sharing his life and the love that he called a "deeper compassion."

Mother Teresa was compassion incarnate, not only for India's poor but for people from Tanzania to Tirana and from Russia to Rome. Hers was an active compassion, not simply an act of compassion. "Love in action is service," she said. "Try to give unconditionally whatever a person needs in the moment. The point is to do something, however small, and show you care through your actions by giving your time."

At her vows in 1931, Mother Teresa took the name of St. Theresa of Lisieux, who was known as the Little Flower of Jesus. Theresa was a French Carmelite sister who lived in the latter part of the nineteenth century. She felt called into prayer for missionaries; due to illness, she was unable to become a missionary herself. But she also taught "the ways of a healthy spirituality which was simple, full of generosity and sacrificial spirit." Another model for Mother Teresa's compassion was the twelfth-century St. Francis of Assisi. Although born into the family of a wealthy Italian merchant, Francis renounced all material property, choosing instead to dedicate his life to caring for the poor and the sick. Mother Teresa wrote that her Missionaries of Charity pray this prayer of supplication, attributed to St. Francis, daily: "Lord, make me a channel of Thy peace, that where there is hatred, I may bring love." St. Francis was canonized in 1228, and in 1980 he was designated the patron saint of ecology.

This deeper compassion, this love, that the outstretched arms of Buddha and the lives of Vanier and Mother Teresa personify, is a hands-on compassion. "Charity and love are the same...don't just give money but reach out your hand instead," Mother Teresa wrote. She recalled visiting homeless people on the streets of London, England: "One man, who was living in a cardboard box, held my hand and said, 'It's been a long time since I felt the warmth of a human hand.'"

That touch of our hands, or that compassion in our hearts, is what we can share in our personal lives. The surgeon who holds the hand of a patient before an operation offers a comfort no chemical sedative can match. The friend who on a miserable, stormy night creates a Chinese food dinner in the hospital lounge, complete with china and chopsticks, reassures one that she is not forgotten. The neighbours who walk, feed and play with a lonely pet lend many a helping hand.

Solace

Canadian singer-songwriter Garnet Rogers consoles most eloquently in "Seeds of Hope": "Take my hand and we will walk together / Take my hand you will not walk alone / Take my hand, this night won't last forever / We'll harvest seeds of hope we've sown."

* * *

Dear Elizabeth:

Today I feel like the tattered birches strewn around here, all sharp points and jagged edges. I've been biting people's heads off and avoiding human contact whenever possible. All I really want is to be left alone, to work off this random fury in the friendly solitude of my garden – probably in the vegetable patch, where I can dig deepest.

Don't ask what's wrong, because I don't know. Maybe I'm panicked by too many deadlines littering those crowded squares on the kitchen calendar (and carefully duplicated in my daybook). Or maybe I feel bereft, having no one to gossip and share things with after your departure last week. It was such a grand visit, wasn't it? In any case, writing it out like this helps – and it's a huge relief to know I don't have to be bright and cheery with you. I can whine and complain, even risk bringing you down with all my angst and carping, and you'll still love and support me. You're right about the writing, too; it's how I express myself. I can no more turn my back on it than I can ignore the people and events that have coloured and shaped my life up to now. Instead, I have to learn to integrate all these diverse parts of myself.

And so to the birches. Birch trees are usually considered graceful and elegant, but there's nothing elegant about the pitiful specimens that remain after last winter's monster ice storm that ripped through much of southeastern Ontario, western Quebec and northern New England. Birches were among the trees worst hit; remember all the ragged, matchstick ends of trunks along the airport parkway? It has been a heartbreaking spectacle for tree-lovers, and many others, too. At least the splintered and sawn-off ends aren't "bleeding" sap now, as they were in the spring, and leaf cover has hidden some of the wounds from sight. Let's pray for speedy and sure new growth!

I wonder if anyone will want to plant birches again, after seeing all that destruction? Granted, that storm was a freak of nature, but the lasting impression is of weakness and waste. When it takes so long from planting to full enjoyment of a sizable tree, who's going to want to invest the time in such a shaky performer? Actually, birches are short-lived among trees at the best of times, averaging only fifty years. But think of the soft shade, the clear gold fall leaves and the sheer, swooping beauty they manage in that time!

Forgive the audaciousness of this next bit, Liz, but I think a birch tree could be the memorial you've been seeking to mark your sister's sadly abbreviated life. Hear me out, please, while I explore some reasons. First, the obvious: despite relatively short life spans, both have had much to offer and have enriched many lives. I know only what little you've told me about Karen, but I'm sure she left quite a legacy. There are her children, the many memories of her humour, her rich relationships with her husband and others. And I've already noted some of the main birch attributes.

It seems to me there's another strong parallel. For all its beauty and strength – and despite its reputation in folklore as a charm against evil – the birch wasn't a strong enough species to bear the weight of all that ice. And in spite of her determination and her faith, Karen ultimately couldn't survive the cancer. But she was here and much loved, and she is remembered. And you carry on, contributing to the pool of medical knowledge that the two of you shared.

There doesn't seem to be much biblical lore about the birch tree, probably because it's a plant of the cooler northern hemispheres. But birch stands for meekness, and the meek shall inherit the earth, right? The Old Irish tree alphabet lists it as symbolic of the start of a new year, and the "besom broom" made of birch twigs was once considered a sure way to drive a witch from the house in Merry Old England. In fact, birch rods have long been used in beatings – to punish bad behaviour, to drive out demons, or to scourge and cleanse the body in a steam bath. There's even a verb "to birch," meaning to flog.

Did you know that oil of wintergreen comes from the stems and bark of some species? Some old medicinal references suggest using birch decoctions for relief of headaches, rheumatism, gas, kidney stones, fevers and abdominal cramps; roasting the cone-like fruits of one type was said to make a smoke that would clear up nasal infections when inhaled. Of course, everyone knows about the peeling white bark of the paper birch, *Betula papyrifera*, also known as canoe or white birch, and its extensive use in canoe-making.

There are several birch species growing in North America and tons of cultivars, and it's hard to choose or distinguish between many of them. So here's my proposal: use the enclosed nursery gift certificate towards Karen's memorial, whatever you decide it should be. But first give some thought to a birch tree. Your property doesn't have any, I know, and I think a dwarf *Betula pendula gracilis* would be wonderful in a corner of your front lawn. Better known as cutleaf weeping birch, it would be right at home in your moist sandy soil, in a spot where there's partial sun. You certainly have room for one, as this type reaches only about fifteen to twenty feet and is no more than half as wide. The finely cut leaves look like miniature maple leaves and turn from summer's dark, glossy green to a lovely fall gold. Don't expect to plant perennials near it, though; the shallow roots are quite dense!

In this "land of the silver birch," can you think of a more fitting memorial? If I've convinced you, or even sparked a few fond memories, then I've done my good deed for today and can go fetch my spade in better humour than I started with!

Anxiously awaiting your reply,

Anne

Dear Annie:

Three things have led me to this missive's topic. First, I had coffee (I know, I know, but morning coffee is a must) on that almost-never-used back porch and watched the leaves of our rusty red oak shiver in the cool air. (I could see my breath!)

Then, while cleaning out our catch-all memorabilia cabinet, made of oak, I came across the two acorns I picked up on the last walk I took with my dad twenty years ago. I'd forgotten all about them but had tucked them safely away for another time – I guess today was that time. I had Quartette on the stereo, so I couldn't help but think of their singer-songwriter Colleen Peterson as I heard her singing. I remembered that she died from ovarian cancer just days before I was diagnosed. And I remembered the stillness in your voice when you called with the news of her death. The juxtaposition made me shiver.

Like a sudden wind on a whisper of a day, memories of an oak tree and Colleen caught my mind. Several filing boxes later I found the material you sent about a planned living memorial to this Canadian country-folk troubadour. It was an oak, *Quercus palustris* or pin oak. Guess what you're about to read? Yep, the inestimable oaks!

The pin oak was considered an ideal tree to withstand the test of time because it is flexible, has handsome, glossy, dark green leaves in summer and russet, bronze or red ones in fall, and adopts an overall pleasing conical shape. I notice that Colleen's tribute tree is planted in a park near a river – and close to your house, so we must visit it during my next trip. These oaks prefer moist, rich, well-drained soils.

Pin oaks, also called swamp oaks, and red oaks are easily transplanted because of shallow, fibrous root systems. Avoid the bur oak, *Quercus macrocarpa*, and the Chinquapin oak, *Quercus muehlenbergii*, as they're trouble to transplant. Annie, you'll be interested in this: the inner bark of the black oak, *Quercus velutina* (found in Southern Ontario) can be boiled to extract a yellow dye for most natural fibres.

The pin oak is also tolerant of windy city conditions. "Winds of time blew my innocence away. / Made a woman from a child as every season changed," Colleen and Nancy Simmonds wrote in "Just Like a Woman."

Park visitors in years to come can expect to see this memorial grow to between sixty and seventy feet, with a spread of twenty-five to forty feet. Some even top one hundred feet. Pin oak likely acquired its common name from the many small branchlets that stick out like pins or hang from the trunk or bigger branches. "Possibly the most attractive of all the oaks we can grow is the pin oak.... This has lower branches that weep back to the ground and a rounded crown," writes Trevor Cole.

Given that there are about eighty species of oak in North America, I'd say that's high praise for the pin oak! More than four hundred and fifty species can be found worldwide, and about ten are native to Canada. Oaks can be either deciduous or evergreen: generally, deciduous on the eastern side of North America and evergreen in the West. The oak is one of about ten members of the beech family.

Interestingly, the galls – growths caused by insects, fungi or bacteria – on the pin oak are used to make a black ink. The galls are steeped in a bit of water with iron filings added. Gives new meaning to the word "pinpoint" doesn't it, pen pal?

Oak is in demand – for furniture and flooring like mine – as the wood is hard, heavy and strong (in most species). I know you, Brian, Maggie and your gardens suffered in the aftermath of that ice storm that cut a swath through eastern Canada and United States. You, much better than I, can appreciate this attribute of the oaks: their branches are almost parallel to the ground, and as Trevor Cole reminds us, this makes for stronger trees. "They are worth considering when it comes time to replant," he says.

Although red oak, or *Quercus rubra*, is native to the shoreline of Lake Superior, mine looks suspiciously planted. The cedar hedge behind the oak gives it away – in its natural habitat, neighbours would likely be trembling aspen or the eastern white pine. My oak is about thirty feet tall and may be only half-grown.

This brings me to one of the myths about oaks: that they are slow-growers. While this is true of white oak, *Quercus alba*, which grows about a foot a year, the pin and red oaks shoot up quite smartly, averaging about two feet a year over a ten-year period. (The famous Wye oak, a white oak in Maryland, at four hundred years of age, is ninety-five feet tall and one hundred and sixty-five feet wide!)

Hundreds of types of insects call oaks "home," which attracts a variety of birds. Wood ducks, jays and pigeons (those scavengers!) also find the acorns tasty treats (more on edible acorns later).

The white oak keeps company in the forest with sugar maple, black cherry or eastern hemlock, as well as other oaks. Its remarkable wood can be crafted into ships or barrels to age fine wine and whiskey. The thick, spongy bark of the Mediterranean cork oak is used for – corks! Ah, Annie, to age in such agreeable surroundings! Red oak is lovely for decking, as I can attest from our old veranda. And Michael can attest to the need to pre-drill the heavy wood if you or Brian use it for any outdoor work.

The Garry oak, *Quercus garryana*, is the only oak native to British Columbia. I think of singer-songwriter John Prine's phrase "a crooked piece of time" when I look at this oak. The wood from this stubby, small, twisted tree was used for fence posts – guaranteed for twenty years, no less – and stirrups. "Limited commercial value" comes to mind.

But Annie, I think the value of the oak rests more in the lore and legend of its lineage than in any attached dollar figure. Ages and ages ago, it's been argued, Diana, the Roman goddess of fertility, had an oak as her sacred tree. Virbius, a bit player in the god/goddess hierarchy, has been associated with Diana and is "a local manifestation of Jupiter, god of the oak and the sky." (In Greek mythology, Artemis is Diana and Zeus is Jupiter.)

A primeval oak forest covered much of what we know as Europe, long before recorded history. These towering trunks, sometimes fourteen feet in diameter, no doubt inspired awe and fear in our very early ancestors as the oaks provided shelter and sustenance. Spanish mountaineers subsisted on acorn bread for much of the year. Raw or roasted, sweet or succulent, the acorns were considered luxury enough to be served as a second course in the mucky-muck circles of the day. Even the duchess in *Don Quixote* sent for acorns. And, of course, these fruits had healing properties. English oak, *Quercus robur*, was used to treat depression "in those who battle courageously," notes Sue Minter in *The Healing Garden.*

It's no surprise the oaks were incorporated into religion, as tree gods and goddesses took root. Mistletoe found growing on an oak certainly enhanced the tree's status as sacred in the lives of the Druids. This was the faith of the ancient inhabitants of the British Isles, from the second century B.C. and well into the second century A.D. They revered the oak: its groves were used for services and the leaves were part of all sacred rites. I guess it's also no surprise that when the Bible speaks of oaks it scolds God's people about tree worship. "You will know that I am [the LORD] when their corpses, cut to pieces, lie there among their idols, all around their altars, on every high hill, on every mountain top, under every spreading tree, under every leafy oak, in fact wherever they offer an appeasing fragrance to all their idols" (Ezekiel 6:13, JB). Tough words to fight well-rooted religious beliefs!

Supposedly, the golden bough that Aeneas had to find as a condition to visit his father in Hades was from an evergreen oak. Aeneas needed the bough to bury his comrade, Misenus, and then had to give it to Sibyl, prophetess of Apollo.

Even today the oak is part of some Canadian military funerals. The theme of life after death is echoed in the music of requiems. "The Slow March from Saul" is played as the cortège approaches the graveyard. Once the service is over and the escort party leaves the gravesite in quick march, the accompanying band breaks into a regimental march, or in the case of the navy, the uplifting "Heart of Oak," with the lines, "Come, cheer up, my lads, 'tis to glory we steer." In the United States military, an oak cluster sitting atop a medal ribbon means that the medal has been awarded again.

In one birthday book, oak represents hospitality. I think true hospitality offers a welcome of warm caring and concern for the traveller. I know that you represent that age-old tradition. Many patients have no family or friends when they must visit hospital clinics in far-off cities. I am grateful to have you, Brian and Maggie welcome me with such compassion (and patience in ferrying me around to the various appointments) into what has become my second home. To paraphrase the Tennessee Williams character Blanche Dubois in *A Streetcar Named Desire*, "I have always depended on the kindness of strangers" – and beloved friends.

So, Annie, I will close for now with one last note: may we age like fine old oaken barrels, well flavoured, well seasoned and well appreciated, not like old oakum, the ratty rope that's used to stuff cracked seams in ships! Take good care…

Elizabeth

P.S. The enclosed owl bookmarks are made of oak. Please tuck one into the book Maggie is reading now and keep one for yourself.

Dearest Liz:

I promise, I'll never give you lettuce! I've been reading reams about its history and significance, and it's one plant I'll definitely not be sending your way. It signifies coldness, you see, and I can't imagine ever feeling chilly towards you. So though I may serve you some of my best greens, fresh from the garden in a salad one day, you won't be getting the plant itself.

In fact, you are the very antithesis of lettuce, to my mind. Where it is cool and crisp, you (almost always) exude warmth and charm. I often think it's that compassionate interest in others that keeps you going through the rough spells. Where would we all be without you, our caring connecting link?

Of course, you can easily grow lettuce for yourself; it's such an easy cool-season annual that it's often recommended for kids' gardens (but I can't interest Maggie). And I suspect you could use a few more greens in your diet – woman does not live by coffee and toast alone! Some iceberg lettuce might work miracles on those hot flashes of yours, too.

Yes, I'll quit lecturing now. Actually, I'm taking a break from garden rearranging to enjoy an iced tea on the patio, where I can admire the ornamental artemisia-and-leaf lettuce combination I tried in two planters this year. It's been very different, fairly successful and quite captivating! I just have to keep the containers well watered, and be thankful our patio is in shade for half the day.

It's considered a sign of middle-class affluence to be able to buy and eat a generous array of lettuce-like greens, according to Canadian social researcher and commentator Margaret Visser. A look at the prices of fancier ones such as radicchio and arugula seem to confirm her opinion, but she says lettuce was once counted among the lowly potherbs, hardly worthy of mention. Lettuce has been in cultivation for at least two thousand years. It was believed to be one of the "bitter herbs" eaten at the inaugural Passover meal celebrated by the Jews in biblical Egypt. There are Greek myths associated with lettuce, too. The handsome young hunter Adonis apparently died after being gored by a boar in a lettuce bed where the goddess Aphrodite, his lover, had hidden him. In another related tale, the ferryman Phaon was made young and beautiful by Aphrodite (she got around, didn't she?) and went on to cuckold many men due to his irresistible charms, which he augmented with sweet perfumes. When Aphrodite hid him from the enraged husbands in a lettuce patch, he died among plants often considered herbs of impotency. Oh, the irony!

Lettuce's reputation as a quencher of sexual passion seems to be bolstered by its roots: the word comes from the Latin *lactuca*, meaning "milky." And lettuces, members of the daisy family, have a cloudy white sap that resembles milk. Nursing a newborn with breast milk is supposed to be a form of natural birth control; thus, fertility is at least temporarily thwarted. "The plant was often given in order to help a mother's milk come after giving birth," Visser wrote in *Much Depends on Dinner*, " [and] interestingly enough, the American prickly lettuce was called 'milk leaf' by the Meskwaki Indians and prescribed by them for the same purpose. The calming effect of lettuce latex may indeed have helped."

But there is also much folklore about the aphrodisiac powers of lettuce juice, *lactucarium*. In ancient Egypt, it was associated with semen and ritually grown and offered to the god Min.

Maybe the age-old use of lettuce as a calmant and sleep inducer would be of more interest to you right now. The sap of wild lettuce, *Lactuca virosa*, acts much like opium, and its sedative effect has been confirmed by modern chemists. Among the ills lettuce juice was said to cure were colic, insomnia, nervous disorders and seasickness. The dried leaves of one wild type are still used by herbalists to help control nervous coughs.

I've never had much luck with head lettuce, but one looseleaf type I really enjoy growing is called 'Red Sails', of the garden lettuce group *Lactuca sativa*. This is a fast and frilly little plant that matures in just forty-five days to loose, deeply cut, tongue-shaped leaves that are tipped with reddish-bronze. Ideal in salads, it's just as good to look at as it is to eat! You harvest the leaves young, because the colour fades with age and older leaves begin to taste bitter as the plant turns to seed production. Plant in spring or early fall to make the most of cooler temperatures. This is no run-of-the-mill selection; it was an All America winner in its class a few years back! Head lettuce and romaine types are great, too, but take longer – in the sixty- to eighty-day range – and I can't seem to keep the slugs out of them.

Lettuce seed is tiny, so you have to sprinkle it on top of the soil with abandon and then wait. When leaf lettuce seedlings are a few inches high, you thin them to six inches apart. The seeds need light to germinate, so they shouldn't be covered. Started plants can be sown one-quarter inch deeper and will get going sooner, but seed is much cheaper, so why not use it and save the "lettuce"? (Sorry, I couldn't resist.) Any rich, moist and well-drained soil is fine, but container-grown lettuce needs regular fertilizing and extra care to ensure soil doesn't dry out. Lettuce is, after all, about ninety-five per cent water – and that's why salad dressing wilts it so quickly. Water in each plant cell keeps the leaf erect, and vinegar or lemon juice mixed with oil destroys the cell's ability to retain water. The depth of planting container is important, too; six inches is a minimum. Lettuce likes sun, but some shade during the hottest part of the growing season helps.

Several grubs and flying pests like lettuce, so it's worth keeping a good pesticide handy – or interplanting with insect-repelling, daisy-like flower *pyrethrum* (*Tanacetum coccineum*) and onions, as I do. By the same token, head lettuce is said to discourage the flea beetle that attacks radishes.

Solace

Well, I've strayed far enough into the lettuce fields. Back to work, but I'll close with a kind of bedtime blessing – and hope you eat your lettuce tonight and sleep well after. A verse from Dave Mallet's "Garden Song" promises: "Plant your rows straight and long / Temper them with prayer and song / Mother Earth will make you strong if you give her love and care." And "lettuce" look forward to our next crop of letters!

Anne

Dear Annie:

So, old chum, what's "turniped" in your life lately? I'm into vegetable talk with this letter, as you can guess! The brook has dried up, the sun is weaker and the smell of fall is in the air. Twin treats today are that I'm not wearing a coat and my sedum tops are in full, purply bloom.

(As I write this, my mind and nose are distracted by the intoxicating smell and sound of the coffeemaker struggling to fill my cup. Will it ever finish? Indulge me as I attempt to divert my attention and ruminate about rutabagas for a while!)

I was rooting around for an edible vegetable yesterday and unearthed a few wrinkled carrots, a couple of pinched parsnips, a shrivelled lime and that trusted old standby – the turnip.

Though I buy these hardy root vegetables with every good intention, it's such an effort to get beyond their thick skins that they often wither away in the basement of my fridge, in that kitchen oxymoron – the crisper. But I'd captured this turnip in time! My hands can't peel anymore but I watched as Pearl's hands patiently pared away the layers of wax, like the curlicues from apple skins. (You haven't met Pearl yet; she's my new home support worker.) I know you turn up your nose at turnip, but I like it baked with a bit of brown sugar and a dribble of maple syrup – a comfort food. Pearl prefers hers with drizzles of honey – another sweet treat.

What we call a turnip is likely its culinary cousin, the rutabaga – thought to be a cross between a cabbage and a turnip. Hang onto your hat – "rutabaga" literally means "root bag" in Swedish! Can't you just hear the backyard vegetable bullies? "Hey, you cabbage-head! Your mother was a root bag!" Tell Maggie that one – she might get some schoolyard mileage out of it!

But there's more: turnips, *Brassica rapa*, and rutabagas, *Brassica napus*, are both biennial herbs that belong to the *Cruciferae*, or mustard, family. It's no wonder you don't like the smell – that family is known for its strong, pungent odours! Mustard family plants have flowers with four petals that form a rounded Maltese cross.

Some types of mustard seeds have been valued since ancient Greek civilization for their medicinal uses and spicy flavourings. Mustard plasters were my mom's favourite remedy for the colds and pneumonia I contracted. When black mustard seeds are mixed with water, they form an essential oil that helps open the lungs for easier breathing. The concoction was wrapped in soft cloths and left on my chest or back until the skin got hot – several long minutes. I hated those plasters because of the smell, but I'd trade five years of my life to feel Mom's hands comforting me again. Enough of mustard – I don't think Mom used any turnip in those plasters!

Both turnips and rutabagas are cool-season vegetables that need to be planted either very early or very late in the growing season. Most turnip roots are white-fleshed and smaller than the yellow-fleshed, larger rutabaga. The rutabaga's Nordic heritage lends its name to a popular variety, the 'White Swede'. 'Purple Top' and 'Just Right' are turnips on the top-ten list.

Turnips and rutabagas should be planted about three quarters of an inch deep, in rows that are a good nine inches apart. You'll have to keep an eye on them after sowing – and I just know you'll try them. Once the tops are growing, thin them to about six inches apart. That way you'll get a decent-sized edible root, but do keep the tops for tasty salad treats. Maybe you could interest Maggie in a rutabaga garden if you tell her the products are for show-and-tell. Who knows what works with kids sometimes? Just don't be so fussy about cooking them, Annie!

You can harvest early turnips after about five weeks, regular turnips from six to ten weeks, while rutabagas take up to twenty-six weeks. The hardy root bags can be left in the ground until after the first frost, but turnips need to be lifted on time to ensure they don't become woody – or else I'd agree with you that the taste becomes a touch too wild. Although turnips and rutabagas are native to the temperate areas of Europe and Asia, the turnip was popular in the gardens of settlers living at Hudson's Bay Company posts by the 1760s. "Perhaps the turnips and the cabbages lessened the incidence of scurvy," notes a company journal entry mentioned in E.E. Rich's *Hudson Bay Company 1670–1870, Vol. 1.*

Turnips also turn up in nineteenth-century literature with Mr. Barkis, that quirky character in Dickens's *David Copperfield*, who used the vegetable as a testimonial. "It was as true …as turnips is. It was as true…as taxes is. And nothing's truer than them." One birthday book says turnip is a symbol of charity – and I like that in the "kindness" sense of the word, meaning loving your fellow human being and not being too quick to judge. That's something I know I must work on, but I'm lucky to know quite a few kind and true "turnip" people.

That brings me to Karen and the phrase she used the day we sat in my neurologist's office, awaiting his diagnosis of her symptoms that were so frighteningly like my MS. "I didn't just fall off the turnip wagon yesterday, you know," she told him. We held hands as he confirmed that we were indeed MS sisters. Little did we know that a decade later we would become cancer sisters, too. As Gilda Radner (who died of ovarian cancer) quipped, "It's always something!"

Annie, take it from me – you never know what's going to "turnip," and as one old garden proverb says, "There's no getting blood out of a turnip."

Elizabeth

Remembrance

I n a small town in eastern Holland, elementary school children care for little flower plots tucked around the 1,355 graves in a Second World War cemetery. And every May 4 – the Dutch remembrance day – the children place bouquets of lilies-of-the-valley and red poppies, wrapped in ribbons of red, white and blue, in front of the gravestones. Those buried were eighteen, nineteen, maybe twenty-two – at most a dozen years older than the young gardeners. This act of remembrance is helping students learn about the cost of war and the price of peace. By tidying the gardens, the children are taking care not to forget – one dictionary definition of remembrance. Holland's memorial day is observed a day before the festive liberation day because "We must remember before we can celebrate," says one teacher.

Old soldiers know the bittersweet taste of remembrance. A bagpiper plays the haunting, familiar chords of "Amazing Grace." Veterans defy their age to stand and honour fallen friends. "They shall grow not old, as we that are left grow old: / Age shall not weary them, nor the years condemn, / At the going down of the sun and in the morning / We will remember them," wrote the nineteenth-century English poet Laurence Binyon. This epitaph, from the poem "For the Fallen," is inscribed on memorials throughout the British Commonwealth.

Veterans don't talk of some ill-gotten glory of war. They talk of the thumpety-thumps of nighttime barrages, the stinking cold of sodden clothes, the utter exhaustion, and the fear of what lay in the hours ahead. "From little towns in a far land we came / To save our honour and a world aflame / By little towns in a far land we sleep / And trust those things we won to you to keep," penned Rudyard Kipling for a First World War memorial in Sault Ste. Marie, Ontario. (This civic war memorial is believed to be the only one in Canada to carry an inscription by Rudyard Kipling. In 1924, Kipling replied to a letter to the local daily newspaper that called for a fitting epitaph, according to *The Sault Star*, Jan. 20, 1997.)

We can never, ever forget the evil of Hitler; nor should we ever forget the tremendous compassion of Mother Teresa. Both examples must be impressed into our archives of memory. "Ours is now a common destiny and that is something we must not forget...my words will have to be so many hammer-strokes with which to beat out the story of our fate and of a piece of history as it is and never was before," Etty Hillesum wrote in her diary in 1942. Etty, a Dutch Jewish student, was deported to the Auschwitz concentration camp in September 1943. She died there at age twenty-nine.

Emotional aches and pains seem to sweep into our hearts when remembrance is linked with melancholy longings. A scent, sight or sound easily takes us elsewhere. "Music, when soft voices die, / Vibrates in the memory; / Odours, when sweet violets sicken, / Live within the sense they quicken," wrote Percy Bysshe Shelley.

Some memories of loved ones, relationships, places or even pets need to be stashed away until there's strength to remember, then slowly measured out in small portions. Perhaps remembering things in this piecemeal fashion is our way of managing what our souls can bear.

A romantic love is often recalled as having a sweet charm. Remember this *Casablanca* treasure: "You must remember this, a kiss is still a kiss, / A sigh is just a sigh; / The fundamental things apply, / As time goes by."

Remembering faraway friends in thought or prayer is one way we express warm wishes. "And always I remember you in my prayers; I remember your tears and long to see you again to complete my happiness," writes the biblical author of a letter to Timothy (2 Timothy 1:3, JB).

Dreams can bring delightful gifts of memory. A man with paralyzed legs almost feels the cold splashes of water as he dreams of waterskiing; a blind woman dreams of a vase of springtime tulips and daffodils sparkling in the sunlight. These are dreams to wish for! "The days may come, the days may go, / But still the hands of memory weave / The blissful dreams of long ago," observed George Cooper in 1877.

Mothers' voices seem clear and present, even in retrospect: "Always wear clean underwear. Don't do that. It's going to be okay. I love you more." Our fond recollections can make us smile, feel loved or make our lives seem of value – and they can ease pain, if only for a moment. In fact, a 1982 study indicated that when people remembered times when someone had taken care of them, their immune systems were actually strengthened, Dr. Bernie Siegel says in *Love, Medicine and Miracles*.

Remembering is also a step along the road to forgiving, recovering and moving forward. It fosters strength and the spiritual healing that leads to a lasting peace. My mom, Evelyn, remembered this song lyric that expresses that thought in a different way: "Memories that bless and burn, I count them over one by one."

Memories are like gold and silver threads woven into the stuff of which we are made. The gold glistens with the times of sunshine yellows, while the silver softens to pewter some of the darker days. As Irish poet W.B. Yeats wrote, "The things a man has heard and seen are threads of life, and if he pulls them carefully from the confused distaff of memory, any who will can weave them into whatever garment of belief pleases them best."

* * *

Dear Anne:
Every so often I pop open an art book or dictionary and find forgotten flowers I had pressed. You know how I like to make

Christmas gift sets of pressed-flower notepaper. Last week I flipped through all the obvious heavy books, rounding up any stragglers to finish this year's job. Or so I thought.

Then, yesterday morning I was hunting for an old university text when I came across a dear little book, *An English Cottage Year*. I didn't recognize it. As I opened the cover, one perfectly pressed blue forget-me-not fluttered out. The inscription said the book was a birthday gift from Karen four years ago. I have no idea who pressed the forget-me-not. I felt sick, really heartsick. I don't remember Karen giving it to me. How can that be? Did I even thank her? I felt so tired, maybe so old, that I had to sit and almost catch my breath. "There was a pause – just long enough for an angel to pass, flying slowly," as Ronald Firbank noticed in *A Host of Angels*.

Karen and I were so different – even in our looks, as I'm the taller, freckled redhead and she was so dark and petite. No one believed we were sisters, yet that sibling connection was there. "Asked to relate the same story from your childhood, you and your siblings would probably sound like characters from the Japanese play *Rashomon*, in which eyewitnesses to a crime give wildly differing accounts," says the *Women's Encyclopedia of Health and Emotional Healing*. That was us.

I wanted to talk to Mom – but in a nanosecond remembered I couldn't. Part of me wishes these unexpected "heart surprises" would just stop. No more. Nada. But what would I do if they did?

The house felt too cramped for my raw confusion. I didn't want to sit near the garden – it looked too tidy for my topsy-turvy feelings. So Biz and I, and the book, headed for the creek, where dozens of late forget-me-nots still cover the bank. The light shade and moist soil there definitely help them bloom from spring through early autumn. The wind kept me company as I had a good cry. Karen's flower was pressed between two pages of familiar garden verses, including this one by William Blake that I'd meant to send ages ago when I wrote of the bleeding heart. Now it fits the tiny forget-me-not: "To create a little flower is the labor of ages." From whence this amazing synchronicity?

For such a midget, the forget-me-not carries a heavy weight in its name, as Laura C. Martin writes in *Wildflower Folklore*. German lore tells of a man who took gold and silver treasures from a cave but left behind the little blue flowers he found there. And this was after he was warned, "Forget not the best." Are you surprised to read that the man met an untimely death? I wonder if men ever read these folk tales.

"Still another story…is that when God was naming all the plants, the little blue flower with the yellow eye could not remember the name given to it. Finally God whispered to it, 'Forget me not, that is your name,'" recounts Martin.

Forget-me-nots are herbs that belong to the borage family. My blue creek forget-me-nots are likely *Myosotis sylvatica*. However, various small, blue spring flowers – annual, biennial or perennial – are sold as forget-me-nots, explains *The Reluctant Gardener*. *Myosotis* means "mouse's ear" in Greek and refers to the shape of the plant's leaf.

Given the profusion of these hardy self-seeders, I imagine some formal gardeners rue the season forget-me-nots take root. "Once you have flowered forget-me-nots, you will have them forever," writes Trevor Cole.

They barely top eight inches in my yard, but some varieties can stretch two feet tall. Forget-me-nots don't spread much more than six inches, but the plants grow so tightly together they look like one contiguous plant. "Groundcover plants take life easy by sprawling around on their bellies," writes Marianne Binetti in *Tips for Carefree Landscapes*. Michael wants to transplant some from the creek to the hill near the brook next spring. I know what he's up to – trying to avoid mowing the hill by planting more wildflowers. But Binetti has a reminder: "The lazy gardener needs to understand right now that groundcover plants cannot be planted and then ignored…. they need to be watered, weeded, and pampered along." It benefits from a haircut between flowerings, too, as it gets very scraggly looking in midsummer.

Although native to Europe and Asia, the forget-me-not covers the North American continent from coast to coast. It is also the

Alaskan state flower. On Canada's east coast, Newfoundlanders often pin sprays to their lapels to remember the First Newfoundland Regiment's sacrifice at Beaumont-Hamel during the First World War. More than seven hundred regimental soldiers were killed or injured during one morning battle, leaving fewer than seventy by day's end. "It has been said...Canada came of age during the Great War. However, the life of Newfoundland was nearly extinguished. Almost a generation of its potential leaders was lost at Beaumont-Hamel and in subsequent actions," says one account. After Beaumont-Hamel, King George V granted the honorific "Royal" to the regiment – now the Royal Newfoundland Regiment – in recognition of its tremendous sacrifices.

You must have read *The Secret Garden*, by Frances Hodgson Burnett. The famous author of *Little Lord Fauntleroy* had rented a manor house in the English countryside in 1898 to escape the outcry after her divorce and relationship with a younger man. Over the years she would retreat there for the quiet of her gardens. In fact, she created a garden with more than three hundred coral-pink roses. In 1911, a few years after she returned to the United States, *The Secret Garden* was published, with its setting an English country manor. Is this art imitating life? Remember near the end of the book when Colin's distant father, Archibald Craven, recognized how he'd allowed grief to keep him from living and loving his son? "[H]e had let his soul fill itself with blackness and had refused obstinately to allow any rift of light to pierce through. He had forgotten and deserted his home." The father sat beside a creek and "his eyes began to see things growing at its edge. There was one lovely mass of blue forget-me-nots growing so close to the stream...at these he found himself looking as he remembered."

Now I'll always think of the small blue forget-me-nots as Karen's. With that I'll close – thank you again, dear friend, for listening. Enclosed is a photocopy of the pressed flower I found. I hope it helps you remember something your heart has foolishly forgotten.

Elizabeth

Dear Liz:

I'm a couple of letters behind after my trip to the East Coast, I know, but I've just been rereading your last few – and I think you've been smoking too many turnip greens! Time to come in out of the sun, dear. Really, parts of your "rooty ruminations" had me snickering in foolish delight as I perched on the porch. Just the pick-me-up I needed after a gruelling morning of back-to-school projects and freelance assignments – all due later this week.

I love getting your faxes and letters; I rip them off the fax or snatch them from the mailbox and dart off to enjoy them in peace, or squirrel them away until a quieter moment presents itself. They're all so interesting that they get my complete attention – and you have a knack for pulling me out of myself long enough to get a grip on reality again. A letter from you always clears my head and adjusts my perspective. Does it work that way for you, I wonder?

Now to the contents of this package. The courier certainly sniffed warily; was Bizzie interested in it too? By now you know it's a scent-filled pillow that is said to ensure sweet dreams. Here's the recipe, from *Secrets of the Garden* by Emilie Barnes.

Dream Pillows
1/2 cup hops – to encourage sleep
1/8 cup lavender blooms – to make dreams pleasant
1/8 cup rosemary leaves – to help you remember dreams
1/8 cup thyme – to prevent nightmares
2 tbsp. mugwort leaves – to instill dreams
1/8 cup rose petals – for dreams of love

Carefully dry all ingredients, then blend and sew into small muslin pillows. Tuck under pillow at night. When given as a gift, include a card of explanation.

I'll bet you've guessed that my plant-of-the-week is one of the above! It's lavender, so aptly described by Shakespeare and our writing "friend" Louise Beebe Wilder as a "nose herb." Truly, lavender's evocative scent makes it memorable. So many people think of it nostalgically, and have happy memories associated with it. Mine is of a rare daylong bus trip to Toronto with my dad to visit the Canadian National Exhibition. I was probably no more than seven or eight, yet I recall basking in Dad's company and full attention for the whole thrilling day. There was so much to see and do and taste! (Yep, I adored the food building.) Near the end of the day, we stopped at a splendiferous souvenir stand where I picked out a lavender sachet for my mom. It was so small and delicate, and I was enthralled by the hinged wicker container that held the precious present. It had bands of pink, mauve and blue around the middle and a silky mauve tassel hanging from one end. I'm not sure whether I really chose it for her or for me.

Lavender gets a bad rap from the birthday books, I'm afraid. They say it is a symbol of mistrust because the asp was believed to have nested in lavender bushes. But in our climate, where only the most hardy varieties of the plant survive as perennials, I hardly think that's a concern! For me, lavender speaks of remembrance – though not the kind you might think. Like the old, loved children's song "Lavender's Blue," I like to think we were given this soulful plant to remind us to remain children at heart. The song's lyrics don't say much, but there's a simple charm and naïveté there that I sometimes ache for us all to rediscover. "Lavender's blue, dilly dilly, lavender's green / When I am king, dilly dilly, you shall be queen / Who told you so, dilly dilly, who told you so? /'Twas my own heart, dilly dilly, that told me so."

A children's poet you may not be familiar with, the late Shel Silverstein, knew well how to keep the wonder of childhood alive in our souls. In his poem "Put Something In," he advises us to draw silly pictures, write inane poetry, dance, act like a kid and otherwise lighten up. His goofy poems and zany illustrations never fail to put a smile on my face and inspire a frivolous thought or two.

I have Maggie to thank for my exposure to all this, of course, just as you have Biz and Michael's kids for many of the crazier moments in your life.

Lavender is a bushy shrub. Its long, slim, grey-green leaves grow in circular groups or opposite pairs along square stems. The leaves are softly furred, but the pleasing scent comes from small, tubular violet-blue flowers that appear in clusters around six- to eight-inch spikes. Plants range from about eight inches to almost three feet.

There are more than twenty-five types of lavender, originating mainly in England and the Mediterranean. The English like to claim that they have the one and only best type for fragrance, but in fact several species can be considered English lavender. The one usually identified is *Lavandula angustifolia*, but there is a French species, *Lavandula stoechas*, that is finely scented and widely distributed on hillsides throughout France, Spain and Portugal.

My luck with lavender has run the gamut from miserable to glorious. This year's pailful of the compact 'Munstead' cultivar (*Lavandula angustifolia* 'Munstead') was the best yet, so that's the kind I'll tell you about.

Lavender craves full sun and good drainage, so my metal pail with its bottom layer of small stones works well. I can't overwinter the plant this way, though. Instead, I'm taking a few cuttings from the foot-high, woody mound to plant in my sunniest border spot. There they will be tucked under thick mulch or some evergreen boughs to ensure winter survival. After flowering, mature plants should be cut back to about half the year's growth to keep them vigorous.

I've been harvesting many of the beautiful purple-blue flower stalks as they reach their peak. That's when the scent is strongest, and best for drying to use in dried flower bouquets, pillows and potpourris or as long wands that can be hung in closets to fight moths and give clothes or linens a memorable fragrance.

Lavandula comes from Latin, meaning "to wash" – and that's a good clue to one popular use for this plant. The oil from its flowers is distilled to scent bath soaps and oils, as well as perfumes. It was also used in massaging oils in the past, when rubbing the oil into the temples was believed to alleviate tension headaches and depression. Medicinally, infusing the flowers for compresses was used to relieve chest congestion, and the Chinese have lavender in a cure-all called white flower oil. (Wouldn't we like some of that?)

Lavender's soothing properties make it ideal for calming teas, and it's a common ingredient in facial treatments. It has even been used in embalming and for lion-taming! Various foods are improved by adding a dash of lavender, among them apple jelly, raspberry jam and various vinegars.

Native writer Loren Cruden says in *Medicine Grove: A Shamanic Herbal* that lavender is respected in birthing rooms as a "peace-bringer" and a "quiet guardian, but not a faltering one." She notes that lavender flowers can be hung in the doorway, or the delivery room can be washed with a lavender infusion before labour begins.

Here's a lovely closing thought from Patrick Lima, who puts spikes of what has been called the queen of herbs between important pages of reference books: "And in winter I am surprised by a sudden sweet scent of summer."

Anne

Hi Annie:

Happy, happy birthday! Here it is your week and I received a gift – thank you so much for the dream pillow! I don't know if it is the lavender or the hops, but falling asleep sure smells good. The antique linen is so pretty and soft. And yes, Biz had her nose in the air when your package arrived. I assume she caught your scent as much as the sweet ingredients.

This is a birthday care package for body and soul. You should find inside, and I hope intact, lemon bath salts; "unseasoned" gardening kneepads; evening primrose capsules (just to remind you of your age!); a new copy of *The Wind in the Willows* (I think Maggie will enjoy Toad); a CD gift certificate to pick something for your listening pleasure; a dozen Hazelnut Crumble Muffins (the courier promised this would arrive overnight); and two dozen narcissus bulbs for that spot you want to naturalize. (Lest I forget, Michael insisted on sending you the weighty bag of clover seed. Do with it what you will.)

Gardening expert Patricia Thorpe says in *Growing Pains: Time and Changes in the Garden* that the definition of naturalizing is pretty loose: "some catalogues urge us to throw bulbs across the lawn like a game of boccie." Although squirrels aren't likely to eat the narcissi, which are poisonous to them, they might dig them up for that game of boccie. Mine have. "[N]aturalizing generally means using plants outside beds and borders in an informal way, a way that we secretly hope will require no work," Thorpe adds. Oh, but it does! She suggests preparing the soil before planting by clearing weeds, rocks and grass – preferably in a lightly shaded area, such as under the trees on your side border.

Narcissi are such common, sunny harbingers of spring, but these bulbs are associated by name with a shadow of tragic Greek mythology. Narcissus, a son of the river god Cephius, was simply beautiful – and he knew it. Echo, a wood nymph, fell in love with him. But she couldn't tell him, because her voice could only mimic the last words she heard. After a disastrous encounter Narcissus spurned Echo's love. Soon after, Narcissus saw his reflection in a still pond and "was captivated by the…beauty that he saw," notes *Classical Mythology*.

This is a tale of unrequited love, as Narcissus couldn't cease his adoration of the image in the pond, nor could he touch it. Poor Echo could not stop loving Narcissus and she literally pined away, until all that was left was her voice. Narcissus languished by the water's edge with his "love" until dying, but there wasn't a corpse. "They found instead a yellow flower with a circle of white petals in its center," notes one mythology text. The myth is thought by some to warn against looking at one's own reflection. I think we should remember Echo and how she lost her life over a very self-absorbed man!

There's a biblical poem that may refer to the narcissus. The plant is native to the Mediterranean region and is thought to be one of three possibilities for the rose of Sharon. Crocus, tulip and narcissus are all contenders, as the translated Hebrew indicates a plant with a bulbous root. The prophet Isaiah trumpets the glory of God, saying, "Let the wilderness and the dry lands exult, / let the wasteland rejoice and bloom, / let it bring forth flowers like the jonquil, / let it rejoice and sing for joy" (Isaiah 35:1, JB).

I've read that the greatest concentration of narcissus is found around the Mediterranean, and that *Narcissus tazetta* grows profusely on the plain of Sharon. (Louise Beebe Wilder says this variety has a "somewhat too overpowering odor – the only narcissus scent I do not like.") *Narcissus tazetta* is found right across the continent to Japan, a testament of its charm and durability; it was carried from land to land centuries ago.

Narcissus is the species, although the terms narcissus, daffodil and jonquil have been used as common names of the eight thousand(!) varieties of this member of the amaryllis family. The common names seem pretty mixed up, but one book says narcissus, generally, have smaller clusters of flowers, while daffodils have larger blooms. However, the term "jonquil" should be used only when describing *Narcissus jonquilla*, which has rush-like leaves and clusters of fragrant flowers.

By and large, narcissus bulbs should be planted five to six inches deep and half a foot apart, in well-drained soil. These bulbs, like crocuses, are super for forcing. You can cram up to five bulbs in a seven-inch pot. You might want to force some of the 'King Alfred' I've sent. I remember with such gratitude the friend who sent me a pot stuffed with sprightly daffodils after my third cancer surgery. That pot sure brightened my dreary February hospital corner!

"Pebbles and water is the simplest medium for forcing bulbs," suggest the authors of *Growing Flowers*. I've not tried this technique, but it sounds simple – do let me know how it goes. Use at least a three-inch-deep pot, with one inch of charcoal in the bottom. Then add about one half inch of clean pebbles. Place the bulbs and fill around them with more pebbles. Add just enough water to reach the bottom of the bulbs. Oh, and if the pot has a drainage hole, be sure to plug it with a cork.

The jaunty daffodils that bob along to the tune of the wind in my early spring garden just pop up year after year. They have single, bright yellow blooms with inch-long trumpets and stand about a foot high. While many narcissi have these distinctive trumpets, others have cup-shaped blooms. Colours range from white, pink, yellow and gold to orange. What a riot the latter would be on a snowy March day! I tried to find a pot of the delicate paperwhites that so often appear around Easter, but I know they aren't hardy over the winter here. As to naming, forget it. "[W]e come to the narcissi; and here again we find ourselves in a confusion. I cannot here cope with the innumerable sorts," comments Vita Sackville-West.

With apologies to God for taking a verse out of context, I'll close with some advice from Isaiah we should remember during this planting season: "Strengthen all weary hands, / steady all trembling knees" (Isaiah 35:3, JB). Enjoy!

Elizabeth

Dear Elizabeth:
There's a raw wind today, so I've been rummaging in closets for cold-weather clothes. I got out my lined leather jacket, too, and found it still wore last year's poppy. I guess that means I don't need to get another one for this Remembrance Day, though I will. The money contributed goes to help old veterans remain comfortable in their twilight years, and that's such a noble cause that I usually pick up enough poppies for each coat in the household.

Maggie will be learning about the poppy at school this year, so I started doing some of my own research. We all know that the red poppy worn on November 11 signifies sadness at the losses and ravages of war; it's our way of saying, "We remember." But how many people know about the plant itself, or the origins of the remembrance association? I was fascinated by what I learned, and want to share some of it with you.

Although my dad was too young to have served in all but the tail end of the Second World War, I know your father did – and suffered war's effects long after its end.

Did you know it was the terrible bombing and devastation of the First World War that created the conditions that allowed the blood-red Flanders poppy to flourish? The plant, *Papaver commutatum*, likes gritty soil, and the tremendous wartime bombardments reduced so many buildings to rubble that massive quantities of the necessary lime and grit were pounded into the soil. Flanders poppies, native to much of Europe, North Africa and West Asia, quickly proliferated on the churned-up battlefields. Their presence seemed mute testimony to all that spilled blood, prompting Canadian soldier-physician John McCrae in 1915 to write his immortal poem, "In Flanders Fields."

Land, however, tends to return to its original state over time, and the Flanders poppies began to dwindle in number over the next decade. By 1937, one writer was calling on naturalists and concerned others to band together and add lime to Belgian soils to preserve what he termed "the greatest War Memorial the world has known." Eric Hardy pleaded in the November 1937 issue of veterans' magazine *The Legionary*, "Are we to see them vanish without an effort to preserve them from becoming no more than mere memory?" How tragic that the events of the next decade would bring terrible international conflict to those fields once again, giving rise to new generations of the beautiful remembrance flower.

There are red poppies growing in Flanders still; I was lucky enough to pluck one in person a few years ago. I pressed it carefully, and brought it home to tuck between the pages of a favourite book (but, of course, I forget which one). Like my stone from the beach at Dieppe, it is a history lesson I never want to forget.

Excuse the repetition if you know all this, Liz, but I like the fact that two women first put the poppy to work as an emblem of remembrance. American canteen worker Moira Michael started wearing a poppy in memory of fallen soldiers at the end of the First World War in New York City, and a visiting Frenchwoman named Madame Guérin learned of the custom in 1920. Returning home, Mme. Guérin began selling homemade poppies to help orphans and others left destitute by what was then called the Great War. She brought her idea to Canada in 1921, the same year poppy sales were launched in the United States, and the tradition soon spread among Allied nations. People have been wearing poppies as a tribute to the fallen ever since.

It's so hard to explain war to a child, especially since we've never had to endure it on a multinational scale on this continent. And we're so many years removed from those all-encompassing wars that our generation is quickly losing any sense of what it means. Some of the music written by Scot-turned-Australian Eric Bogle helps me with that. He has earned international recognition for his 1972 song "And the Band Played Waltzing Matilda"; it's a heartbreaking, searing indictment of war. And his words in "No Man's Land" paint a stark picture of their own: "[T]he sun shining now on these green fields of France / The warm wind blows gently and the red poppies dance… / But here in this graveyard it's still no man's land / The countless white crosses in mute witness stand / To man's blind indifference to his fellow man… / [I]t all happened again and again…."

After all that, it seems sacrilegious to talk about plant culture, but I'd like to try growing a Flanders-type poppy next year. On the off chance that you would, too, here's what I've learned.

Poppies want a sunny location with coarse, well-drained soil. It's recommended that you plant poppies among more beautifully leaved and long-lived flowers, because the poppy's leaves die back to ugly shreds after flowering is finished. The Flanders poppy is just eighteen inches tall, with a single bowl-shaped blossom atop each wiry stem. There are black blotches at the centre of each of the four papery crimson petals. Though each flower lasts only a day or two, a plant will bear several between late June and sometime in August. Removing spent flowers encourages new blooms, but a couple of the distinctive urn-shaped pods (which look like pepper pots) should be left alone in the fall if you want the plant to self-seed. That's the only way to get it back (short of buying new starter plants), because these poppies are annuals.

Many people say the fragile blooms of the poppy won't survive cutting, but garden writer and expert the late Lois Hole said you can prevent wilting by immersing recut stem ends in boiling water for half a minute or singeing them in a candle flame.

I'd like to try a showy black-spotted Flanders cultivar called 'Ladybird', but it may not be easy to find. Many catalogues and garden centres are pushing a cultivar called 'Allegro' as a remembrance poppy, but it's really a dwarf version of the perennial Oriental poppy, *Papaver orientale*. Oriental types are close cousins, as is the well-known opium poppy, *Papaver somniferum*. The latter symbolizes oblivion, according to some sources, and its use as a sedative or pain-reliever and to treat nervousness, coughs and diarrhea is noted.

The edible non-narcotic seeds of the Oriental poppy are the ones used in toothsome breads, baked goods and other savoury foods. The petals of the Flanders poppy, though, were at one time favoured to colour or sweeten medicines. And in the Middle Ages, herbalists used this smallest poppy as a cure for pleurisy and the "ague" – a vicious fever with sweating and chills. I hope my pressed flower serves as a cure for forgetfulness, and floats out from its hiding place one day with a message for its finder.

Failing a real Flanders poppy, I guess I could live with the closely related corn poppy, *Papaver rhoeas*. It's an annual, too, that comes in shades of rose, salmon and scarlet, sometimes with unusual shapes or edges, or with white throats. This type is sometimes known as the Shirley poppy, apparently named by a British clergyman who bred new colours for the traditional red field poppy. He gave the new strain the name of the village in which he was vicar.

One more quote to close this letter, from a celebrated, wily Scot. Sounds to me like Robbie Burns knew what he was talking about: "But pleasures are like poppies spread – / You seize the flow'r, its bloom is shed; / Or like the snow falls in the river – / A moment white – then meets forever."

Anne

Dear Anne:

I hope this package survives the journey to your house. The wreath is scented (still, I hope) with sprigs of rosemary in honour of your new year of horticultural studies. In ancient Greece, students would wear garlands or amulets of rosemary to improve their memories while studying for exams. I don't expect you to don this wreath, but perhaps it will help to have it adorn your office door.

I confess that the rosemary is as much for me as you. This perfumed herb represents remembrance. Two years ago, you gave me rosemary oil and a clay lamp ring for my birthday, but I put it away after Mom died. The scent sickened me, as it reminded me of her bath oil. Only now is it comforting; in fact, it is wafting around me as I write by lamplight through these early hours. "Fragrance has a way of lifting our spirits and stirring good memories as nothing else can," says Michael MacCaskey in *Gardening for Dummies*.

But I think fragrance is equally proficient at stirring painful memories. Scent is in the nose of the sniffer! "For a perfume that is a delight to one individual may be a horror to another," comments Louise Beebe Wilder. It takes time, and that means distance, to remember without surrendering to sobs. I call it learning how to "remember right." It's acknowledging an emotion that's much richer than any fleeting sentimentality. That "right" remembrance chafes at my heart but it's better, most times I think, than slippery tears that just slide by. "Pain we obey," Proust said, and I think that only by confronting soul pain can we learn to remember right. It's always struck me as foolish when people say they have no regrets. How preposterous or arrogant! Have they lived such a perfect life that no one has been hurt by them, or have they been so blind or so shallow as to not see the pain? I think we constantly make choices when we remember. We can choose to remember the good, the bad or (what's more likely true) all that in-between grey. As Tom Robbins writes in *Still Life with Woodpecker*, choice is "the word that throws a window open after the final door is closed... the word that separates that which is dead from that which is living." We have to choose to come to grips with the guilt.

While rosemary holds both bitter and sweet fragrant memories for me, this greyish-green shrub is lush in legend. Originally found in the Mediterranean hills and a member of the mint family, *Rosmarinus officinalis* is replete with religious meaning. The blue flowers supposedly originated with the blue of Mary's cloak, one she hung on a rosemary bush while fleeing from Herod with the infant Jesus. Then, for hundreds of years it was believed the shrub grew no taller than six feet within a thirty-three-year period, revering Christ's abbreviated life, notes that superb reference *Rodale's Illustrated Encyclopedia of Herbs*. Of course, the herb's name honours Mary.

Sir Thomas More, the head of the English church who lost his own head in 1535 (although he was canonized four hundred years later, in 1935), once said of rosemary, "I lett it runne all over my garden wall, not onlie because my bees love it, but because 'tis the herb sacred to remembrance, and therefore to friendship." He sounds like just our sort of live-and-let-live type of gardener.

Also in the sixteenth century, the well-heeled would hire perfumers to scent their homes with rosemary incense. The perfumer would whisk the herb with sugar and heat it over hot coals. In fact, my herbal encyclopedia suggests tossing a handful of rosemary into barbecue coals during the last five to ten minutes of cooking to add extra flavour to the food – sweetish but mint-like. Get Brian to try that the next time you grill lamb chops. It might be nice for whitefish or salmon steaks, too.

Sprinkling rosemary on orange sections or adding some of the chopped herb to biscuits or dumplings are other culinary tips suggested by a garden catalogue. What we used to hum in the '70s, "parsley, sage, rosemary and thyme," is now de rigueur for poultry stuffing.

Medicinally, an ointment made from the oil of rosemary reportedly helps ease the pain of rheumatism, bruises and wounds. I was most interested to read it was used to treat muscle spasms – they're a bummer, as anyone with MS can attest. And a bath in rosemary oil is said to make the old young again. Perhaps the oil will ease some of the sensory distortions I'm troubled with from the MS. It's worth a try.

Vita Sackville-West recommends rosemary for a bee garden, but my crocuses, beebalm, sage and forget-me-nots already attract enough bees to keep Bizzie on the run for hours.

Herbs are plants – either soft or woody – with scented leaves. "Herb growing combines the delights of the flower garden with the productivity of the vegetable plot," notes the *Practical Guide to Gardening in Canada*. Rosemary should be started from cuttings, as seeds take ages to germinate. Given our winter conditions, try planting it in a porous container. The roots, like those of other evergreen plants, are prime for root rot, so they need good drainage. Rosemary is tricky: it needs full sun but doesn't like to dry out, either. 'Tis a challenge to be sure, but its rich history seems worth the trouble.

I think some leaves would be delicious in your foccacia bread. You can pick the leaves anytime to use immediately.

Cultivars with pink or white flowers are also available. Whatever you choose, rosemary has to winter indoors, as it can "tolerate frost, but not freezing of the roots," notes Patricia Thorpe in *Growing Pains*.

"There's rosemary, that's for remembrance; pray you, love, remember. And there is pansies, that's for thoughts," said Ophelia in Shakespeare's *Hamlet*. On that note I'll close, sending you thoughts for good studying. Please remember me to Brian and Maggie, and give hugs all around to that ragtag collection of kittens you've acquired!

Elizabeth

Healing

You've heard the phrase that something takes its own sweet time. So does healing. Here, "sweet" time means the right, appropriate or fitting time. We may wish to rush the process, but we simply can't. Healing is attuned to the intransigent timepiece of the soul.

Healing is much more than closing physical wounds or mending emotional fences. Healing tick-tocks through the pain and grief of a loss to a new time of acceptance, hope and honest remembrance. Healing can balance all the uneven, jagged pains in our lives, moving inexorably like a precision clock. Back and forth, back and forth, until the rhythm is right.

Our minds and souls need to be repaired or restored to health, just like our bodies. Shortly after a tragic cycling accident left a young man I know paralyzed, he reassured his mom, "Look, I'm not dead, I'm just different." Wow! His mind was positioning his body and soul for a time of health.

Sometimes the physical or emotional injuries don't go away. The demands on our soul are so great that health seems impossible. Visualization can help. Suffering can be like a shadow: one that stalks you, or one that flourishes and then fades. Certainly, a shadow is always present. Sometimes it hides during the height of day, but mostly it falls behind. Picture yourself walking into the sunlight and look to see where the shadow lies. Healing can be described as freedom from anything bad – as we walk into the sunlight, we leave darkness behind.

At times a shadow will loom larger than you, but you learn to trust – to really believe in the farthest cranny of your mind – that it will recede. Accept the times when the shadow does "overshadow" you; don't feel you are giving up or giving in! You are still worthy – you're just resting, with the confidence that this lurking darkness shall soon withdraw once again. Your mind is your best ally as you battle for health. Read books! "[T]he mind exerts the deepest influence on the body. Freedom from sickness…depends on finding that all-important balanced awareness from within," notes Dr. Deepak Chopra's Internet site.

Use your mind to help your body handle pain. "Memory is where the proof of life is stored," wrote Norman Cousins, a man who overcame serious heart disease by believing in the life-sustaining properties of hope, faith, love and laughter. It's said that laughter is the music of life; watching half a dozen John Candy videos can indeed make the "unbearable bearable," as Dr. Bernie Siegel predicts in his book *Love, Medicine and Miracles*.

Memories of a garden abloom with the subtle corals and pinks of summer phlox can help calm many kinds of anxiety. The phrase "and this too shall pass" gets one through any number of sticky situations. Ted Kipping, an American tree trimmer and master horticulturist, explains how the garden helps him heal: "I don't think gardening is important; I'd say it's crucial," he writes. "Whatever jagged little waves there were in my day, whatever turmoil was pecking away at my foundations or spirit, just evaporate in grooming and caring for the garden and being exposed to the spirits of all those plants. Their companionship is a balm to the spirit."

In the times of skulking shadows, family and friends can step in with welcome help. Containers of beef-and-barley soup that arrive at your door, "I'm thinking of you" cards and phone calls, inspirational tapes and bestseller mysteries, or remembrances in prayer circles all express love and concern. And a pot of green hyacinth buds forces one to look forward to the future! Will they be solid mauve or tinged with white? Remember their scent? At times like this, it is good to think of the old maxim: God is in the details. Hang your hope on the small stuff.

The most important person in your recovery team is you, not the medical personnel, counsellors, lawyers or even your friends and family. Take whatever measure of control you can over what's happening around you. Learn everything you can about your trouble. Learn so much that you drive the experts crazy. Read, ask questions, read some more and ask more questions. It is your life, your time. "The way we choose to live and the depth of our feelings, our ability to love and be loved and to take in all the colours of the world around us – these determine the worth and true extent of whatever time we have," adds Cousins.

Physicians can profoundly affect our relationship with suffering – and thus with healing. Tossing aside the cloak of impartiality lets a physician share the mantle of pain. "I can feel their pain as they describe it. I can understand them without blame, and want them to get well because I will be getting well myself," comments Chopra in *Return of the Rishi: A Doctor's Search for the Ultimate*. Luke, the "beloved physician" and author of the third gospel, wrote that part of Jesus' prophetic mission was to "heal the broken-hearted" (Luke 4:18, KJB).

Healing means reaching the point when you know you can shuck the illness in your soul. "What we once enjoyed and deeply loved we can never lose, for all that we love deeply becomes part of us," remarked Helen Keller. A relationship may be over, a loved one may be dead or you may be stuck with a serious disease, but your soul is no longer sick; you recognize the joy of a new day again. "Just because you were ill a moment, a month, or a year ago does not mean that you are necessarily ill right now. What you need is to free yourself from the belief that your present reality is so firmly connected to the past. Only then can you create a future in the shape you desire," observes Dr. Irving Oyle.

Choose to be at peace with your future. Healing is about coming to terms with life and acknowledging real fear – it is not just about getting better physically, adds Siegel in *Love, Medicine and Miracles.*

There is "a time to heal" (Ecclesiastes 3:3, KJB), and in that time we will find a touch of the peace that "passes all understanding."

Dear Elizabeth:

I can't believe we've both stumbled onto Yeats at almost the same time! On the beautiful card enclosed you will find a poignant spiritual poem by that quirky Irish poet. And the little bag has herbal throat drops containing angelica, another kind of healer that I'll explain shortly

Though I'm no student of poetry, "The Two Trees" seems written for you and me, and for anyone launched on a journey of personal exploration and healing. It came my way recently and I just had to hand-letter it for you. Thoughts like this are meant to be shared among companions of the soul. The accompanying tape has a haunting version of the poem set to music by Loreena McKennitt. It's her 1994 release *The Mask and Mirror* – consider it an early Christmas present.

Yeats wrote this poem for Maud Gonne, the beautiful actress and Irish nationalist he adored. It became one of their favourites, though their love affair ultimately fizzled. In the poem, he gives her some age-old advice that I seem to see in some form in every women's magazine or self-help book: Look for the good inside and rejoice in it. Ah, but he says it so much more eloquently: "Gaze no more in the bitter glass. / Beloved, gaze in thine own heart, / The holy tree is growing there; / From joy the holy branches start, / And all the trembling flowers they bear... / Thine eyes grow full of tender care...."

It seems Yeats was talking about how a state of unbalance or disquiet can disrupt a life or hinder true enjoyment. The trees of the poem are said to symbolize two things: the Tree of Knowledge mentioned in the Bible, and the Tree of Life that in ancient Hebrew tradition (*cabala*) expresses the planes through which one travels to attain full wisdom and the sublime state of being.

Using symbols from nature helps us to call on special powers to harmonize experiences of our everyday world and yearnings of our spirits, in Yeats's view. Pretty heavy stuff, but I like the poetry and can relate to some of what he's getting at – I think!

Wouldn't you like a plant with reputed divine powers and associations on your side? With his lifelong interest in mysticism and enchantment, Yeats might well have been drawn to the treelike angelica, a six-foot herb that was considered in medieval times to be a charm against witches and evil spirits. It is named *Angelica archangelica*, because legend has it the plant always blooms on May 8, the feast day of the archangel Michael.

Angelica has been considered a healing plant for thousands of years, and it's a towering focal point in any garden. I've never grown it, but my neighbour had a beauty in a sunny corner of her front garden this year. At about three feet wide, it was massive enough to discourage kids and paperboys from trying to hop the flowerbed and cut across the yard, and it shaded lovely pink impatiens beneath. It bloomed in early summer, floating clouds of tiny white flowers in perfect spheres above the divided, toothed leaves that make it look like a dark, brooding giant celery.

While it's an annual in our climate, angelica is described by *Rodale's Illustrated Encyclopedia of Herbs* as a "perennial biennial" because it lasts longer in warm places. Flowering and seed-setting generally occur in the plant's second or third year, but cutting the fading blooms off right away prevents seed production, thus prolonging the main root's life by a few years.

This herb is best started from fresh seed tossed on top of moist, fertile soil and left uncovered so the sun can start it. I guess that means July or August sowing. I confess I'm tempted, but where would I put a regal giant like angelica? Maybe I can talk Brian's mother into trying it at the back of her generous, sun-soaked vegetable garden. It sounds easy enough to grow, and is usually not troubled by pests.

I could point out to Brian's mom the culinary possibilities, since she loves to cook and is always experimenting. Angelica imparts a licorice flavour. The dried root is powdered and can enhance breads, muffins and cookies, while fresh leaves will punch up soups, stews and salads. The stalks are sometimes stewed early in the season and eaten as a vegetable. Dried leaves are a flavouring herb; they can also make a soothing tea.

I'd love to have sent you candied angelica, a sweet mouthful I've had a few times on fine cakes, but the sugary purplish-green stem bits are as rare as hen's teeth around here. A liqueur like Benedictine or chartreuse would do, since angelica flavours these drinks, but I know you don't drink anymore. Instead, I'm sharing some comforting, mild throat lozenges that I've found. They include angelica and menthol, so maybe they'll help calm that scratchy throat I heard on the phone this week. The herb of the angels is featured in tons of other products, too, from bath oils and soaps to creams and perfumes.

Here's an incredible piece of plant trivia for you: angelica's honourable Chinese ancestor is *Angelica sinensis* – the Dong quai we see in health food stores everywhere. "No herb has so many documented medicinal uses," one herb catalogue gushes. Dong quai is said to lower blood pressure, strengthen the heart, regulate menstruation, relieve menopausal symptoms, and who knows what else? Definitely a herb for these hectic lives of ours!

Necklaces of angelica were draped around peasant children's necks in days gone by to protect them from harm. A potion called Carmelite water was brewed from angelica's roots, to ensure long life and guard against poisons and evil spells. Angelica water was the principal ingredient in another decoction that combined it with nutmeg and treacle in a preparation recommended by the College of Physicians in London to curb the terrible plague of 1665. According to *Rodale's Illustrated Encyclopedia of Herbs*, "Legend has it that...a monk met an angel in his dreams. The angel told him that angelica would cure the plague." Deafness, poor eyesight, rabies and colic were among other ills treated by the herb in syrups, poultices and tinctures.

Today, medicinal uses of angelica mirror many of the folk remedies but focus mainly on those associated with regulating and assisting the female reproductive system, and on bronchial and digestive complaints. It's a winter warmer too, boosting circulation and fighting off coughs and colds. Angelica is not recommended for use by pregnant women or diabetics, though – the former because it promotes bleeding and the latter because it may increase blood sugar.

Native writer Loren Cruden says angelica is allied in the heavens with Venus and the sun. Lyrically, she writes: "Angelica, through a nature that attracts goodness and encourages wisdom, gives little room for ill.... It is a positive, strong, and sweet presence."

Moderation may be wise, though. Despite its uses in healing and widespread acceptance as a herb safe for use, angelica has a suspected dark side. At least one authority has stated it is a carcinogen that should be avoided, says *Rodale's*.

Too bad Yeats died in 1939. I think he would have relished the lively challenge in these lines from a song by the Indigo Girls: "I went to the doctor, I went to the mountains / I looked to the children, I drank from the fountain / There's more than one answer to these questions pointing me in a crooked line / The less I seek my source for some definitive / The closer I am to fine."

Anne

Dear Anne:

Yippee, yippee – my cyclamen has bloomed!

Small stuff to you, my dear horticulture chum, but I've never kept one of those gift plants alive long enough for a second round of blooms. This *Cyclamen persicum* was a cheery, white welcome home after my third cancer surgery. I enjoyed it for a good month before I had to snip its sagging stems.

That plant has struggled to sustain life amidst considerable adversity: there were times the soil was too wet or too dry, the location was too sunny or too shady, the temperature too hot or too cool. Consequently, the soggy stems collapsed – fainted, really – or the leaves yellowed, seemingly in an angry snarl at my ineptitude.

Ah, but Tuesday morning as I opened the blinds along the east-facing bow window – where the cyclamen has been for several months – I was delightfully surprised by one crisp white bloom. And there's a second flower stem sneaking up the middle. I felt like a child as I twirled the pot around, gazing at the solitary flower!

I know Michael, and no doubt anyone who entered our living room, wondered why I kept this bedraggled-looking plant in full view. I don't think I even knew, until I saw it bloom again. It calls to mind my third surgery – not the incisions and infections, but those weeks I spent on the gynecological oncology ward. The plant is a potent reminder of how very, very lucky I am. I came home. "The miracle is not to walk on water. The miracle is to walk on the green earth, dwelling deeply in the present moment and feeling truly alive," wrote Thich Nhat Hanh.

Although I've been in hospitals often with the MS, no ward was like that cancer floor. It was full of startlingly young women, all there to fight terrifying "female" cancers. In Canada, it's estimated that more than 2,100 women will get ovarian cancer this year and almost 1,400 will die. In the United States that figure is multiplied by ten. Diagnosis of this particular cancer is very difficult, because many symptoms are vague until the devastating later stages. Did I tell you I'm in another research program – this one at a California university – to help doctors detect ovarian cancer earlier? Faster diagnoses mean better chances to heal bodies and souls. "The body and the soul make a living creature," Aristotle remarked so many centuries ago.

I've told Michael that for Christmas I want a new card file, to keep track of the various MS and cancer research programs I'm in. It is crucial that people volunteer for research studies. It's the only way we will learn the causes, study possible treatments and in the end, offer help. Annie, I can hear you saying, "Liz is on her soapbox again!" So I'll humbly turn back to cyclamen.

With this "modest" plant (as Vita Sackville-West calls it) we travel back to the Mediterranean, where so many of the plants we've explored originated. Wild cyclamen range from Italy to Israel, from Turkey to Tunisia and from Albania to Algeria. In fact, some experts think cyclamen is the lily referred to by Jesus: "Consider the lilies how they grow: they toil not, they spin not; and yet I say unto you, that Solomon in all his glory was not arrayed like one of these" (Luke 12:27, KJB). But these delicate white- or bright-pink-flowered plants are also called Solomon's crown, in honour of the Jewish king who built the first temple to the Lord in Jerusalem. I think that tells us how well rooted cyclamen is in the landscape. It is a true roadside attraction, as the plant grows in meadows, on hillsides and along old walls – any well shaded and sheltered location will do.

Although I think of cyclamen as a winter-flowering houseplant, there are types that have flowering times covering every month of the year. In fact, there are nineteen species of this plant of the primrose family.

Cyclamen plants are partial to moderate temperatures with indirect sun. For my cyclamen, things started looking up, so to speak, once I took the pot out of its fancy foil wrapper, placed it in a decorative ceramic pot, and started watering from the bottom. I poked a couple of extra holes in the original plastic pot, just to ensure the water had several seepage sites. I kept the soil moist, as I learned that overwatering causes root rot. After that I stopped fussing. My eastern window is well away from any heat vents – something to avoid with cyclamen.

Then came that magical morning when it bloomed! The satiny-petalled flowers have been called "miniature butterflies." Their appearance atop a thin, almost transparent stem gives the illusion of a butterfly floating among the heart-shaped leaves. It's not hard to thrill an amateur gardener, is it?

This cyclamen has been a companion on my road to health. Not surprisingly, it really was a plant used for healing. In the seventeenth century, its tuberous roots were crushed into a skin ointment to prevent pitting and disfiguring after smallpox. They were also ground into little cakes and eaten for reported aphrodisiac properties – all in the name of good health, I'm sure!

The enclosed midget birdbath is for next year's summer garden. Please give it to Maggie – she might enjoy birds visiting the garden, even if she doesn't go there much herself. I picked it up at an end-of-season discount day, along with a new CD-ROM landscape program. Aren't you proud of me for taking root in this land of health and planning next year's new garden? "Elizabeth's Hardy Herbs for Health," I'll name the collection in tribute to all we've learned through these letters. I'll close, raising my glass of club soda in salute – *skoal*, to your health, dear friend!

Elizabeth

Dear Liz:

Well, we're all set here to fend off any vampires, demons or witches lurking about. Not only do I have a potted garlic plant growing near a sunny window, but a friend has generously treated me to one of those long ropes of braided garlic you see in the markets each fall. She knows I won't pay the $20 or more they're asking, but also knows how much I appreciate the "reeking rose." She surprised me with some last week to repay a favour. Don't you just love unexpected kindnesses like that?

It seems the B-grade movies and cartoons didn't just invent the theory that garlic will hold many ills at bay; it has been a recognized healer for two thousand years. Legend has bestowed on the lowly bulb the power to protect against vampires or turn off an unwanted suitor. But a Russian tale declares that garlic grew up in the left footprint of the Devil. And in some parts of India, the garlic plant is believed to signal the presence of evil spirits. That's the trouble with these folk tales, too many contradictions and not enough straight answers – like life, eh?

The healing properties of this plant seem more straightforward, thank goodness. Garlic has long been a diuretic, digestive stimulant and antispasmodic. Tuberculosis and whooping cough were once treated with garlic in various applications. It is a proven antiseptic that was valued in both world wars, where it was applied to wounds to prevent them turning septic. It has been proven to lower blood pressure, and a possible role in preventing tumour formation is under investigation. In China, it is believed that eating garlic may help prevent stomach cancer. "Our apothecary's shop is our garden full of potherbs, and our doctor is a clove of garlic," some kindly scribe noted in 1615.

Do you feed garlic to Bizzie? I read that garlic is a time-honoured cure for worms and parasites in pets. Gives a whole new meaning to the phrase "dog breath," doesn't it?

I'm sure you're wondering – and yes, I did find a musical allusion for us to enjoy. You know how I love to spice up these letters with quotations from some of my best-loved music. I admit this was a tough one, since there's no time in my life right now to indulge in hours at the library, on the Internet or at the music archives to satisfy idle curiosities. But my schoolwork requires plant research quite often, so that serves as my excuse. In the spirit of garlic cure-alls, here's a gem I remembered from an old Steve Goodman CD. In the rollicking nonsense song "The Barnyard Dance" (written by Carl Martin), he burbles: "And old man garlic dropped dead of the colic / Down at the barnyard dance – this mornin'!" But in fact, colic is severe pain caused by muscle spasms in the abdomen, and herbalist Michael Tierra in *The Way of Herbs* recommends: "For nervous spasms, cramps and seizures, crush one clove of garlic in hot milk [and drink it]."

Good old garlic fed the slaves as they built the pyramids in Egypt, and the Bible mentions the Israelites pining for it after enjoying it in Egypt and then escaping into the desert – where garlic wasn't. Earliest Sanskrit writings refer to the pungent bulb, which comes from central Asia. Writing about plants of the Bible, garden writer and consultant Allan Swenson says it's no wonder this plant was so important to the people of those times; there are more than sixty species of onion and garlic known there. It's considered the herb of Mars, the Roman war god, so Roman troops ate garlic to gird their strength for battle.

One of the things I admire about garlic is how it's a friend to other plants, actually promoting their good health. The book title *Roses Love Garlic* says it all – or almost all. Garden writer Louise Riotte tells us how garlic and other lily family members guard against mildew and black spot on roses, as well as repelling moles.

The garlic plants make a kind of living mulch to conserve moisture around the rose roots, too, if you plant them thick enough. Garlic chases off fruit tree borers. And here's a fact that has my curiosity piqued – garlic planted among any sort of scented, flowering plants often increases their fragrance. Self-defence, maybe? (It's so aggravating: none of my references has explained why.)

Garlic's pesticidal properties are enough to discourage most insects, says Patrick Lima, and garden guru Marjorie Harris reports on an organic pesticide she uses to banish ants, cabbageworms, spiders and caterpillars that mixes water with the juices of garlic and hot peppers. Another good spray can be made of pureed garlic and onion, she writes in *Ecological Gardening*. She has a caution you might want to note, Liz: "Never plant garlic near gladioli – they don't like each other at all."

The common kitchen garlic is called *Allium sativum*, and it's very easy to grow. I have carelessly tucked a few cloves – the individual sections of the whole, papery multipart bulb – into the ground in late summer or early fall, and they seem to flourish around my roses. A heavy leaf-and-soil mulch protects them over the winter, and the two-foot grass-like foliage reappears early each spring. Garlic wants rich, dryish soil in a sheltered, sunny spot. Regular watering and the twice-a-season bone meal dressing I give both roses and garlic certainly are appreciated!

It's worth keeping the area weed-free, Lima adds. The plant can be grown in pots, as well. My indoor plant is an experiment; I had saved for fall planting a few garlic bulbs from the market that had begun to go soft. And when I found an extra one sprouting in the cupboard a week or so later, I couldn't bear to throw it away so I popped it into a pot and placed it in my only really sunny window. It's small, but fine so far! I wonder how declining light will affect it, and whether it will produce the typical rounded cluster of whitish-pink flowers? I'm well stocked for winter, at any rate.

With all the Caesar salads and garlic bread you and I have shared at lunches and dinners in Italian restaurants over the years, I know you have the same affection for garlic that I do – so I'll skip the myriad ways the plant revs up foods from many cultures.

There are whole shelves of books on that subject. It's great that the Eastern and Mediterranean culinary cultures make more of it than our timid Western societies do. They cook and use garlic as a whole vegetable, rather than just as a seasoning or flavour-enhancer. Unfortunately, some authorities suggest garlic's healing potency is lost or greatly diminished when cooked – so let's keep some of the real, raw thing prominent in our diets through our salads and dips.

I've never grown enough of it to bother harvesting, and I've never tried the related, milder but bigger *Allium ampeloprasum* (elephant garlic), so I can't comment on those. I've read that you can dig up garlic when the flat leaves go brown in fall, though, and hang bulbs in a cool, dry place to use over the winter. Sounds good, but why bother when we can get lovely jars of minced garlic preserved in oil from the Asian groceries for about $2 a bottle? (I hope this one for you arrived intact in its foam and popcorn packing.)

Bye for now and *bon appétit*!

Anne

Dear Annie:

Bizzie brings you this letter's plant, as peppermint paws now perfume my writing room. Apparently she's been digging around the mint under the lilac bushes – likely after a squirrel. So thoughtful of her to send you her sweetest wishes, isn't it?

Biz certainly did what Pluto intended. The Greek god of the underworld fell in love with Minthe (also known as Mentha), one of the nymphs. When Persephone (Pluto's wife and a formidable goddess as daughter of Zeus and queen of the lower world) found out, she took sweet revenge. "O Persephone, you were allowed at one time to change the limbs of the maiden Mentha into the fragrant mint," wrote Ovid, the Roman poet, two thousand years ago. Pluto could not reverse this vengeful spell but he tempered it: the more Minthe was stepped on, the sweeter she'd smell. Pliny, the great first-century Roman writer of natural history, wrote of mint that "the very smell of it reanimates the spirit."

My mint mushroomed, so to speak, this past spring, providing a fragrant undergrowth for the lilacs. After Mom's death, I searched her garden for the mint I remembered. A neighbour watched me wander the yard in vain for a whiff of the herb. On hearing the object of my quest, she recalled that Mom lost her mint (not her mind!) one very dry summer.

Several days after our discussion, I found a clump of moist mint tucked into a bag on my doorstep. A note told me the neighbour had sniffed out her old patch of this perennial Mom had given her eons ago. There's no disguising the sharply sweet scent of mint; its aromatic aura extends for quite a radius. So, via that kindly neighbour, Mom's mint – *Mentha piperita* – is now mine. Mints are native to Europe and Asia, but many have been naturalized throughout North America.

Mint belongs to the plant family *Lamiaceae*, which has more than 3,500 species. Far too many to discuss, but here are a few tidbits. Basil, sage, rosemary, thyme and lavender are family members, and all have been valued for their commercial, culinary and medicinal properties for centuries. The Romans made peppermint crowns, notes *Rodale's Illustrated Encyclopedia of Herbs*. Remember how fond Greek students were of rosemary garlands? Matthew and Luke scold the Pharisees – New Testament legal eagles – for faithfully paying their taxes with mint. That was the letter of the law, I guess, but the levy ignored the spirit of God's law. "But alas for you Pharisees! You who pay your tithe of mint and rue and all sorts of garden herbs and overlook justice and the love of God! These you should have practised, without leaving the others undone" (Luke 11:42, JB).

Peppermint's tang reminds me of the pan of dessert squares a colleague sent when I came home from one of my surgeries. So appropriate, as mint is a symbol of hospitality – surely an early step to friendship! And, like friendship, peppermint must be cultivated with care. It's a sterile hybrid of water mint and spearmint, so it can be reproduced only with cuttings. And menthol – the soothing ingredient found in cough and scratchy-throat remedies – comes from peppermint. I've used peppermint cream for the leg pain I have from the MS. It doesn't ease spasms but it helps cool the burning sensory distortions I have. As you know, the abdominal surgeries left me with cranky bowels. Although it tastes strong, peppermint tea, fortunately, does soothe that discomfort. Even "I-never-drink-tea" Michael takes a cup when his stomach turns twitchy. So, does this mean those chocolate-covered after-dinner mints are gastronomically guilt-free? I don't think so!

If you steep spearmint's grey-green leaves, you'll get a tea that's good for insomnia. Washing chapped hands in spearmint tea will comfort them, adds *Rodale's*. And spearmint's rich nectar makes it a butterfly favourite. Caterpillars, the culprits in many a garden disaster, like to nibble on garden foliage. But butterflies don't always enjoy the same plants they did when they were young. "This means that in our efforts to attract butterflies to the backyard, we need to plant both caterpillar favorites and nectar plants for the adults," observes gardening author Jeff Cox in *Landscaping with Nature*.

Mints prefer moist, partly shady areas, and profit from frequent brush cuts throughout the summer. This encourages what Shakespeare called a plant of "middle summer" to spread. Mom made a delicious mint jelly from the leaves (these should be picked young to preserve their taste) that she served with pork dishes. Jars were tucked away in the pantry to present to visiting aunts, friends or neighbours.

Emile Verhaeren, a late nineteenth-century Belgian poet, penned that, "within the garden there is healthfulness." Excuse me for taking this literally, but there's evidence that mints are healthy for our gardens. Marjorie Harris writes in *Favorite Garden Tips* that peppermint keeps red ants away from shrubs, while spearmint keeps aphids off neighbouring plants. Apparently, the mints will discourage mice or other rodents from visiting compost piles, too.

Along with gardening, I've been walking daily to strengthen my jelly-weak legs. "Use them or lose them," is my adage. I'll close with these words from Agatha Christie that I read in Sarah Ban Breathnach's *Simple Abundance* – words that have been filtering through my consciousness all week. "I like living. I have sometimes been wildly, despairingly, acutely miserable, racked with sorrow, but through it all I still know quite certainly that just to be alive is a grand thing." Despite the pain I feel I must say, Yes!

Please put this box of peppermints on your dining room table to share with all who visit…

Elizabeth

Elizabeth, "master-gardener-in-the-making":

How fine and strong you're sounding these days! I am proud – you're becoming a true sister of the trowel, and just look what you've accomplished spiritually. Neither of us knows enough yet to lay claim to the horticultural title "master gardener," of course – not for a long while. But you sound so competent, and very much in charge in your spiritual garden.

Thank you, thank you for the beautiful binder. The floral watercolour cover is so inspiring – and how did you know I'm floundering under the weight of all that plant lore we've been sharing? I kept rummaging through my personal correspondence files to look things up all summer, and knew I'd have to consolidate all my horticultural stuff soon. Now these "plant letters" have a place of honour on the bookshelf between my school notes and textbooks. It's a good thing one of us is organized!

After these positive remarks, I hate to break the mood, but I'm knee-deep in blues. Some days I'm fine, then on others a kind of unspecified despair washes over me. I wander around, looking over all the garden areas but taking no pleasure in them. Instead of beautiful seed pods, surprising late blooms and exceptional fall colour, I just see more work. This needs dividing, that needs cutting back, over there are some perennials that need tucking in. When you add these tasks to the list of endless work, school, parenting and personal responsibilities, it quickly seems overwhelming and I shrink back, exhausted. Where did the joy go? Now I know exactly what Joni Mitchell meant when she sang "and the day goes dismal" on her 1970s *For the Roses* release.

My doctor is concerned, but not overly alarmed. She works in a family health centre where the practitioners of several related disciplines share office space and resources. She is referring me to the naturopath there to see if some diet changes or herbal remedies might help, and she mentioned St. John's wort as one possible way to lift my spirits. Don't worry; it's all closely monitored and done in consultation with other healing team members there, and I'll ask lots of questions if I go for it.

Ironically, I have St. John's wort – a sunny yellow-flowering plant – growing along the side fence. I hadn't bothered to identify it until this year, when I was driven to do so by visitors who kept asking, "What is that weedy thing over there?" I don't have enough to make my own herbal remedy, and wouldn't try it if I did. I don't have a clue as to how it's done, and the extract is easily available in capsule form, anyway. (It's a touch pricey, though; about $16 to $20 for a month's supply. But then I guess that's cheaper than Scotch.)

St. John's wort is a recognized antidepressant that has been in use for centuries. The Crusaders brought the shrubby perennial, of the botanical order that includes tea, back from the East. It was traditionally hung above doorways to protect the inhabitants of a house from harm. The common name links this plant with June 24, the feast day of St. John and a time well suited to decorating and safeguarding the home. "Wort" is just an old-fashioned word for plant. Other common names are Aaron's beard and St. Andrew's cross. *Hypericum perforatum*, the botanical name, reinforces that protective theme; the first word literally means "above an icon" and refers to the custom of hanging sprigs above pictures or images to keep bad stuff at a distance. The second word, *perforatum*, describes the oil glands that resemble pinpricked holes in the leaves. That oil is effective when rubbed on the skin to relieve muscular pain, stiff joints, bruises and swellings. *Hypericin* is the active ingredient in St. John's wort. It is an antiviral agent that has been proven in medical studies to reduce anxiety and depression.

The leaves and petals of St. John's wort look like they're bleeding when crushed, so Greek and Roman physicians of long ago believed this meant it was a good topical dressing for wounds. Other past St. John's wort treatments have reputedly aided gastric disorders, bedwetting and urinary problems, nervous coughs, anemia and worms. However, there are cautions in the literature about prolonged use if you're light-skinned, because it increases sensitivity to the sun.

It's not hard to grow this fifteen- to eighteen-inch-tall herb at home; it can take sun or partial shade. Soil quality isn't important, and the plant can tolerate some drought. It's easily started by fall cuttings or division, and you can expect a mature plant to spread two or three feet. Clumps should be divided every three or four years – unless you want to wait long enough for the area to slowly fill in with "babies" created by runners from the root system. Pests are rarely a problem.

The small, five-petalled blossoms with fluffy tufts of stamens at their centres are true garden brighteners from late June through early fall. The smooth-edged, elliptical leaves are interesting, too, because they grow in neat pairs along ridged stems. And when you pluck one and hold it up to the light, the oil glands show up as tiny, translucent portholes!

Winter protection for the roots and a spring trim are all the care this charitable plant needs. It won't live many years, but it doesn't sound hard to keep a supply of new plants ready to fill in the gaps.

While I'm in this mood, Joan Baez is on the CD player, and her rendition of "The Swallow Song" (written by her brother-in-law, Richard Farina) seems to be reminding me that this, too, shall pass. "[W]ill the breezes blow the petals from your hand / And will some loving ease your pain / And will the silence strike confusion from your soul / And will the swallows come again?"

On that note, I'll close for today. Maybe I'll start on the St. John's wort soon, and hope it delivers on a legend that was popular on the Isle of Wight long ago. If you stepped on the plant at twilight, it was believed you might be whisked away by a magic fairy horse and return only at daylight – with who knows what secrets? Do you think it works only if you step on the spot where the plant is actually in bloom, or should I stomp on a capsule or two?

Anne

Love

Love is a winding river that ebbs and flows through our days. Sometimes it cradles and soothes us, and we are like fallen leaves floating gently upon the eddies of time. On other occasions, love is a roaring torrent that catapults us recklessly through rapids, over waterfalls and against unyielding rocks – until we're giddy and stunned by the unchannelled force of it all. Love is raw, untamed, unknowable and unpredictable.

Best – and worst – of all, it seems utterly beyond our control. That is what thrills us, maddens us, elates us, coddles us and thrusts us abruptly into despair. We can channel, parcel out and try to influence love. We can give it a comfortable home, but in the end none can predict where love will blossom or when it will go.

And yet, love is ultimately what defines us and shapes our lives. It is the emotion and intellectual connection that makes us whole. (Nor should we assume we're the only species to feel love. In the 1995 bestseller *When Elephants Weep*, co-authors Jeffrey Moussaieff Masson and Susan McCarthy present many convincing arguments about animals' ability to feel, including this description of a gander's behaviour when his mate was killed by a fox: "He stood silently by her partly eaten body, which lay across their nest. In the following days he hunched his body and hung his head. His eyes became sunken. His status in the flock plummeted, since he did not have the heart to defend himself from…attacks." His mourning period lasted a year, they note.) Love is always with us, one way or another. It is what carries and sustains us.

If you are among the faithful, you see the symbols of love among the icons, creeds, prayers and rituals that have marked our passage and our belief for hundreds and thousands of years. If you are unmoved or unconvinced by the faiths and religions of our times, love comes in other forms. Look for it in the touch of a friend who wipes a fevered brow, the lover's caress, the trusting nudge of a bird or animal venturing close, in the kindness of a stranger or the eyes of a child. Find it in the dewdrops glistening on a delicate rosebud.

Love is truly our destiny and our life preserver; we are nothing without it. And we need only reach for it. Never assume that you are without love – it is all around you. "A God so smart / We were born with two hands reaching out / A heart that knows the joys of love / The stars above / The lucky ones / Oh, the lucky ones / to have these dreams to dream at all," croons Willie P. Bennett in his 1989 recording called *The Lucky Ones*. But Alannah Myles snarls: "Love is what you want it to be, / Love is heaven to the lonely," on her self-titled 1989 release, from the song "Love Is," written by Christopher Ward and David Tyson.

We will not speak here of the spark of sexual attraction or the precious, perhaps fleeting, beauty of romantic love. There are countless other places for those discussions, from far more qualified authorities. Rather, we write here of love on a different scale – as the rare, unqualified and embracing depth of affection that can grow up between very close friends, and between souls that recognize a unique resonance and embrace one another. We explore, too, the vast world that opens up when one's love for humanity begins to expand to encompass all others. Who can forget how American humorist and children's author Theodore Geisel, alias Dr. Seuss, portrayed this phenomenon in *How the Grinch Stole Christmas*! After seeing that Christmas had still come to the Whos, despite his stealing the trees, presents, treats and trimmings, the Grinch stopped to mull over his astonishment: "Well…in Who-ville they say / That the Grinch's small heart / Grew three sizes that day! /

And the minute his heart didn't feel quite so tight, / He whizzed with his load through the bright morning light...."

The apostle Paul in his letter to the Galatians said that in serving one another we show our love, and "all the law is fulfilled in one word, even in this; Thou shalt love thy neighbour as thyself" (Galatians 5:14, KJB).

Love is essential to finding true meaning for our existence, declares Mary Jo Leddy, a tireless and well-known Canadian social commentator, defender of human rights and peace activist. In her 1990 book *Say to the Darkness, We Beg to Differ*, she writes: "Real commitment begins when the heart is broken open by love.... In love one becomes compelled and free, driven and desiring.... Each day I am awakened by a sound. Sometimes it is an alarm signalling that now is the moment to differ from the darkness. At other times it is a bell ringing out that now is the hour to defer to the light."

No one is saying it will be easy. It can, in fact, be terrifying to those unused to being open, sharing and trusting, to venture outside the small circle of home and hearth – whether to give or to receive. On the other hand, once started it's a hard habit to break. (And why would you? Like concentric circles rippling ever outward when a stone is tossed into a still pool, your act of love flows out to touch someone else – who in turn does a kindness, until all the ripples intersect and goodness flows back from whence it came.) We all know how to do this, it's just been conditioned out of many among us. Whenever you give of yourself, you are contributing to love.

It's the tiny things that can open doors to love and rewarding friendships. The extra cookies you bake so that a tin of them can go to school or the office for sharing, the clothes you turn over to the second-hand shops, the tiny mittens you knit or the lap quilts you sew for hospitalized souls who need to keep warm – these are examples of opening your heart to a universal kind of love. So, too, are the fresh garden vegetables you prepare and take to a soup kitchen or food depot.

Three women who wrote what became a classic reference in the world of vegetarian cookery know about this kind of personal growth. Laurel Robertson, Carol Flinders and Bronwen Godfrey wrote in their 1976 bestseller *Laurel's Kitchen* about a radical change in attitude that led them to see housework, food preparation and other aspects of keeping house as a rich, vital part of the world they aspired to – a form of worship, even: "As soon as we take into our own hands some of the tasks we'd previously consigned to machines and manufacturers, our work becomes vastly more gratifying…. To lead lives of artistry, we have only to slow down, to simplify, to start making wise choices."

Through our closest friends, we can find the courage to take the plunge. Kahlil Gibran in *The Prophet* says a friend is "your needs answered." He continues, "He is your field which you sow with love and reap with thanksgiving…. For you come to him with your hunger, and you seek him for peace…. And in the sweetness of friendship let there be laughter, and sharing of pleasures. For in the dew of little things the heart finds its morning and is refreshed."

* * *

Hi, Annie:

I hear the sadness in your voice these days. As you have reached me with these garden letters of our souls, I wish to help you. Depression is such a slippery emotion, isn't it? It's here one hour, seemingly gone the next, only to return an hour later. Please do not feel that your angst is any less worthy than mine, just because you're not stuck with some ominous-sounding brand-name disease! You are struggling with this malaise, and it is as valid as any other condition or experience. No one is judging you – least of all me.

Enclosed are a few raspberry/lemon tea bags – make a pot now, then find a seat in the autumn sun to rest and read this letter. The laundry can tumble a bit longer, Maggie will be fine, and that deadline will stretch a few more minutes. Consider this line from Emerson as you relax in your garden: "A friend may well be reckoned the masterpiece of Nature."

Do you remember the pot of ivy I had on top of the piano? You don't? Well, it doesn't really matter, but it gave up the "root" this week. After a month of intense plant mothering, I let it go. I felt somewhat sad, as I'd had that ivy for fifteen years. It truly was an English ivy. I brought it back – don't ask how – from the grounds of Winchester Cathedral. After successfully rooting it, the ivy moved around the country with me. I don't know what I did wrong; maybe we should start researching our houseplants next.

Ivy is such a popular ground cover – it certainly carpeted the area around the cathedral, softening the landscape against such a splendid monolithic piece of architecture.

Ivies are woody vines belonging to the ginseng family, and "their adventurous rootlets attach to trees or bare walls," notes my computer encyclopedia, *Encarta*. English ivy, *Hedera helix*, is between six and eight inches tall when used as a ground cover, but when trained to climb walls, fences or trellises it can reach ninety feet. Annie, no surprise here, that's where the term "Ivy League" comes from; it refers to the ivy-covered buildings in a group of eight old, prestigious universities in the eastern United States.

The dark green leaves have three to five lobes, with whitish veins showing in the young leaves. Although very pretty to look at, its berry-like fruit is poisonous – I've noticed that the birds and squirrels avoid it.

The Greek god Dionysus was so touched by someone that he turned her into ivy. After one adoring worshipper danced herself to death before him, he transformed her body into ivy, the plant that entwines and embraces its support. Dionysus, you may remember, is also known by his Roman name, Bacchus, the god of wine. So, do you think he was in his right mind when he transformed her? In any case, Dionysus wore a crown of ivy and the plant was considered a charm against inebriation! Ye "gads" – was this an acronym for Gods Against DrunkS – the god of wine wearing a charm against drunkenness? You are so right, Annie, I am feeling far feistier these weeks! Ooh, I'm on a roll: WOW – perhaps this should be Watch Out Weeds week! Okay, I'll stop.

Ivy really has been cultivated since ancient times, and there are many varieties to prove it. I've read that *Hedera helix* is native to the Caucasus Mountains, which are between the Black and

Caspian seas in southeast Europe. *Hedera cananensis*, Algerian ivy, is a warm-weather type native to the Canary Islands, Spain, the Azores, Portugal and Algeria. Then there's the cultivars 'Bulgaria', 'Hebron', 'Rochester', 'Romania', 'Baltica', 'Hibernica' – you get the drift.

Ivy has long been known to represent friendship. It is a true friend to the walls it climbs, as it shields the buildings against weathering. (However, rootlets can be irksome if they take hold in cracks in the wall. Let's think of the plant's therapeutic attributes!) Meanwhile, the ground ivy that so often gilds the ground isn't really an ivy at all, but a mint. *Glechoma hederacea* is that small, creeping "ivy" that is usually regarded as a weed in our gardens or lawns. It is the plethora of common names and the abundance of the plant on our acre of Eden that attracted me.

Probably best known among the common names is creeping charlie. According to Pamela Jones in *Just Weeds: History, Myths and Uses*, it's also known as gill-creep-by-the-ground, blue runner, devil's candlestick, field balm, cat's foot (thought you'd like that) or a personal favourite, Lizzie-run-up-the-hedge! Whatever the name, it is a runaway root to be sure. It's everywhere because the plant takes root (in shallow soil) and produces stems wherever leaf nodes meet the earth. I suppose it is often called a weed because it is perennial, roots easily, and is invasive and hard to control. But Gerard, the sixteenth-century English herbalist and surgeon, would argue that ground ivy is a herb: "Ground ivy…a low or base herbe; it creepeth and spreads upon the ground hither and thither all about, with many stalkes of an uncertaine length, slender and like those of the Vine: whereupon grow leaves something broad and round; among which come forth the floures gaping like little hoods," Jones tells us.

Ground ivy's little, lipped, purplish flowers may be responsible for the "gill" in some of the common names, she writes. The old word *gile*, meaning "lip," could refer to the small flower. On the other hand, she adds, gill could come from the French word *guiller*, meaning "to ferment beer." My Gage dictionary notes that gill is a unit for measuring liquids and comes from an old French word, *gille*, referring to wine measure. "In brief only one thing seems certain: the origin of the 'gill' names is uncertain," comments Jones.

I must lend you her book; you will thoroughly enjoy the discussion of weeds, herbs and "wild things" in the introduction. Weeds are generally regarded as plants growing where they are not wanted, useless or pesky plants. Haven't you felt sorry for weeds at times? Here we are yanking, chopping and discarding plants that in other times and places held value. The ground ivy was used for treating everything from bronchitis to boils to bowel troubles. Rather a wholesome, useful plant to have at the end of a trowel, wouldn't you say?

Enclosed is a gift certificate for ice cream. Consider this a new twist on Job's verse: "Friendship's sweetness comforts the soul" (Proverbs 27:9, JB). Call me collect when you want to talk...

Elizabeth

Dear Elizabeth:

You know, I've been puzzling about relationships – among people, between people and animals, even between people and plants. While some people just slap a few annuals into the garden, others among us choose the plants we do for particular reasons, albeit sometimes prompted by motivations that are subtle or even subconscious. I was thinking that if there could be floral symbols to represent specific people, I guess mine might have to be a rose.

Don't get me wrong – it has nothing to do with any notion of beauty! I voice this fledgling theory grudgingly because I'm not enamoured of some of those demanding and gaudy garden showpieces. But one of the shrub or wild rose types might be just the ticket. Here's why: the rose is universally recognized as a symbol of love, but there's usually a thorn at the heart of its beauty. And, like the rose, I know I'm often prickly with those I love. I'm a woman who needs to be alone, often, and I know how hard that can be on those closest to me. Maybe over time my garden is helping to at least blunt the pricks of those thorny moments.

A special birthday gift has sparked this train of thought. I probably didn't tell you about it earlier, but it's worth giving it its due now, because it was so unexpected – and so thoughtful. It arrived via a card from an aunt I haven't seen or spoken with in a long while. Tucked into the envelope was a generous money order that came with strict instructions to "buy a great, glorious rosebush you've been hankering after." What a treat!

My aunt had heard from Mom about my horticulture studies and wanted to encourage me. She says I'm upholding a fine family tradition, and it reminds her of my grandmother's beautiful gardens of years gone by. My two grandmothers (gardeners both) are dead now, and I only dimly recall their gardens, but I sure wish I could talk flowers, herbs and vegetables with them, now that I'm old enough to appreciate their accumulated wisdom.

Choosing the perfect rose was tough. The variety of colours, sizes, styles, species and cultivars was dizzying. And you know how I am about roses: they must be utterly hardy, very low maintenance, able to get by without chemicals and friendly enough to grow alongside the five others that grace my only sunny fence. Any newcomer must have a positively delicious fragrance, too. None of those elegant, long-blooming but scentless modern hybrids for me. I'm with Robert Browning on this one: "Any nose / May ravage with impunity the rose." Louise Beebe Wilder once sniffed, "A trend towards mere beauty of person in roses is greatly to be deplored."

So all that narrowed the search. I was looking for an old-fashioned rose, it turned out, one of those often referred to as shrub roses. They have some of the best scents going. Thanks to my plant studies and our correspondence there was yet another criterion: the rose should be useful in some way, a healer or a plant that would bear fruit that people or wildlife could use. The philosophy of the Shakers, with their barebones lifestyle and shared property, appeals to me on this point: "[I]t was strongly impressed on us that a rose was useful, not ornamental.... Its mission was to be made into rosewater, and if we thought of it in any other way we were making an idol of it and thereby imperilling our souls," says one "sister in a Shaker community (American)," according to Kathleen Bronzert and Bruce Sherwin's book *The Glory of the Garden*.

Finally, I found what I was looking for in an out-of-town specialty nursery. It's *Rosa gallica officinalis*, the French apothecary rose that has been in cultivation and used medicinally for more than a century. Next year, let's hope I'll be gathering apothecary rose petals for a potpourri for your desk. (The fragrance is in the petals, I've read, as opposed to the leaves, stems or seeds where some other plants harbour their individual scents. Did you know that?)

I've christened my new rose Katharine, after my aunt, and it should delight me in July with several rich crimson blossoms cupping bright yellow stamens. Old-fashioned roses like this one have big, blowsy open flowers with many overlapping petals; this type is considered a semi-double. It probably won't flower more than once a season, unless I'm lucky enough to get a second brief show in the fall. That's not likely until it's had a year or two to settle in. Blazing red round fruits – the nutritious rose hips – will appear sometime in August and delight the birds well into winter.

Those lovely hips are the source of rich supplies of vitamin C, as well as some other vitamins – such as E – and acids. Vitamin C fights a number of viral and bacterial diseases and forms collagen, so important to heal wounds. Rose-hip tea can be a mild laxative or diuretic. In the Second World War, when fresh fruit was rarely available in Britain, the plentiful native rose hips were collected and made into a vitamin-packed syrup for both civilians and the military. Other medicinal uses for roses have been as eyewashes, throat gargles and cough syrups. To quote Native writer Loren Cruden, "Nongrasping love is rose's vision of well-being. It is an herb that refreshes and rejuvenates, calming stress and pain."

That's how Canadian rocker Neil Young saw it in his song "Love Is a Rose," warbled on our CD player by Linda Ronstadt on her *Greatest Hits* recording. "Love is a rose but you'd better not pick it / Only grows when it's on the vine / Handful of thorns and you know you've missed it, / Lose your love when you say the word 'mine.'"

Liz, there's so much lore connected with the rose that I hardly know where to begin! Instead, I'll just relate a few of my favourites.

It's mentioned in the Bible, though it's not always clear what flower is really being referred to. Apparently, the rose was in the Garden of Eden, and developed thorns only after Adam and Eve's departure from that celebrated place.

One adorable legend has roses turning red after Cupid spilled wine over one of them, while another says Venus's bleeding feet stained the blossoms as she stepped on thorns when chasing after Adonis! Roses usually represent female beauty, and the flower is often painted with the Virgin Mary. But in Arab lore, the white rose emerged from the tears of Mohammed as he made his way to heaven. The colour of the blossom is significant: tradition has dictated that the white rose stands for innocence and purity; the yellow for jealousy or perfect accomplishment; the pink for simplicity or happy love; and the red for passion or desire. White roses were once used to denote a virgin's grave, and fallen rose petals are seen as reminders of our mortality. My *Rosa gallica officinalis* is said to signify "union."

Roses appeal to cooks, too, but in the interest of brevity I'll leave you to explore that angle at your leisure. Do try the enclosed rose petal jelly, though, and let us give thanks for old dears who will take the time to make this treasure for the rest of us to find at church bazaars. It's excellent on a toasted English muffin.

Modern rose culture can be so demanding that I feel vindicated by the remarks of the authors of *The Reluctant Gardener*: "Roses are the stars of the garden, but you pay for the show they put on. They are expensive, high-maintenance plants, susceptible to bugs, diseases and severe winters. You will need the temperament of a gambler and the discipline of a soldier to enjoy growing roses in a cold climate."

Where angelica is known as the angels' herb, roses are often called the queen of flowers. That sounds both impressive and intimidating, but for the sake of my little apothecary rose I'll try to become the "Queen mum." I've given it my best shot while planting: heavy (but not wet or clod-forming) clay-based soil, compost and bone meal enrichment to more than a foot deep in the planting hole; full sun; annual manure or compost mulching; winter protection in the form of mounded soil and evergreen boughs. Many roses require severe spring pruning, but old-fashioned roses should be left alone until after flowering – and then just trimmed for size, shape and to remove weaker canes. Canadian gardening expert Mark Cullen says this is because they bloom on last year's growth. My kind of maintenance, for sure! (Even better, mine is prickle-free.)

My rosebush will reach three to five feet in height – eventually. There's a related cultivar you might fancy called 'Rosa Mundi' that looks like candy with its white–pink–deep-pink mottled, semi-double blossoms. These shrubs are winter hardy and heat tolerant, so with regular care I don't anticipate any big problems. You can check back with me in a year to see how my little *Rosa* is.

The vultures are circling, so it must be close to dinnertime. I'll have to close, but not before noting that I think it's high time you and I do what the poet Edna St. Vincent Millay advised: "Oh, little rose tree, bloom! / Summer is nearly over. / The dahlias bleed, and the phlox is seed. / Nothing's left of the clover. / And the path of the poppy no one knows. / I would blossom if I were a rose." As for those signature flowers I mentioned, I'm still thinking about what yours would be. Something like a bronzed perennial autumn chrysanthemum, perhaps, or a blazing butterscotch blanket flower of the *Gaillardia* group. What do you think?

Anne

Dear Anne:

"Sage and rosemary together work better than either alone," says *Rodale's Illustrated Encyclopedia of Herbs*. Isn't that so true about friends? When my world collapsed two years ago, it was family and friends who pieced together a patchwork of love strong enough for me to hold on to. As Robert Fulghum said in *All I Really Need to Know I Learned in Kindergarten*, "When you go out into the world, watch out for traffic, hold hands, and stick together."

I am grateful for all those helping hands – and for the foil-wrapped peanut-butter-and-jam toast my big brother would deliver daily to the hospital for my dinner; the meal roster my colleagues organized so that Michael and I were fed for months; the gifts of long-distance phone cards while I was in the Ottawa hospital; the visits, calls and letters from faraway friends; the handheld signs saying More Ice, Book Please, Make This a Tube-free Zone, Call a Nurse and Go Away! that you and Maggie made so I could "talk" with those blasted tubes down my throat. And, of course, I give thanks for all the flowers and plants that brightened my corner!

As I was yanking out some sage that had run amok in the garden this year, I remembered what the garden looked like when we moved here. In three years, the garden and I have changed – so much so that I don't recognize either. "Illness forces one to care for oneself.... In illness, finally comes permission to rest, permission to treat with love and kindness the base matter of one's own body," writes Judith Duerk in *Circle of Stones*, a commentary and compilation of meditative thoughts from women who have struggled to find their inner selves.

I've had to rest for so long. And for so long I had to abandon the garden. "I would spend long hours sitting in a chair.... I sat at the window by the garden, watching the birds at the feeder. We had a simple relationship, the birds and I.... they ate...I watched. Time passed," writes one woman in Duerk's book.

As time passed, the garden plants struggled for some balance – as I did, I suppose. The sage firmly took root, commandeering the sandy, sunny portion of the flower bed. I recall a much smaller tuft of sage that first year!

Yesterday, as I carted armfuls of the tangy herb to a composter, I had to admire the tenacity of this perennial. But it's time to rein it in. The whorls of purple flowers look dramatic against the backdrop of orange tiger lilies, but I don't want the sage crowding out the fainter, pale delphiniums nearby that have, at best, a tenuous hold on life in my garden. In the same vein, I can't let the tougher grief overwhelm that twinge of gentle joy in my soul. It seems that grief, even two years later, must be acknowledged like the morning fog we often have in this Great Lakes city. I hear ships on those early, foggy mornings blowing five short whistles to let other ships know their locations. But soon, the sun burns off the fog. Then I hear the ships blow one long and two short whistles as the captains recognize other ships around them and say "hello." The ships see where they are and I see garden colours. "It finally feels as if I am finding my way to my own life…. There is a hush, a sense of waiting…as I watch my life unfold itself to me newly each day and beckon me onward to its unfoldment," writes another woman in *Circle of Stones*.

I'm sure you aren't surprised to read that today's plant has something to do with health and where that leads. My garden's common sage, *Salvia officinalis*, has been revered for centuries for its curative powers. Flowers, leaves and oils from this plant have given it such a healthy reputation. *Salvia* comes from a Latin word meaning to save or heal. Not surprisingly, this herb – another hardy member of the mint family – is associated with immortality and longevity. It has even been called *Salvia salvatrix*, Sage the Saviour. Rodale's records that a tenth-century Italian medical school is credited with this phrase: "Why should a man die, when he can go to his garden for sage?"

Why indeed? Gargling with sage is said to soothe a sore throat, relax inflamed tonsils or ease bleeding gums. Rubbing fresh leaves on your teeth supposedly cleanses them while strengthening the gums. Leaves steeped in boiling water, then strained, were used to darken hair. "Good for diseases of the liver and to make blood," wrote Culpeper, adding, "and Pliny saith it cureth stinging and biting serpents." Sage tea was used to treat everything from headaches to hemorrhages and was valued so highly that the Chinese would trade their superb green tea at a four-to-one ratio. (Now, I would not part with my green tea!)

And sage spices up soups or casseroles with its lemony, bittersweet taste. Of course, Christmas dinner would not be complete without sage dressing, would it? In Holland, the leaves and flowers of *Salvia glutinosa* are used to flavour wine. I've learned that sage is a flavour to savour – just a sprinkle can add a pungent punch. Perhaps the Psalmist was acknowledging the power of sage in this verse of thanksgiving: "He causeth the grass to grow for the cattle, and herb for the service of man: that he may bring forth food out of the earth" (Psalms 104:14, KJB).

Biblically, some scholars liken *Salvia judaica*, the sage that grows throughout Israel, to the Jewish menorah, notes Allan Swenson in *Your Biblical Garden*. When sage is dried flat it looks like it could be the natural model for this seven-branched candlestick used in temple services.

What do you think "domestic virtues" are? I've read that sage represents them, too. I imagine it means caring for hearth and home, but I like to think it means also caring for others, for family and friends. Could this be stretched to caring for the gardens that help heal our bodies and souls? Seems plausible, as in one area of France sage is supposed to lessen grief – whether physical or mental.

On our side of the pond, sage (and cedar, too) is often used for smudging – a traditional Native way of purifying air by using smouldering plants to drive away undesirable influences or to welcome good ones. I've attended many Native ceremonies where smudging was used, and I remember a sense of wonder – and even holiness – as different herbs burned at various stages of the ceremonies. The ritual is so soothing to one's senses, watching as the smoke is gently waved throughout the air, and then inhaling various scents. "Herbs can be used to maintain the integrity of sacred space during ceremony," writes Loren Cruden in *Medicine Grove*.

Along with sage's association with longevity, Cruden adds that the herb has properties very useful to menopausal women. "Sage expresses a sensible wisdom and perspective, a long-range consideration," she notes. Perhaps we need a bit more sage in our lives to achieve that sensible wisdom, that long-range perception we both must muster. "Only by prevailing against her guilt and dread can a woman bring her life situations, one by one, under her own jurisdiction and authority. Only by prevailing can she relate to her life through her own wisdom…a woman comes to her own grounding, a sense of her own substance," writes Duerk.

On that note, Annie, I'll close. Be sure to check around the enclosed sweetgrass braid (to scent your kitchen or office) for a small packet of sage – as it does last forever...

Elizabeth

P.S. Thank you for that minced garlic you sent weeks ago. I've used about a quarter of the jar already – it is much easier for these hands than pressing clove after clove. To paraphrase Chaucer, "well loved she garlic, onions and leeks!"

Hi, Liz:

The midnight fax wizard strikes again! I'm restless tonight, so I started rummaging through garden catalogues and reference books on your behalf. Your query about a ground cover (other than your ivy) for a shady lot under evergreens was tricky, because the plant I had in mind wasn't in my main school text. But never fear – I found it elsewhere.

I'm impressed, by the way, that you're getting quizzed by friends and neighbours about gardening. Word of your horticultural prowess must be spreading!

You can tell your friend from theological college days that she can create a beautiful, low green mat under her churchyard's old spruces with *Vinca minor*, better known as periwinkle. Charming, starry blue flowers will dot the carpet in late spring. It spreads slowly, though, so recommend that she get a few flats of this perennial early next spring. Then she can set them out over a wide area, well spaced, and "layer" some of the creeping runners later in summer to fill in the spaces. Periwinkle is hardy to your area and can thrive even in deep shade, as long as it has good fertility and is kept moist through droughts.

Here's what I know you will value most about periwinkle – it contains alkaloids used to treat some forms of cancer. A related annual type called Madagascar or Rosy periwinkle, *Catharanthus roseus*, is a traditional African treatment for diabetes. Periwinkle has been employed medicinally to stop bleeding, and as an astringent. Medieval herbalists thought it could cure fear, envy and demonic possession. (Just right for a church, eh?)

Your friend might be interested to learn that this spring beauty stands for sincere friendship in France, but the Italians call it the "flower of death" and used to place periwinkle wreaths on the graves of their deceased children. In Germany, it's a sign of immortality because its small, leathery leaves remain green all year – even under snow. My favourite legend comes from England, where the plant means tender memories but was also known as the sorcerer's violet that could be tucked into charms and love potions.

Originally from Europe and Western Asia, periwinkle has been grown since ancient times and is widely planted in North America.

I have two kinds of *vinca* in my yard, both growing in a dark corner beneath a young walnut tree and sprawling mallow shrubs. One is the regular periwinkle, with its graceful pairs of glossy, deep green leaves on runners that spread every which way. Only a few blue blooms have appeared so far; it's still a fairly new planting. For variety, I was given a cutting by a friend last summer. It is the 'Ralph Shugert' cultivar, which has creamy white leaf edges. Both types are spreading, but during the growing season I try to hurry them along by pinning the long stems down at various intervals under soil and some small rocks. They root at the leaf nodes then, creating new plants. You can also take a cutting, strip it of all leaves except a pair at each end, and bury them in a shallow trench wherever you want. This is the "layering" technique I mentioned earlier. (I learned these tricks at school.) Many other types offer white, rosy pink, sky blue and plum blossoms. *Vinca major* is almost identical but is larger and possibly less able to cope with extended hot and dry periods.

It's worth digging the planting bed well before establishing a ground cover, because you won't be digging a few years down the road. There should be lots of organic material, such as compost, worked in to nourish the plants. New plants should be placed a foot apart. Winter protection will save the evergreen leaves from drying out and discolouring, and weeding is important in the first couple of seasons.

Because periwinkle is so shallow-rooted, your friend could improve the spring picture by tucking some bulbs in here and there – daffodils and snowdrops would be gorgeous.

Maybe you'll want to share this with "the rev," courtesy of William Wordsworth: "Through primrose tufts in that green bower, / The periwinkle trailed its wreaths; / And 'tis my faith that every flower / Enjoys the air it breathes."

And in the spirit of sincere friendship, I'd like to share some wise words from a children's author that you and I – and Maggie – adore, Jean Little. In her 1970 work of children's fiction, *Look Through My Window*, Little explained how true friends can endure despite their differences. "'We mustn't be careful. If we say the wrong thing, we must just forget it. Maybe we'll learn. But we mustn't be watching out all the time. We might end up talking about things like the weather. Safe things….' She looked ahead… and saw the two of them, grown up, still friends, still different, still talking about real things and not minding hurts because they had so much that was good."

Anne

Joy

"Weeping may endure for a night, but joy cometh in the morning," the Psalmist wrote of God's covenant – promise – to his people (Psalm 30:5, KJB). It seems that joy is so inextricably juxtaposed with anguish that one cannot know a true meter of ecstasy without experiencing some measure of suffering. Perhaps it's a condition of our humanity that we can compare only the most obvious of emotions or experiences. As Canadian artist Missakian expressed it, "Through my paintings, I celebrate life with ecstasy over passivity, movement over inertia and joy over melancholic outlook."

Joy is often described as happiness or pleasure, while its opposite is "dismal" – a word that means "dark." So, joy – light – is contrasted with what is dismal – dark. Jesus is often described as light in the Gospel of John: "I, the light, have come into the world, so that whoever believes in me need not stay in the dark any more" (John 12:46, JB). Joy must be as powerful as light to overcome darkness. Sydney Carter's lyrics in the ballad-like hymn "Lord of the Dance" capture this power of joy over darkness in the last verse: "They cut me down but I leaped up high / For I am the dance that can never, never die / I'll live in you if you'll live in me / For I am the Lord of the Dance, said he!"

How we experience joy seems twofold. It can be like a wave of intense, however brief, happiness regardless of circumstances, or it can be a state of perpetual joy, something we deliberately cultivate in our lives. Observe how it bursts forth when you follow a generous impulse, as in the breathtaking yellow of spring daffodils bought with your last few dollars, money that was intended for bread or milk but is instead exuberantly cast upon the waters of cancer society fundraising.

In their book *The Pleasure Connection*, Deva and James Beck write of how endorphins can naturally encourage joy in our lives. "Have you ever felt a fleeting sense of bliss? It happens like a slight mist... phantom feeling.... This phantom is a good example of the quick bliss which tiny endorphins can bring to us. You might have felt this joy while listening to a glorious birdsong, smelling a flower's fragrance...."

Nineteenth-century French writer Gerard de Nerval opined, "Every flower is a soul blossoming out to nature." To which we would reply, "Every garden is a soul coming into flower." Garden enthusiast Vivian Elisabeth Glyck exulted in her 1997 book *12 Lessons on Life I Learned from My Garden*: "And when the sun finally shone on my soul again, when I could allow love, sexuality, passion, and grace to touch me once more, I discovered that I had emerged a more resilient being than ever before. The winter of my soul helped me to find my spirit, and so I have blossomed into a self-reliant, intuitive captain of my own destiny."

If we choose to find joy in our lives, it cannot depend on circumstances. Viktor E. Frankl was a renowned psychiatrist who survived years of almost unbearable horror in Nazi death camps. In his classic book *Man's Search for Meaning*, he wrote that we can say "yes" to life in spite of pain, guilt and death. "If...one cannot change a situation that causes his suffering, he can still choose his attitude." We can find meaning for our lives, some measure of that deliberate, determined joy. Frankl continued, "People tend to see only the stubble fields of transitoriness but overlook and forget the full granaries of the past into which they have brought the harvest of their lives: the deeds done, the loves loved, and last but not least, the sufferings they have gone through with courage...."

In his 1996 book *Would You Believe?*, Tom Harpur writes of the keen interest in spirituality – "the name we give to the dimension of seeing and living that goes far beyond the material world to deeper truths and eternal values" – in the years before the new millennium. "Something is definitely stirring in the human soul as we approach the year 2000 A.D.," he says.

Harpur contends that the spiritual challenge in the coming years is to find a "form for a spirituality that moves beyond anything our species as a whole has before thought of, or practised." This "cosmic consciousness" is something Richard Maurice Bucke, a Canadian doctor, wrote about at the turn of the twentieth century. One night, while in London, England, Bucke had a profound spiritual experience that led to this insight of cosmic consciousness. Harpur describes the event: "At once, there came upon him a 'sense of exultation, of immense joyousness accompanied…by an intellectual illumination quite impossible to describe.' Into his brain 'streamed one momentary lightning-flash of Brahmic [divine] Splendor which has ever since enlightened his life. Upon his heart fell one drop of Brahmic bliss….'"

This is not some faraway place that Bucke and Harpur are referring to. Rather, all is possible in this world, in our land pockmarked by pain, stripped bare with grief, if we work at understanding and recognizing this universal awareness. As the nineteenth-century American poet, diplomat and abolitionist James Russell Lowell wrote, "Great truths are portions of the soul of man; Great souls are portions of eternity."

So joy is also about triumphing today over the infinite fears of tomorrow, and the guilts and regrets of yesterday. It is about choosing to find meaning in the face of adversity, about shouting "yes!" more times than snapping "no," and about dreaming despite despair. Marathon of Hope runner Terry Fox said in 1980, after the cancer that had taken his leg returned and he was forced to stop his one-legged run across Canada: "How many people do something they really believe in? I just wish people would realize that anything's possible if you try, dreams are made if people try. When I started this run, I said that if we all gave one dollar, we'd have $22 million for cancer research, and I don't care, man, there's no reason that isn't possible…. I'd like to see everybody go kind of wild, inspired with the fund-raising." Canadians said yes, and Terry's dream realized $23.4 million for cancer research before he died in 1981.

Terry's famous hip-hop run with his artificial leg has been cast in bronze statues in mid-stride, like a dancer caught in a moment of motion. In dance we express our dreams, our hopes, our joyous celebration over hardship. The author of Ecclesiastes affirms that yes, indeed, there is a time to mourn and there really is a time to dance.

The Lord of the Dance is a figure who transcends religions, from a Hindu god who dances to the ordered movement of the universe to the hero of an Irish legend who defeats an evil foe. The hymn "Lord of the Dance" can get the most hardened soul toe-tapping in time as the lyrics skip through the air – a powerful testament to how joy overcomes suffering: "I danced on a Friday, when the sky turned black / It's hard to dance with the devil on your back / They buried my body and they thought I was gone / But I am the dance and I still go on."

Canadian novelist and ardent peace activist Margaret Laurence touched on this theme in 1987 when, not long before her death from cancer, she wrote in her memoir *Dance on the Earth*: "I believe we have to live, as long as we live, in the expectation and hope of changing the world for the better…. What are we to live for, except life itself? And, with all our doubts, with all our flaws, with all our problems, I believe that we will carry on, with God's help…. May the dance go on."

Like the song's refrain, joy is something that should lead us through a lifetime. "Dance, dance wherever you may be / I am the Lord of the Dance, said he / And I'll lead you all wherever you may be / And I'll lead you all in the dance, said he."

* * *

Dear Elizabeth:

I've been thinking a lot lately about spontaneity, and its role in our capacity to experience joy. At a time when you are beginning to enjoy life again and I am coming to terms with and finding calm acceptance about my choices over the past few years, it seems to me we should be on top of the world. We're finally free of so many old demons, ready at last to take chances and explore new horizons, to open ourselves to even deeper emotions. But I'm feeling a reluctance and malaise that I can't explain – and I'm wondering whether the inability to be spontaneous has something to do with it. Do you have it, too?

I learned at an early age not to feel or expect too much, because then disappointments wouldn't cut as deeply. Later, I guess I squelched every instinctive response so that I'd have time to assess, gauge reactions or second-guess the situation. That protected my core, and helped me try to meet all those expectations life throws at us. Am I doing it still, waiting for external permission or an outside reaction to tell me how I feel about things? Kind of ridiculous at this age, don't you think?

But we speak often of masks, shells, walls – aren't they all part of the same thing?

Fortunately, with you I can be impulsive and unrestrained, and that is what I value most from my garden – the chance to succumb to some grander design without fear or hesitation. Laura Smith, another Canadian songwriter we both admire, has said joy is "a personal thing," and that resonates. So does something I read about the revered French Impressionist painter Claude Monet; he said in his later years that working in his garden was what he relished most. "I wanted to stay put here, where I'm happy. I've grown used to the flowers in my garden in the spring and to the water lilies in my pond…in the summertime: they give flavor to my life every day." More than a decade earlier, when he was sixty-four, Monet had told a visitor to Giverny: "Aside from painting and gardening, I'm good for nothing."

That must be what I want from my grubbing in dirt – the chance to finally be happy with myself, sure of who I am and what I'm doing. One day soon, I want to love me as much as I love the things I nurture and celebrate in nature.

A pretty roundabout way of introducing the rhizome I've sent along this time, isn't it? I've always admired those people who feel secure enough to meet life with a "Damn the torpedoes! Full speed ahead!" defiance. For me, the flower that best exemplifies this is the iris – a breathtaking flourish of brilliant colour atop a strong stem.

Iris means "rainbow" in Greek, named for the messenger goddess who brought only good news. A mounted poster of one of Van Gogh's famous iris paintings has presided in my bedroom for decades, grandly eloquent.

Let's consider this humble root your rainbow and mine. It's *Iris reticulata*, or netted iris, a treat I picked up at a horticultural society sale yesterday and something I've always wanted to grow. Come early spring, it should be a deep purple, dwarf plant with fragrant blooms and yellow or orange markings on wide-reaching falls. It likes full sun and slightly alkaline, well-drained soil. The tiny bulblets multiply well and can be lifted to divide in the fall. A few clumps would look lovely along your creek.

There are so many types, colours and varieties of iris – literally hundreds – that entire horticultural societies are devoted to them. You can peruse catalogues that sell only iris, and there are at least six main classifications – so I won't presume to describe the family in any detail. Just savour them as I do, applaud their variety and explore ever further if you want to add to your collection.

One floral book I have says the flower's three petals represent faith, wisdom and valour; what an uplifting trinity!

Anne

Oh, Annie!

I am prickling like one of your high-brow roses at the thought of a chrysanthemum being "my" flower, as you suggested recently! Really, Anne.

I chanced upon the letter while sifting through the spoor on my desk. (Who knows when I'll need that carpet-cleaning coupon for my hardwood, or when I'll order a complete set of country-

and-western commemorative silver spoons, or leap at the offer of a two-for-one walking trip in the Scottish highlands! The detritus that clutters our day-to-day lives, eh?)

But how could you, dear garden soul, think of me as one of those tidy, perfectly formed puffballs! Ugh…those are not adjectives this pen would ink to describe my life! That said, you impelled me to check the floral lore – I do appreciate the love, truth and cheerfulness attributed to these sunny-coloured globes.

As I read of your rosebush, my heart stung – just a bit – remembering *The Little Prince* by Antoine de Saint-Exupéry. The tiny prince loved and cared for the one rose in his world, even after he learned there were many like it in another world. He said of his beloved flower: "But in herself alone she is more important than all the hundreds of you other roses: …because it is she that I have sheltered…because it is she that I have listened to, when she grumbled, or boasted, or even sometimes when she said nothing. Because she is my rose." Doesn't that celebrate the uniqueness of being cherished, treasured and loved?

In this, my next rush of thoughts, I offer a floral tribute to you – a packet of borage. I know its name sounds so harsh, and perhaps that accounts for its hard message of "bluntness." But you have always been straight with me, Annie. Some would say blunt, others would say forthright, even honest. Sugar-coating isn't your style, thank God. Remember the phone call telling you I had cancer? After that dreadful pause, your voice struggling, you told me, "Okay, I'll get working on the Net. We need to find out about this." You knew that we had to put our research skills to work. You knew that naming the disease and learning the lingo would help me contain the fear. As the author of Ecclesiastes penned, "If for want of sharpening the ax is blunt, you have to strike very hard, but the reward given by wisdom is success" (Ecclesiastes 10:10, JB). Oh, we succeeded, didn't we? Remember the pages of questions I'd have for the doctors? Yikes, they must have cringed seeing me gimping along the halls, files spilling over my arms! We sure learned more than we ever thought we'd need to know about ovarian cancer. Breaking it down into a research project helped me tackle it – and handle it – bit by bit. It is a lesson well appreciated for the next crisis, whatever it may turn out to be.

Now with borage in my garden, like you as a friend, I have even more help. *Borago officinalis*, the culinary herb, is a plant of sweet surprise. Royal purply-blue faces look down from the tops of the hairy stems of this self-seeder, lending credence to the notion this plant represents courage. Celtic warriors reportedly drank borage-flavoured wine to imbue them with courage before battle, notes *Rodale's Illustrated Encyclopedia of Herbs*. There's one suggestion that its name actually comes from an old Celtic word meaning courage. Borage, like any stalwart companion, strengthens neighbouring plants against pesky insects or disease.

Borage might also be a corruption of the Latin word *cor*, referring to "heart." And here I found an ancillary significance for this common potherb. It is good for our hearts and our souls. As the sixteenth-century herbalist Gerard noted, the flowers were used to make the mind glad. "There be also many things made of these used everywhere for the comfort of the heart, for the driving away of sorrow and increasing the joy of the minde."

That joy is something I have found so ephemeral. Just when I thought I'd grasped it, a phone call with more bad news ripped it from me. Looking back, that's when I turned to the garden. I was looking for the joy that my mom found buried there. I'll never know if I discovered what she treasured even in the scrappiest plots, but I have unearthed my own bit of joy. As Carole Giangrande wrote of gardening: "It is only a beginning, the limited solution to a few limited problems. But it is a powerful antidote to the feeling of helplessness that assails so many of us so much of the time. Above all, the garden is…often beyond what we ever hoped for or planned."

Instead of trying to clench my joy, I've learned to let it drift over me and ebb when it must. Like the pain I know will recede during an MS exacerbation, joy is the gentle warming wave I know will return even in the driest of times. I also know I have a responsibility to work at joy. If I sat back waiting or just wishing for it, I don't think it would roll in! Sharing times with Michael, my family and my friends, quiet time in the garden and reading are investments in future joy, I think. "Grief can take care of itself; but to get the full value of joy you must have somebody to divide it with," said Mark Twain. Perhaps sharing that joy is a bit of what God's love is, maybe even where it is.

So here I've shared my borage thoughts of joy with you, but I must bring you back to cultivation tips. With such extraordinarily joyful symbolism, you might be surprised that borage does just fine, thank you very much, in ordinary soil. Be sure to plant it in a sunny spot with lots of space (perhaps your west wall?), as the individual clumps will need about two feet each. These dear, bobbing babies will remember to reseed themselves (Like the joy, right? It will come back!), so it's no surprise borage and forget-me-nots belong to the same family.

Your herbs should bloom next May if you get the seeds tamped in this fall, but don't worry if they take a second year to bloom. In our grandmothers' times the flowers were candied to treat those with lung ailments. Water distilled with the flowers was used to treat eye inflammations. As Jeanne Rose writes in her herbal guide, "Borage is said to have a wondrous effect on the body…and mind." French king Charlemagne thought so too, as he had a royal herb garden planted in the ninth century. Herbs were believed key to better lives even then, writes Sarah Ban Breathnach in *Simple Abundance: A Daybook of Comfort and Joy.*

Annie, I have read so many biblical passages about this elusive joy. Some speak of gladness, happiness or completeness of a joyful heart. But I've found some comfort in the accompanying verses – the ones that address mourning or sadness. They've affirmed what I've experienced – that to know that briefest bit of heartfelt joy, one must have lived the heartache of grief. "I will change their mourning into gladness, comfort them, give them joy after their troubles," wrote Jeremiah (Jeremiah 31:13, JB); "You will be sorrowful, but your sorrow will turn to joy," says the Gospel of John (John 16:20, JB). I particularly appreciate the simple honesty of this, another verse from John, and one I've said over and over again in my mind: "In the world you will have trouble, but be brave" (John 16:33, JB).

I see I've ended this letter in a much different spot than where I started. Maybe that says something about joy, grief or life. And there is precious little for you in this package this time – just some seeds, and a few cherished verses. Savour both and keep well, dear friend. I hope for a bit of joy in your life this day. As one of our favourite authors, Emily Dickinson, wrote, "The soul should always stand ajar, ready to welcome the ecstatic experience."

Elizabeth

P.S. Thank you for the iris – Michael planted it by the creek, as requested.

My dear Elizabeth:

God, it's good to hear you in fighting form again! I've missed our occasional verbal jousting matches. This means you really are regaining your old strength – and doesn't it feel fabulous? (As you may have guessed, I'm feeling somewhat perkier myself; maybe it's the St. John's wort.) It's clear you've no more than a cursory acquaintance with chrysanthemums, though. Allow me to extend your horticultural horizons just a little further.

I'll have you know the humble mum has been grown in China since 500 B.C., and it comes in literally hundreds of colours, shapes and sizes. At the annual "mum show" my mom and I used to attend at the Central Experimental Farm, before government cutbacks closed it, I can recall blooms ranging from miniature bronze buttons to big, white daisy types to huge, stringy pastel confections resembling spider asters. Certainly there were the "puffballs," but so much more! Shasta and painted daisies and the small, medicinal feverfew have at times been classified with the mums, too, but not anymore. It's a genus in transition, to say the least! (Most catalogues and nurseries shun the new family name *Dendranthema*, though, and continue to sell wagonloads of plain, old hardy chrysanthemums each fall – and that's what gardeners look for.)

Joy

My school textbook says this flower has been described as "the last smile of the departing year," and I have a fact sheet that praises its late-fall colour and christens the plant the "October Rose." A book I'm reading notes another bizarre quality: according to *Feng Shui in the Garden,* the houseplant-type mum is excellent for clearing toxins such as ammonia, benzene and formaldehyde from household air, but also honours the past. The name "chrysanthemum" comes from the Greek words for golden flower; it is an emblem of Japan and is revered throughout Asia as a symbol of purity and longevity. One legend has it that a spring rising up from a bed of chrysanthemums can give new life. Those qualities, along with the warm tones and special beauty of this late flower, were what I had in mind when I suggested it could be your floral signature – not any misconceptions about a perfect pompon life. The vibrant chrysanthemum is something to be cherished, in my view, as is your golden friendship. Take it or leave it, at least now you know what was intended. And be forewarned – I'm dragging you to a good greenhouse or fall flower show the first chance I get, to show you some real mums!

But enough about mums; they aren't even what I intended to write about today. Consider this a bonus letter, because you're getting information about two plants in one package. The true subject of today's missive is a much more magical garden treasure, the captivating lady's mantle. All I can send right now is this lush photo from the clump that grew in my garden last season, but come spring I'll rush out and pot up a cutting or two so you can share in the "miraculous cures" that *Lois Hole's Perennial Favorites* says Arab legends have promised. Note the breathtaking raindrops that glisten in the centre of each leaf in my photo: therein lies the magic that I'll explain shortly.

Just over a foot tall, this perennial is best recognized by its elegant scalloped leaves, but veteran gardeners also seek it out for the unusual chartreuse colour of its flowering clusters. The one-eighth-inch blossoms that appear in late spring have no petals but pack many four- or five-sepaled greenish-yellow balls into a dense, spreading flower head. *Alchemilla mollis,* as it is botanically known, tolerates either full sun or partial shade in cooler climes like ours. It likes moist soil and good fertility, and will reward the accommodating gardener by self-sowing. The plant's soft green, velvety leaves and two-foot rounded shape make it an excellent edging for garden beds or pathways. It is sometimes used as a ground cover in low-traffic areas. Lady's mantle provides beautiful dried flowers, and the fresh-cut blooms will last at least a week in bouquets. Few pests or diseases bother the plant.

It's said the lovely leaves gave lady's mantle its common name, because they represent the cloak worn by the Virgin Mary. In Arab countries, some believe a tea made from the leaves can restore beauty and youth. The description in one of my herbal catalogues doesn't hold out quite the same hope; it says the plant can be used to treat rheumatism, failing appetite, stomach ills, muscle problems and menstrual disorders. This is also an astringent herb, so adding it to your bath helps to heal skin inflammation. In Native medicine, lady's mantle is considered a love herb and is sometimes called upon to aid in birthing.

For me, though, there is irresistible charm in the notion that drinking the dewdrops collected in the centre of each leaf imparts some magical quality or special wisdom. The Latin names get closer to the spirit of the plant's uniqueness, I think. *Alchemilla* means alchemy, the mysterious process whereby one thing is transformed into another. And *mollis* refers to the silky whitish-grey hairs that give the leaves their frosted, silvery appearance. In other words, soft and gentle transformation. And isn't that what we're aiming for, you and I?

Songwriter Dar Williams has a verse in "You're Aging Well" that I think lays it all out for us: "[T]he woman of voices...gave me the language that keeps me alive. She said: / 'I'm so glad that you finally made it here, / With all things you know now that only time can tell, / Looking back, seeing far, landing right where we are, / and ooohhh...aren't we aging well?'"

On that mellow note, I'll close for now. But here's another bit of wisdom we can appreciate, from Shel Silverstein. Pulled from his poem "How Many? How Much?" it seems to fit the friendly tone of this letter. "How much good inside a day? / Depends how good you live 'em. / How much love inside a friend? / Depends how much you give 'em."

Anne

P.S. I got so carried away with my plant writings that I forgot to tell you my exceptionally good news. One of my teachers has asked me to be an apprentice in her landscaping business next summer! She says the pay isn't great, but it will be a remarkable chance to learn, a break from classes and a time to put what she calls my "strong sense of theme and design" to work. Can you believe it? More than ever, I can hardly wait for spring...

Dear Annie:

Congratulations on your new job! As you get ready for this landscaping venture consider these 1935 thoughts from H.B. Dunington-Grubb: "The Canadian landscape architect works day and night for six weeks in the spring; snores gently through the short, hot summer; finds his autumn golf interrupted by the occasional job; and hibernates during the winter." But I know you, dear soul: autumn finds you grubbing in the dirt, padding and tucking everything in for the cold months ahead. I can't imagine you hibernating; instead, you'll probably take more courses so that next season your gardening skills will be that much richer. You have so much to offer with the sensitivity you bring to your gardening. I could say you have a gift for gardening, but I won't, because I know how you have scraped to reach this point, putting heart and soul into that sometimes heavy and always difficult work.

To sum up our weather this week, I quote Peter Mayle's *A Year in Provence*: "We went to bed in one season and woke up in another." The dew stays longer these chilly days. Before I dream of next year's new plants, there's lots of mucking around to do – and high on the list is consigning to the compost this year's outtakes! But first...

The birch you suggested for the front lawn survived. Skinny and scrawny as it looks now, I can picture it growing to grace the scene around it. Anne, I have lost a bit more sight in my good eye, but I am holding close the hope I'll continue to see my garden, birch included. Michael had the front garden extended out to the birch, mainly so he can mow the lawn more easily but also so that I could have a larger morning shade / afternoon sun flower bed. The birch was a fine choice, as it accepted its move with little visible angst – just a few yellowed leaves. No doubt it will bow to that winter north wind, but I don't think it will snap. It just needs time to settle into its space. As Ella M. Harcourt wrote, "[N]o one should be permitted to view our gardens – and especially mine, – who has no imagination; whose soul is so dead that he cannot gaze ecstatically at a vast waste of earth…and see beautiful visions like the pictures in the catalogues."

One "vast waste" in my garden that certainly did not turn into an ethereal vision was my sweet marjoram. After playing with sage and rosemary, it seemed almost de rigueur to try *Origanum majorana*. (There's "thyme" for next year! Ha ha!) A perennial in warm places but an annual or a rangy houseplant here, marjoram is known as a "prosperity" herb. And prospering is a verb you and I could use in our lives, right? "Along with luck is the grouping of herbs linked with prosperity. These herbs in their various ways embody a truth of abundance or of the thriving that is possible in the interconnection of giving and receiving. The prosperity herbs help perspective to be open, positive and accepting of good," writes Loren Cruden.

While I successfully started the marjoram seedlings indoors with moist soil near my sunniest, warmest window, the transplants didn't thrive. They need lots of sun in well-drained soil, something I thought I had given them. Perhaps those hot July days I spent at camp sapped their strength. I know, I know, I should have kept a closer eye on them, but I honestly forgot about these small mint family members that I had moved into the far southwest corner of the garden. Until I can reseed in spring, there are always the few dried young leaves I harvested that are delicious in poultry dressing and almost any soup – creamed, strained or pureed. A herb catalogue we both have notes that it's essential for a German potato soup. (Yum!) But Patrick Lima declares in *The Harrowsmith*

Joy

Illustrated Book of Herbs, "This is a herb I like to smell but not taste...a little too perfumy for foods...."

Medicinally, marjoram – primarily wild marjoram – has been used for various complaints from toothaches to cancer. Marjoram is reputed to benefit the skin and can be added to herbal bath mixtures, recommends herbalist Jeanne Rose.

Just as sweet as its oregano-balsam taste is its Greek lore. Native to Eurasia but naturalized across the Mediterranean, the Greeks called marjoram "the joy of the mountains." One myth says that marjoram was really a youth named Amarakos, who was in service to the king of Cyprus. One day Amarakos, fearing retaliation, fainted after dropping a jar of the king's favourite perfume. While he was still unconscious, those ever-thoughtful gods changed him into marjoram so that he would forever sweetly perfume the palace. Capricious or what?

Marjoram was also considered dear to the goddess of love, Aphrodite, and that is what makes the herb so gentle, notes *Rodale's Illustrated Encyclopedia of Herbs*. Maybe that's why one birthday book says it is a symbol for blushes. This herb was thought to comfort the dead when grown on graves. One could dream of a future spouse if anointed with marjoram before retiring, adds Rodale's. Sweet dreams, perhaps, but I think of a dear verse from Proverbs: "When thou liest down, thou shalt not be afraid: yea, thou shalt lie down, and thy sleep shall be sweet" (Proverbs 3:24, KJB). That is peaceful, isn't it? And, yes, marjoram can be used in dream pillows!

Annie, you know how bereft of professional help I was during those god-awful dark days of grief, then the loneliness of cancer. I really felt I was travelling in some foreign land where I didn't know the language or customs. Canadian author Penelope Williams apparently felt the same way. She wrote in her compelling 1993 account of her experiences with breast cancer, aptly titled *That Other Place*: "I wanted to stump along alone; well, alone except for my own personal support group.... But alone in the sense that I was the only traveller; my family and friends cheered and encouraged from the border."

But Williams did find solace, strength and release as she began sharing her feelings with other cancer patients in an informal self-help group – she found fellow travellers who, unfortunately, knew the route. There's so much that can be done to help people with "grief work" that I want to look into educational programs this year with an eye perhaps to a millennium pastoral project. Yes, Annie, I'm willing to push the envelope of health one more time. "We'll see," so to speak!

Michael understands that the family deaths and the cancer took my soul to a different place. God knows, it felt frozen for months as I tried to cope with the day-to-day surgery stuff. But my soul is ticking again. The intensity of all that pain has lessened to the point that Michael and I are back to our bickering and bantering. Thank God! One – or two – can only tiptoe around life so long and then it's time to shout, to scream, to holler, "I'm alive!" Like the last few leaves in the backyard today, the golds, russets and crimson reds are startlingly alive. Autumn's colours aren't spring's, but they can dazzle me any day – that's enough.

Michael bought us a new "professional standard" rake with the widest fan I've ever seen and I'm itching to get out and totter around with it. I'll close with these words from the late art critic Bernard Berenson: "I walk in the garden, I look at the flowers and shrubs and trees and discover in them an exquisiteness of contour, a vitality of edge…. Each day, as I look, I wonder where my eyes were yesterday."

And that quote, at last, should offer some hint as to this package. (Yes, you can open it now. You didn't cheat by peeking before checking out the "Open Me First" envelope, did you?) Ta-da! Do you like it? If you turn the painting over, you'll see it is titled *The Garden of Our Souls*. All our plants are there, Annie – that's what I requested when I commissioned it. If you need courage, find the Madonna lily, see the snowdrop for some hope, look to the oak sapling for patience, and like the purple sage that weaves throughout the canvas or the periwinkle that dots its corners, please know I'll crop up when you need me, my garden friend!

Elizabeth

Cultivating Friendship

Fast-forward seven years. Thankfully, Anne and Elizabeth are still playing in the dirt and revelling in their gardens – though now often on cantankerous, creaking knees. But these are newer, smaller gardens, the products of changed circumstances.

While there has been much to celebrate, especially in terms of personal growth, there have also been sorrows and setbacks. Elizabeth has soldiered through several new periods of illness: cancer scares, increasingly serious MS attacks, an infection that wouldn't heal and eventually destroyed the lymphatic system in one leg. And the ever-present fear that the cancer will return, someplace clse.

For Anne, money worries and some less-than-rewarding work experiences have taken their toll. An aging body and flagging spirits often challenge her dream of working in landscaping. A motor vehicle accident three years ago affected two of Anne's most essential gardening tools: the strength in her back and, sadly, her stamina.

Lifestyles and relationships have altered for both women. Each confesses to periods of emptiness when nothing seems worthwhile. Sometimes they laugh, haltingly, that age 60 is closer than 30.

The friendship that sustained them through so much has been scarred by a time when each felt abandoned and the bond came close to breaking. Trust that the two thought rock-solid has been fractured. While Anne and Elizabeth continue to care and reach out to one another, more effort is now involved. There's an edge of doubt, and a readiness to hold back in self-defence. They acknowledge that hesitation and Elizabeth, perhaps more than Anne, is frightened. Several friendships Elizabeth thought whole have been scarred by her actions in the last few years; some will not heal.

It seems like a return to the bleak days when they first started exchanging the "garden" letters – but with fewer expectations. Elizabeth is revisiting her spiritual roots, exploring in many new fields for enlightenment and reassurance. Anne is more cynical. She's just searching – wherever the road takes her.

* * *

Dear Anne:

I hope you and Maggie kicked back and kicked up your heels on summer vacation. (Remember the John Candy movie?) Three weeks in Prince Edward Island! It's been decades since I scooped clams or ate fresh lobster at an island church.

Do lupines still skirt the highways in their pinks, blues and mauves? They are striking in bloom. Okay, we won't speak of the toppled stalks.

Annie, I didn't want to leave this message on your voice mail. I'd be crying, and that would frighten you. And I didn't want it jumbled in e-mails you'd be scurrying through as you got back into work mode. No, my heart said this news required an old-fashioned, handwritten letter.

A few weeks ago, Bizzie died. She was 14 years and one month.

She came into my life one year after Michael did. Remember how he and I used to be so careful about splitting our finances, half and half? Well, she was the best $200 I ever spent. Bizzie was with me for one third of my life. I knew she guarded me, but she always thought it was her job to protect our house, too. In fact, the one time our home was vandalized Bizzie was away with me at camp. (I never told her about the break-in!)

This past winter was horrid for all of us. Essentially, Bizzie lived in the bungalow's short hallway; I couldn't get her out for walks because of the strep in my left leg. That lack of exercise, in turn, exacerbated my MS. Her arthritis was bothering her, so she wasn't too eager to go far anyway. I promised her a good summer – but then it poured cats and dogs all June and July. One rare clear day, Bizzie was out in the garden. Unbeknownst to me she got into the foxglove that had been so carefully tended by the previous owner of this house.

Anne, I knew nothing about foxglove, but that night Bizzie's breathing was laboured. She couldn't follow commands, and despite always being such a lady, she didn't notice her incontinence. We got to the vet early the next day, and I was told to think of putting Bizzie down. Killing Bizzie! To paraphrase Churchill, it wasn't the end but the beginning of the end. Those dainty violet bells Bizzie ate signalled an ominous decline.

The guilt I feel about that foxglove will haunt me for a very long time. Within two weeks she was gone.

Please, however stunning and gentle the trumpets appear, do not plant foxglove if you still want to encourage your neighbour's puppy to visit. This biennial is infused with digitalis, the drug used to fight heart disease. In fact, its Latin name is *Digitalis purpurea*.

I learned from reading *The Harrowsmith Perennial Garden* that foxglove usually enjoys moist soil. I think I'll give that area an intended drought. Author Patrick Lima encourages gardeners to be patient with the seeds of this plant, cultivating them with peat moss, compost or leaf mould. While my noxious ones grew in full sun, foxglove favours the shade.

Yes, Annie, I recognize the medicinal value of this plant but it has hurt my heart – and our dear Bizzie's.

Apparently, foxglove was used in healing as far back as 1000 A.D. The English turned to it for coughs, epilepsy or swollen glands. Some have speculated that Vincent Van Gogh took it for epilepsy, and that it influenced his art (*not* his heart): various reports have noted patients seeing a yellow aura when the drug is consumed. Go figure.

Solace

You and I have shared intense grief these past years over deaths and illnesses. Broken relationships, too. I understand – in my mind – that I have transferred some of my relationship grief to Bizzie. But I cry all the same.

Remember when we wrote about grief? That it circles back? Yet one more time, one more circle…

I checked *Healthy Healing* and discovered that my garden actually contains plants that make antidotes to the arrhythmia Bizzie exhibited: evening primrose, peppermint, rosemary, sage and hawthorn. Various extracts, teas and oils can ease the irregular heartbeats in people, but probably not in dogs, I realize. And I wasn't about to play home pharmacist.

I've had Bizzie cremated; the urn is in a box near my desk. What do I do with it? When my mom was cremated we buried the urn with my father's casket. But my beloved Bizzie? If I bury her in the garden near a special plant (dogwood?), what happens if we move? Do I dig her up? I haven't considered animal burial rituals before.

I have read part of Axel Munthe's "instead of a preface" to *The Story of San Michele* more than once these past weeks. Can't remember if you know the book. You and I would agree this passage is overwritten, but it was 1936 and perhaps it was the style of the time:

> I can say with a clear conscience that I have not deceived my readers – in my love for animals. I have loved them far more than I have ever loved my fellow-men. All that is best in me I have given to them, and I mean to stand by them to the last and share their fate whatever it may be. If it is true that there is to be no haven of rest for them when their sufferings here are at an end, I, for one, am not going to bargain for any haven for myself. I shall go without fear where they go, and by the side of my brothers and sisters from forests and fields, from skies and seas, lie down to merciful extinction in their mysterious underworld, safe from any further torments inflicted by God or man, safe from any haunting dream of eternity.

Whew. Long to write, long to read, but I feel that way sometimes. Maudlin, but perhaps I'll have Bizzie's ashes sprinkled with mine into Lake Superior.

Okay, enough. I have rambled on without even asking about your health. How is the joint pain – are you still taking devil's claw? And how was the holiday?

Keep well, my dear, and write soonest.

Liz

P.S. Please tell Maggie her drawing of Bizzie remains on my office door.

Dear Elizabeth:

Oh, my poor Bizzie! I've felt so sad since reading your letter. It was hard enough when I called you after learning the news, but worse when I told Maggie. We cried together, then she brought me her best spiral shell from the ones we had collected in P.E.I. She was so solemn. She'd like you to mark Bizzie's resting place with it – a love token for the dog she never got to meet but loved anyway.

I know Biz adored the water, so that might be a good place for her ashes. But a special spot under the dogwoods would be appropriate, too; *The Language of Flowers* says dogwood is a symbol of duration. That was certainly Bizzie – in there for the long haul, no matter what. If you tucked some of those bluebells we both love beneath the shrubs that would also fit: they signify constancy.

It amazed me how well Bizzie and I hit it off, the few times I was able to travel to your house. As you know, I'm a devoted cat person with little experience of dogs as companions. Bizzie's exuberant paws-on-the-shoulders, face-drenching welcome always shook me a bit. But when you looked deep into those expressive brown eyes you couldn't help but see the intelligence and decency of that sweet canine soul. I was just flattered (and relieved) that she accepted me from the start as a worthy friend for her precious Elizabeth. I envied the unqualified devotion she gave you. It was just like what Connie Kaldor describes in her song "I Love That Dog": "And on those days when it seems / like I haven't a friend /

he's so glad to see me / that he wags his whole back end."

Cherish the memories, my dear, and you'll have the best of Bizzie with you forever.

It almost seems too cold to turn to another subject now, but maybe you'll find it apropos. There's a herb I've stumbled upon recently that you might like for your "wilderness" out back. It's called motherwort, *Leonurus cardiaca*, and it has been springing up repeatedly in one of the gardens I look after. My Richter's herb catalogue calls it a "gentle sedative" often prescribed for palpitations and to calm the nervous system. An Internet source (www.purplesage.org.uk) notes the Greek word *leonurus* describes the shaggy, toothed leaves; they were thought to resemble a lion's ear or tail. The common name refers to the plant's use in soothing anxious new mothers and helping the uterus contract after delivery.

The tall, pink-flowered plant I'm finding grows vigorously in bright sun and dry soil, and I let a few plants remain in selected areas because I like their colour, height and wide-branching habit. I'll have to keep rooting out newcomers and cut off all the seed heads, though, or it will soon be everywhere. Many more formal horticulturists consider this a pesky weed!

Our old friend Nicholas Culpeper, the English herbalist of long ago, declared: "There is no better herb to take melancholy vapours from the heart and to strengthen it."

Let's take heart, then. In closing, I must add that I'm very glad we've revived handwritten letters to supplement – or complement – our phone calls and e-mails. It's a quiet, contemplative form of deeper connection that I've truly missed these last couple of years…

Anne

Oh, Annie!

The tucks and folds of your package revealed treats to make my spirit and face smile. That fragile seashell arrived without a chip or crack – so I share a snippet of your P.E.I. trip. Once I get some help lifting that glass from my coffee table I'll place it with my other shells. Maybe next to the tiny seahorse.

Of course, I'll say you shouldn't have sent the money towards Gracie's vet bills, but I am grateful. The vet has not charged for all his services. However, the tally remains substantial; I'll trot your contribution up today. Bizzie's sickness was bad enough, but when Gracie-the-Wonder-Kitty developed heart problems things started to get way out of hand.

Last weekend I walked (er, tripped) my way through a nature path within the city. Bizzie and I used to tramp that trail but I'd scold her for bumbling into burr bushes. Poor girl would cry when I had to pull burrs from her snout. Still, next visit she'd find more burrs. When I arrived home on Saturday, I had prickly burr heads stuck to the oddest places on my clothes. You can imagine. But only my cane had edged off the path – nary a piece of clothing. My, how strong the grip of a burr! No wonder they are said to be the inspiration for Velcro.

What a curiosity burrs are – somewhat like a porcupine's quills transferred to flora. I wondered about their history, and if they had any use other than provoking loads of laundry.

Without question I turned to my weed book, leaving aside perennial garden guides. Sure enough, *Arctium lappa* or the great burdock occupied some substantial four pages. After all your horticulture courses, I'm sure you can translate the name, but just in case, *Arctium* refers to "north" and "bear," while *lappa* refers to those pesky burrs. In fact, an old English term for the burrs meant "robber" or "to seize." Quite appropriate, I think.

Shakespeare agreed. Celia tells Rosalind that "if we walk not in the trodden paths, our very petticoats will catch them" in *As You Like It*.

It isn't difficult to find burdock because it has free rein in ditches, fields and stream banks, and sneaks into many a garden, including mine. The taproot stretches down three feet and the plant can tower eight feet. No wonder I couldn't pull the ones Bizzie found at the back of this yard last year. Burdock's domain is north of the equator throughout Asia, Europe and North America.

I was surprised at the number of medicinal uses for all the parts of the plant. Marg, my homemaker, remembered it being sold as a tonic years ago when she worked in a pharmacy. Sure enough, when I checked *Rodale's Illustrated Encyclopedia of Herbs* I read it has often been used as a diuretic or a general pick-me-up tonic. Maybe we should try it.

Even teenagers can benefit because burdock can help clear up acne. Leaves, roots or seeds boiled with different ratios of water produce the skin toner or the ingestible tonic. Although physicians and pharmacists dispute its effectiveness, they don't question its safety.

Anne, as I wrestled with remnants of burrs that withstood the washer and dryer I thought of the struggles our friendship has suffered. While we have endured long silences – in anger, you must admit – we have "stuck" by each other.

Did you read Canadian writer Joan Barfoot's *Charlotte and Claudia Keeping in Touch*? It's about two seventy-ish women who have been friends since school days. At times, they too experienced emotional distance. My copy is well-worn. I'd like to share a short passage with you, where Claudia muses about her relationship with Charlotte: "Their friendship is a spine that has grown with them, and whatever aches and pains and inflexibilities it has developed here and there, now and then, its absence is not imaginable. What would one be without a spine?"

When I imagine my spine I see spiky vertebrae jutting out and causing pain, for which I keep a back pain pharmaceutical company in business. But without my spine I could not write this letter nor drive my car to post it.

This brought to mind a Keats verse of utter pain, from "Sleep and Poetry":

> But strength alone though of the Muses born
> Is like a fallen angel: trees uptorn,
> Darkness, and worms, and shrouds, and sepulchres
> Delight it; for it feeds upon the burrs
> And thorns of life; forgetting the great end

Of poesy, that it should be a friend
To soothe the cares, and lift the thoughts of man.

Must we always feed upon the burrs and thorns of life? Anne, I am so confused. What sort of Christian am I? Or am I one? What kind of friend am I to you?

I turned again to Shakespeare. Stratford's favourite author offers some advice in *Measure for Measure*. Simply: "I am a kind of burr; I shall stick."

I've been reading James, and a bit of the early church writings in the New Testament. He penned and spoke of deeds being more important than words. His writings speak to me – I feel I am more words than action, especially these last three years. "You see that a person is justified by what he does and by faith alone...so faith without deeds is dead" (James 2:24-26, NIV).

Annie, am I just words, not deeds?

I apologize for sounding so glum, but hey, home is where the heart is...and my heart feels far from home. I know you understand.

Lizzie

Dear Liz:

Well, I'm glad you didn't consider it necessary to include some burrs in your last letter! As you say, they're everywhere. I find them clinging to the bottom half of my garden pants all too often. Maggie has a talent for toting them along, too, from the schoolyard, the park, the bike path, you name it.

Did you know, incidentally, that according to Geoffrey Grigson in *Wild Flowers in Britain*, burdock was apparently named by the English botanist John Gerard in the late 1500s?

You wrote to me recently about the poisonous powers of foxglove, and now I have another toxic plant for you. It's *Aconitum napellus*, better known as monkshood or wolfsbane, and a concern to me this week because it isn't blooming in a nearby garden and a friend has asked me why. Before I get to the plant culture, though,

I hope you'll bear with me while I do some ruminating.

This stately garden perennial has been called one of the protective herbs by herbalist Loren Cruden, in *Medicine Grove: A Shamanic Herbal*. She says these herbs "are allies of discernment and appropriate response." Get yourself a drink, Liz; I've been into the wine and I'm feeling feisty tonight. What I have to say may or may not be "appropriate," but I think it needs to be said. I'll be anxious to hear your response.

Before I go any further, let me assure you that – brief lapses excepted – you have been a stalwart friend and I couldn't do without your continuing support.

I hope you won't consider this a poison pen letter but will take it as it's intended. I need to understand and put things into perspective. You won't be too surprised, I know, because we've skirted around this discussion a few times over the past year, ever since contact was re-established between us.

I'm talking about that long stretch a couple of years ago when you and I drifted so far apart that I thought our friendship was over. Almost overnight it seemed like we went from knowing virtually everything about each other's lives, thoughts and schedules to stilted, infrequent long-distance telephone calls. And then nothing… It's only because we have drawn closer again and agreed to forgive and move on that I dare mention this now. I don't want our friendship to ever reach that point again; it's just too damn lonely!

Remember Lynn Miles, the singer-songwriter from Ottawa who's doing so well now on the international folk circuit? She describes that void so well in the song "Loneliness" on her *Slightly Haunted* recording: "Loneliness sits on the porch of the house you used to live in / It is the distant sound of thunder and trains and loons / It is the hurt that hurts the deepest / It is the ache that you can't cure / It is the desperation of the late night telephone call… It is the cry of the southbound bird in the fall."

Those lines only scratch the surface of how I felt the day I heard a flat mechanical voice telling me over the phone line that the number I knew almost by heart was no longer in service. My e-mails started bouncing back about the same time, and it was weeks before you called to say hello and tell me breezily about how your life had changed. Yes, I was angry, and shocked that contact with me suddenly meant so little.

But I know there's fault on both sides. In fact, I seem to recall that I was the one to pull away first. And I'm sorry if I was brutal or abrupt in how I expressed myself then. It was a tense, unhappy time at our house, and I guess I thought it might be better if I turned my full attention to my own family instead of sharing every last snivel of frustration with you. I knew you were struggling, too, and both our mates had complained about how often you and I talked. I don't think men use their best friends as sounding boards and emotional lifelines the way women do.

In any case, it was a sad, solitary period – and I had my doubts about the new people claiming so much of your time. The Elizabeth I knew just seemed to vanish for awhile. I didn't know what parts of your stories and (mis)adventures to believe when we finally did communicate. Doubt crept in – and you know how I value honesty above almost all else. I can't say my spiritual side filled the void, either. If anything, it has probably receded.

There are likely a ton of psychological and spiritual references that would comfort or explain what we went through, but frankly I'm not interested at this point. It would take too much energy to look them up, or to read and interpret them.

Instead, let's just say that I'm glad you're back and that we're connected again. Like Charlotte and Claudia, Joan Barfoot's wonderful characters, let's keep on talking well into our dotage!

As for the plant, don't ever handle monkshood without gloves, Liz, and don't let kids or animals near it. All parts of it contain poisonous alkaloids. In fact, the name "wolfsbane" comes from an old hunting trick – arrows or parts of traps smeared with its venom whittled down the wolf population quite handily. A drug was once made from monkshood to relieve neuralgia and sciatic pain, but it proved too risky and the plant is now chiefly ornamental. Too bad it has such frightening qualities, because the hooded flower is a lovely late-summer or early fall addition to shadier gardens.

I prefer blue or violet cultivars, but the white and bicolours are also popular.

In case you're wondering, some checking in the reference books may have solved the riddle of my friend's non-flowering plants. They want partial shade and rich, moist soil; the experts warn that monkshood mustn't dry out. But dry roots are inevitable in the spot where Gail has hers planted, by a stone wall and in direct sun.

Here's a happier thought to end with: garden guru Patrick Lima says monkshood is an enduring perennial. That's what I'm wishing for us, too. So, are we good?

Take care and write again soon.

Anne

Dear Anne:

I know you worried about the poisonous nature of your monkshood correspondence, but stop. You wrote the truth. I'll try to respond in kind.

Yes, I was hurt. That said, Annie, I really did disappear. The Liz you knew went someplace dark, for a time that seemed like eternity. Instead of trusting myself, I gave control to someone else and that strained family and friendships. Consequently, my physical and emotional health worsened. I remain ashamed of who I became in my selfishness. What a fool I was, and now I am paying for that self-centredness. Some relationships are irreparably broken and some are tenuous at best. "Like a bad tooth or a lame foot is reliance on the unfaithful in times of trouble," wrote Solomon (Proverbs 25:19, NIV).

I'm afraid I'll run out of time before I run out of opportunities to make amends to people who were just trying to help me. But I so hope, as C.S. Lewis wrote in *Mere Christianity*, that God "does not live in a time-series at all" and will forgive me. Right now I need a lot of help to forgive myself. Thankfully, friends Beulah, Lee, Janis and Joanne are walking with me through this pain.

Thinking about time led me naturally to think about thyme. There is an old adage about this aromatic and tasty herb that seems particularly appropriate for this letter, Anne. "When in doubt, use thyme." Similar to "time heals all things," isn't it?

You will appreciate the possible origins for the name *Thymus vulgaris*. I sure do! *Thymus* was Greek for "courage" – something we both have needed to write these last few letters. However, the word could also mean "fumigate," and that's a scary thought. The herb would be burned to chase stinging insects from a household. Strangely, given that story, thyme remains a favourite treat for bees – and birds.

Here's a delightful tale for Maggie: in days of yore some people thought fairies lived in beds of thyme, so gardeners would set aside a patch like you and I do butterfly or bird houses.

Speaking, er, writing of which, my bright orange butterfly house has faded to a nauseating yellow and is falling apart. I hope the senior citizens' club continues to build them. That would be a great Christmas gift for my garden, wouldn't it?

I recently received *The Complete Book of the Flower Fairies* by Cicely Mary Barker. You would treasure the illustrations that accompany each poem. I checked for thyme and found this dear poem:

Where?
Where are the fairies?
Where can we find them?
We've seen the fairy-rings
They leave behind them!
When they have danced all night,
Where do they go?
Lark, in the sky above,
Say, do you know?
Is it a secret
No one is telling?
Why, in your garden
Surely they're dwelling!
No need for journeying,
Seeking afar:
Where there are flowers,
There fairies are!

My small patch of common thyme has tiny pink flowers, but I read that some bloom in violet. The shrub is small, only about a foot tall, and it flowered in late June this year, continuing well into July. *Rodale's Illustrated Encyclopedia of Herbs* recommends cluster sowing. Plants germinated from seeds indoors can be set outside in a clump for a faster, more stable crop. Thyme is pretty hardy anywhere with some sun and well-drained soil. That said, creeping thyme thrives in poorly drained soil.

Anne, I know you will smile at this next tidbit. Thyme ranges throughout the western Mediterranean but it is believed the wee seed-like nutlets reached North America via sheep's fleece!

The scented pillow you made me years ago is now tucked into my old stuffed animal collection and there is still a hint of thyme. Did you dry the thyme from your garden?

My well-thumbed *Landscaping with Nature* advises using *Thymus serpyllum* – creeping thyme – for the nooks and crannies of natural stone walls and paths. Apparently, this thyme forgives the odd footsteps, too.

Thyme also has a flavourful history. Its taste was found in liqueurs, cheeses and seasoning for beef from Greece to France. The plant's medicinal lore will perk you up: from the fifteenth to the seventeenth century it was thought to cure depression and epilepsy and was used to combat the plagues that swept through Europe. Beer with thyme was thought to be a remedy for shyness, while nightmares were said to be cured with a tea made with thyme. As recently as the First World War, its essential oil was a battlefield antiseptic. Even flatulence was "quieted" with a warm infusion made from the entire plant!

A tinge of thyme is still found in some cough syrups.

Apparently, French cuisine experts consider thyme one of the finest herbs. I can hear you snickering that I am definitely not one to write of recipes, but even I use dried thyme in tomato sauces and soups. Greek gourmet shops stock thyme-flavoured honey.

You have been faithful in keeping a store of bath treats on my shelves, and I still have some lavender bubbles. However, thyme is also used in bath cosmetics, cologne and even laundry detergents. What an all-round handy plant, isn't it?

Perhaps a tea with thyme would help ease my emotional pain. It is so easy to make villains of people whose opinions one doesn't like. Here is where I need the courage of thyme – and time. Thank you for trusting the strength of our friendship enough to tell me your truth. I will try to mend the threads of that trust.

Anne, I'm becoming maudlin, so it's time to put down the pen and turn out the lights.

Elizabeth

Dear Elizabeth:

I can't believe how spectacular these golden fall days are! I've been tucking in my garden beds for the winter and finding it so exhilarating. It was crisp but bright today, with geese flying over every now and then and a cardinal stopping by to visit – just perfect.

You'd think the end of the growing season would be a miserable time for a gardener, but I don't see it that way. It *is* sad to see all those great blooms, scents and textures coming to an end, but it's also a good time to take stock. Sometimes we get so busy with watering, feeding and caring for the garden that we forget to sit still and enjoy what's there. I'm guilty of that: I buzz around like a hummingbird when I'm out there, from task to task and improvement to improvement. Today was more tranquil, with lots of time to marvel at what did well and rejoice in how things have grown or multiplied.

There isn't a lot left in bloom at this point, so any plant still flowering has twice the impact. In my yard it's all purply stuff now: sedums, mums, fall asters and the odd bellflower. But there was one precious little burst of white and yellow in the front bed that caught my eye – and my imagination. It was feverfew, a perennial wildflower/weed that has been around here for a couple of years. I've seen the miniature daisy-like blooms and finely cut foliage before but never paid much attention; it's easily overshadowed by flashier summer flowers. But this was a late show, a second flush created by shearing and deadheading in midsummer.

In a way, I think this rebirth is a bit like our friendship. After a jolt and the pruning of old illusions and unrealistic expectations, we've been lucky enough to find new growth.

All of this is to say that I really appreciated your last letter, Liz. Thank you. I know that we said our apologies and "made up" a while ago; I just felt it was necessary to get some of the hurt out of the way and make sure we each knew how it felt at the other end. That way, I'm hoping we'll never go there again.

I don't want you grovelling or beating yourself up over what has happened in the past. What's done is done, and we both have so much to offer. Let's not waste it wallowing in negativity.

You know, Liz, I've lost friends through miscommunication and neglect before, and it's not nice. I think the worst mistake people can make in a friendship – or any relationship, for that matter – is to fail to respond. It gets misinterpreted, then bad feelings and doubts build up and the connection deteriorates before you know it. A close bond takes effort, and no excuse is good enough for putting it on the back burner indefinitely.

Kids seem to have a handle on this. Maggie and her friends are always on the computer "chatting" after school. I tease her about them being more open and brave in what they say online than they are in person, but at least they're talking! And they don't bother with e-mails that have a built-in delay and can be ignored – they're on real-time chat lines, with everyone contributing at once. (It's almost all in monosyllables and borderline illiterate – but that's another story…)

Back to feverfew, or *Chrysanthemum parthenium*. It's been known as a medicinal plant since at least Roman times, when it was used to treat the chills and fevers of the "ague." Fresh leaves were bound around the poor patient's wrists. One old superstition held that planting feverfew around the homestead would keep disease away, according to Anna Kruger's *Canadian Nature Guides – Herbs*. An online source (www.angelfire.com) says Dioscorides, the Greek herbalist, used it to treat arthritis, and in the 1600s

Culpeper prescribed this plant for strengthening women's wombs and relieving migraines. While I know you don't suffer from migraines – praise be! – you'll be interested to hear two of its more contemporary uses: for treating sleep problems (says Patrick Lima in *The Harrowsmith Illustrated Book of Herbs*) and indigestion (says Kruger).

It's good in the garden, too, warding off many pests because it contains toxic pyrethrin. There's another Latin name, *Tanacetum parthenium*, and a whole bouquet of common names, too many to list and several of them shared with its near-lookalike cousin German chamomile, *Matricaria recutita*. Both are often called "chamomile" as a common name, Kruger states.

Here's the best part – a source on the Web (www.victorianbazaar. com) called "Language of Flowers" gives a terrific meaning for chamomile, saying the plant symbolizes "energy in action." I'm not sure whether this applies to feverfew or to the German chamomile, but who cares? I'm adopting it as my personal motto and flower for the month of October! In the same vein, I've been touched by a song called "October Days" by John Lincoln Wright, a New England country singer, which I heard on a cancer fundraising album. Wright describes the glory of October mornings, filled with "the grace of life." When he talks about having high spirits and feeling full of praise, I know just what he means.

If you'd like to try growing some feverfew, let me know and I'll divide a clump for you. It's not too demanding; it just wants what most herbs crave – warmth, decent soil that drains well, and sun or light shade. Do try the tea; it's supposed to be a calming brew.

That's it for tonight. My tired old bones need a hot soak. Write soon and tell me how those spiritual studies are going, okay? Take care,

Anne

Dear Anne:
Mea culpa for this tardy response. I know it has been weeks since your last letter. But I have a good excuse. My right hand was

tied up – in an intravenous line. Yep, again. The side effects were crappy so I'm hoping the drug's kick stays awhile. Consequently, this has sidelined me from any garden action. I have two bags of bulbs, promising fringed tulips, cooling their roots in my fridge. Want to visit?

Oh, please finish reading before opening the accompanying small packet.

As I gazed out my patio door this morning with coffee in hand, I saw muted oranges, rusts and greens. The tapestry was shot with brilliant yellow and purple autumn crocuses that must have opened overnight. I didn't know they were in the garden. This yard surprises me every season, forgiving my mishandling of its sprouts and stems.

And thank you for the kind words of forgiveness in your letter. I've learned just how painful and lonely it is to take friendships for granted. Perhaps Robert Louis Stevenson knew those feelings before he penned these words in *Across the Plains*: "So long as we love we serve; so long as we are loved by others, I would almost say that we are indispensable; and no man is useless while he has a friend."

Today is another glorious – what you call golden – day. I remember from my Manitoulin Island years that painters Ivan Wheale and A.J. Casson would extol the quality of this autumn light shining on the North Channel. Casson described it to friends there as "the best painting light in the world."

I think of it as the planet's promise: despite the coming winter of pale light and grey horizons, the earth will be reborn with bright skies and green lands. Like the resurrection of Christ. The Gospel of John is replete with images of Jesus as light. "The light shines in the darkness, but the darkness has not understood it" (John 1:5, NIV). Or John's famous phrase that Jesus is the "light of the world" (John 8:12, NIV).

You asked me ages ago about my theology studies. As you can see, I tend to link events to my readings these days. Annie, it feels so good to be back in school, in yet another master's program! Years ago we talked about this possibility, but I never thought it would or could happen. The readings, lectures and class discussions stretch my brain "muscles" to climb hills I have never visited. But it is an incredibly healthy trip thanks to this amazing professor.

I'm taking a course on the biblical meaning of *shalom*, peace, from the Old to New Testament. What a "living" word *shalom* is. Tom, the prof, is excellent at illustrating the various nuances using the barest threads of verses. There are only about a dozen of us in the class, including several ministers. They certainly have me beat finding the references!

I must scold you for something in your feverfew missive: I suffer terribly from wicked migraines. How could you, The Keeper of My Illnesses, forget my whines of tossing my cookies with those wretched headaches? Shame on you! Oral drugs don't work so I land in emerg for IV meds. Then again, I'm on IV so often I bet you just take it all for granted. But perhaps feverfew is the long-hoped-for answer.

You are more adventurous than I in trying non-traditional medicines, so you will perk up at my next report. I am taking large doses of magnesium for my muscles and nerves. A woman in my theology class, who has a grim form of arthritis, urged me to try it.

Not knowing anything except that magnesium is a heavy mineral and used in garden fertilizers, I found an online primer. Apparently, every cell in the body needs magnesium. It is used in more than three hundred biochemical reactions. Get this – it is used to maintain *normal* nerve and muscle function. We both know I am anything but normal. I think I'd like "normal" for a change. Hey, it might be fun, downright hilarious, to have normal functions! Then again, that could be dangerous, as Bruce Cockburn crooned: "The trouble with normal is it always gets worse!"

Magnesium is found in green vegetables such as spinach or broccoli and in seeds and nuts. Would you eat more leafy greens if you grew them yourself, Annie? You, the avid baker, should be pleased to read that whole-wheat bread has twice as much magnesium as white bread. Just don't tell Maggie. (I wish she wouldn't insist on store-bought white bread when you bake such excellent loaves. Would you make some potato bread for my next visit? Please, pretty please?)

Although hard water is tough on our hair, it is rich in my new mineral friend. I am taking 500 mg of magnesium at night, plus whatever is in my multivitamin and water during the day. My pharmacist (yes, the one I've had a crush on for years) said the recommended dose is 50 mg twice a day. Most people meet daily requirements through a normal diet of five servings of fruits and vegetables, with a dark-green leafy vegetable thrown in for good measure. But with my hit-and-miss diet I need supplements of everything, I think.

I've learned that various drugs I take, plus the damned vomiting, may be depleting my magnesium reserves. It was weird to read the signs of deficiency because they include muscle contractions, cramps, tingling and numbness in the extremities. Everything I have with the MS. I have swallowed my way through one bottle of magnesium. Effects? Well, the spasms are marginally better, so I want to give it another month and another bottle. As a pharmacist said, what do I have to lose?

But that's not why I've sent *you* a bottle. The American Food and Drug Administration conducted a study of 30,000 adults with elevated blood pressure who took high doses of magnesium. The results, including four years of follow-up reports, indicated that blood pressure could be significantly lowered with a diet high in magnesium, potassium and calcium. Would you humour me and take the pills for a month to see if it helps your BP? While you and I can't often afford to live on magnesium-rich avocados and cashews, we can afford wheat germ, bran and peanut butter.

As menopausal women, we might benefit from magnesium. Several American studies have suggested that adding extra magnesium could improve bone mineral density. We need all the help we can afford, dear sister soul! As Oscar Wilde wrote, "Nowadays we are all of us so hard up that the only pleasant things to pay are compliments."

Well, it's time for a snack, perhaps a nice mixed cereal with peanut-buttered toast to go with my bedtime meds and minerals. Goodnight, my friend. Write when you can.

Liz

Hello, Liz:

The cornflowers are out and I've been thinking of you, so I was finally moved to write. It's been so long that I hardly know where to start – by acknowledging embarrassment that we let our correspondence lag this badly, I guess. Still, these have been frantic times and I know that writing by hand or on computer is difficult for you as you recover from the mastectomy.

It's not like we've been totally out of touch. The phone calls, e-mails and occasional gift packages are our habit now – a most appreciated lifeline.

It's wonderful that you're doing so well since your surgery. I was so dubious about the necessity for it, and so frightened for you. But obviously your instincts were right, and it was the only way to stave off another brush with cancer and attain some peace of mind. So congratulations once again! Your courage is a continuing source of inspiration for me. I can't wait to see where your religion courses lead, as you grow stronger.

You've been asking how I *really* am, and I haven't known what to say. But I'll try to outline a bit of it for you. I guess you knew before I did that Brian and I wouldn't be able to patch things up. We had grown too far apart. We lead separate lives now, intersecting only where Maggie is concerned. We've kept the arrangements as peaceful, flexible and amicable as possible, but there's always pain in a life change this big.

I think it's been long enough that I'm past the shock of being on my own, but numbness has set in. I see and feel everything from a distance, as if I'm the dispassionate narrator instead of a participant. In fact, that's what's gone from my life – passion. Everything is either by rote or in slo-mo. Emotions hardly ever surface, and when they do they fade quickly. There are great times with Maggie, of course, but that dynamic is also changing. She's had her own anguish to work through – hurts largely brought on by her parents, so we can't help. And she's approaching her teens now (gulp!) and that's a roller coaster on its own.

When she's not here, I seem to prefer solitude. I'm glad you can reach through the façade and give me a good shake every now and again!

No plant talk today, I'm afraid. Instead of viewing each plant as amazing and distinct, often symbolizing something in my life, and worth sharing, I'm seeing fuzzy panoramas. A field of grasses swaying in the breeze, or a lone lighthouse on a wild, rocky point. I still find release in the garden, but it's just a bit too staid and serene.

I know, complaining again – but it all makes me so impatient! And so disappointed with myself. When I look at what other 40- and 50-something women are doing with their lives, at what you are accomplishing against tremendous odds, I feel ashamed. What do I produce, and what do I have to feel sorry about? Or so afraid of? Such fruitless self-pity…

Instead of a lily of the field, I feel more like a common field weed. With more rough edges than ever.

As songwriter Stephen Fearing sings in "Glory Train," "Morning drags itself to town / spreading like a stain / I'm sick of waiting, waiting for the glory train."

A Nova Scotia artist I've been reading about would say I'm stuck in "aridity," a kind of fretful resistance to change and further evolution. I found Regina Coupar's *The Art of Soul: An Artist's Guide to Spirituality* interesting and much of her artwork beautiful, even soothing, but she is much more committed to the spiritual path than I'll ever be. I like her message about forging ahead and giving ourselves permission to grow through creativity – but haven't a clue how that's done, especially when you're bone-weary and sick of the world.

"It is when we turn inward and confront our darkness that the divine light of our soul becomes most visible. The dark moments of our lives provide an opportunity to seek strength, courage and guidance from inside ourselves," she writes. "When we stop fighting them, the experiences of the dark night strengthen our soul and deepen our understanding of the human journey. New life emerges from darkness." Uh-huh, but that doesn't get you out of bed in the morning to head off to work to put food on the table, does it?

The idea of painting has always appealed to me, though. Maybe, when and if I ever retire, I'll have the time and energy to try out watercolours or acrylics. Flowers and landscapes first, of course!

Meanwhile, I hope you enjoy the pocket calendar and bookmark I've enclosed. The painting of the black kitten among the tulips is probably my favourite; it reminded me of Gracie. These are the work of another Nova Scotian painter, who lived in Digby County (1903–1970). Her name was Maud Lewis, and her joy just leaps off the page – or canvas! I hadn't known about Maud until my mom mentioned her to me last year; then I did some research. She was a national treasure of sorts, an untrained, humble folk artist who took great delight in what she saw around her. She was able to express that passion in simple paintings that she sold from her tiny one-room home beside the highway. From what I've read, Maud's marriage, health and personal circumstances were far from ideal, but she transcended her lot in life and managed to pursue the thing she loved most.

One biography, *The Illuminated Life of Maud Lewis*, states: "Maud's inner strength, courage, determination, humour, and optimism illuminated this world so that she transformed something seemingly mundane into brightness and vitality." The same book adds a telling quote from Maud herself: "I'm contented here.... As long as I've got a bit of brush in front of me, I'm all right."

Her legacy is the vivid work she left behind, much of it now housed at the Art Gallery of Nova Scotia in Halifax, along with her remarkable painted house. But what will my legacy be?

For some perverse reason, I'm comforted by Saskatchewan poet Lorna Crozier's take on our irrelevance in the grand scheme of things. She writes in a poem titled "In Moonlight," from her book *The Garden Going on Without Us*: "Something moves / just beyond the mind's / clumsy fingers. / It has to do with seeds. / The earth's insomnia. / The garden going on without us / needing no one / to watch it / not even the moon."

Food for thought…

Anne

My dear Anne:

I am so happy to hear from you, especially after my wearying trip home.

I arrived home early Thursday morning after long flights, delayed connections and stormy weather. My tingly legs told me the MS wasn't happy. Between the west coast and Eastern Ontario I whispered to my legs, only a few more, just a few more hours until sleep. Now, after this travel whine of mine, I assure you the times out west were splendid – both with my girlfriends and then with my California family.

We ate too much, drank too much, but loved and laughed *so* much. You will be jealous to read that my cousin Chris and I saw Donovan in an intimate downstairs San Francisco pub. Donovan arrived curbside as Chris and I, along with a dozen or so other old folkies, waited for the doors to open. Well, the troubadour danced or spoke with each of us. Yes, I have pictures! And get this: we were at the best table, directly in front of the stage, poised perfectly between speakers. Just grit your teeth in envy, girlfriend!

Donovan sang signatory hits such as "Mellow Yellow" and Buffy Sainte-Marie's "The Universal Soldier," noting that the song is as appropriate today in the midst of the war in Iraq as in the days of the Vietnam War.

Thanks to the generosity of family and friends, these summer jaunts really helped. My heart, and perhaps my soul, splintered with the final breakup of my marriage. But I realized I must keep my mind – and my awareness of the "Now" – intact for the ever-present next surgery, my friends, my courses, even my kittens. I guess that is the "Now" of my everyday life. "The quality of your consciousness at this moment is what shapes the future – which, of course, can only be experienced as the Now," writes Eckhart

Tolle in his powerful book *Practicing the Power of Now*.

Although I appreciate your quote from Regina Coupar, I, too, struggle with how to stay focused on the divine light of my soul. She writes of the "dark night," and for me the dark night is literally one of pain, spasms, seizures. You know I agree new life can alight from darkness – but it is not easy. I think it is one of those lifelong lessons, speeding up or slowing down depending on the length of life. Does this make any sense? Your letter expressed what I have recognized over these last few years – you lost your passion. Your eyes revealed as much. I recognized it only because I saw that loss mirrored in my own eyes.

Anne, I so appreciate and understand your feelings of numbness. I describe it as a bleakness and hollowness. I have not let feelings surface. Now I let the tears flow as I discover new writings, allow the good memories to reappear and try to deal with my anguish. It is so difficult and painful, almost like trying to get blood from a stone, to paraphrase a much better soul. But we must do this arduous heart work to make room for a healthier heart. That's my dream.

I hope you understand that I *found* some passion in this season of summer travelling. I found that passion in the intensity of the music with my treasured cousin Chris; the intensity of the love my Aunt Ruth and my cousins Ruthmarie, Chris and Rich gave me; and the richness of spiritual experiences we shared from prayer to attending an evening of dharma talk at Spirit Rock.

Before reading your letter, I e-mailed Chris to say that I had several of those "aha!" passion moments while in Petaluma, about one hour east of San Francisco. It took a while to remember what passion feels like. But when I gazed at – and listened to – 2,000-year-old redwood trees, heard Stephen Foster's "Hard Times" gently played, tasted exquisitely broiled seafood and smiled with exceptional new friends, it tickled my soul, saying "Hey, girl, this is passion!"

Annie, this has been a painful year but I've had so much happiness recently. (Remind me I said this when I start feeling alone again.)

When Cindy and I were on Keats Island in June, we were smitten with the arbutus trees, and the eagles perched atop. Did you know eagles have three finger wings at the tip of each wing? That identifies the high-flying bird as an eagle. The arbutus's slim, smooth red-sleeved trunk stretched to the ocean from rock outcroppings, with arching branches ruffled in bright green leaves.

Cindy gently peeled a few layers of paper-thin bark from the closest trunk, and I've enclosed a piece for you. I hope you can read my inscription. Some passion was reawakening. The arbutus will always signify kindred-soul friendship to Cindy and me, now celebrating 32 years as girlfriends.

After I took that multi-faith course in June, I had no idea my summer travels would further my course experiences. They sure did. While on Quadra Island, off Vancouver Island, Cindy (who is Ojibwe) and I smoked her native pipe. As we sat on the rocky tip of Rebecca Spit, Cindy extended her beautifully handcrafted pipe in four directions: east for new beginnings; south for strength; west for clarity; north for healing.

This reminded me of a passage from *Religion in a New Key*, a book by Darrol Bryant, one of my theology profs:

> For it is important to understand that in the dialogue between religions, we are called not to reduce the intensity or depth of our own faith but to bear witness to it while respecting the faith of the others. So the proper context between believers is not, I believe, in terms of the superiority of my faith over yours, but in the depth of our devotion to the One that Muslims call Allah, that Christians call God, and that Hindus call by many Names. For it is that One and that One alone who should be the object of our striving and our faith.

Something, eh?

Then, while in northern California, family members and I visited Spirit Rock, a meditation centre about 45 kilometres north of San Francisco, for a Monday evening class. It was awesome. The centre hosts classes and retreats exploring meditation and its relation to our society. Jack Kornfield, who runs the class we attended, spoke of the goodness of people and of the peace one can find through self-discipline in studying the words and participating in the works of one's faith.

I juxtaposed his message of goodness with Christianity's core belief in the sinfulness of humanity. This is tricky. But once again, I was reminded of my summer course readings. I'm grateful I took my textbooks "a-travelling."

In *One Earth, Many Religions*, author Paul F. Knitter puts it this way:

> And so my image of the religious Other as a frightening and fascinating Mystery has been complemented by an image of them as *fellow travelers*.... my experience – and my trust – is that as followers of various religious paths, we all can experience a common concern and a common responsibility to respond, as religious persons, to the widespread human and ecological suffering and injustice that are threatening our species and our planet.... But I can say, from my own experience and from reading about the experience of others, that a growing number of believers from most religious paths *are* so concerned – and *are* experiencing themselves as fellow travelers and fellow actors with persons of other faiths.

Anne, I struggle with actions supposedly from my faith, with actions I hope I respect from other faiths, and with pain I try to keep from most people. St. Paul's words in his letter to the Romans confuse me: "But we also rejoice in our suffering; because we know that suffering produces perseverance; perseverance, character; and character, hope. And hope does not disappoint us, because God has poured out his love into our hearts by the Holy Spirit, whom he has given us" (Romans 5:3-5, NIV).

This is rough, because I do not understand the purpose of continued suffering. However, "hope" has become the most powerful word I know. Such a simple, four-letter noun and verb, it encompasses the new beginnings, strength, clarity and healing of Cindy's pipe.

And it speaks to me of action. Don't all of us strive to do what is good or right, in hope of that outcome? Audre Lorde said it so succinctly in "The Black Unicorn," which I read in her book *The Cancer Journals*: "Our labour has become / more important / than our silence."

Poet May Riley Smith wrote a piece called "The Child in Me," reprinted in the book *The Things That Matter: An Anthology of Women's Spiritual Poetry*. My girlfriend Yvonne Yoerger gave me this book of inspirational poems the last time she visited. It is a treasure. This poem haunts yet comforts me. The second stanza says:

> My House of Life is weather-stained with years
> (O Child in Me, I wonder why you stay).
> Its windows are bedimmed with rain of tears,
> Its walls have lost their rose – its thatch is gray:
> One after one its guests depart –
> So dull a host is my old heart –
> O Child in Me, I wonder why *You* stay!

I hope you understand why this comforts me. Despite the pain, I tell myself "this is a perfect day," and dream of love in my life once again.

There is medical news – but let's keep that for another letter. It is time for bed, or so the kittens tell me.

Liz

P.S. Tomorrow I am helping a friend weed her veggie garden. My reward will be a sample basket of everything ripe. Good deal, isn't it?

Dear Liz:

Well, it's happened again! The near-end of another season in my gardens has snuck up and clobbered me. I was doing some maintenance and clean-up outside this past weekend and spotted red tips on the Virginia creeper.

When did *that* happen?

Okay, it's not exactly pumpkin time yet, but there is definitely a winding-down feel to things, isn't there? All the back-to-school promotions are in full swing – with Maggie clamouring for some rad new clothes – while I'm still padding around in shorts and sandals. Out of sync again; what else is new?

Oddly enough, it's not sore knees or aching hip joints that are telling me it's been a long season. Instead, my poor old thumbs have taken the most punishment. One client has several mature, out-of-control shrubs that we've been trying to tame, and, often, my thumbs and knuckles suffer from secateur seizure – too much pruning in a single day. Worse, I'm regularly banging my hands into walls that are closer than I thought, or whacking them accidentally with the spade handle. I guess I'm getting clumsier in my old age. One garden friend who heard me complaining has passed along a great homeopathic remedy, though, that is really helping. Ask your healthcare people about arnica, and if they think it's okay to try some, I'll pick up a tube of the cream for you. It might help your aching joints, too.

We won't be growing this wildflower in our gardens, Liz. It's more suited to the dappled shade of open woodlands, and too plain for most cultivated gardens. The bright yellow daisy-like bloom isn't all that unusual or exciting. But it's still an interesting plant, and it commands great respect for its curative qualities.

Like so many plants we know and love, *Arnica montana* originated in Europe but hitched a ride over to North America. Members of this perennial species range from the Arctic to New Mexico. It's no more than two feet tall, with pairs of coarsely toothed, sometimes heart-shaped leaves. The flowers are about two to three inches wide, appearing in early summer. *Arnica* likes comfortably moist roots – no hot, baking clay.

Common names for this potent plant include mountain tobacco, leopardsbane and wolfsbane (this last shared with monkshood). It is used externally to soothe and heal sunburn, bruises, sprains, swelling and the like – but several sources warn it should not be applied to open wounds because it may cause inflammation, itching or other skin irritations. Internal use by tincture is generally not recommended, except under an experienced homeopath's direction. The plant can prompt severe allergic reactions in some people, so users proceed with caution. *Arnica* has been associated with side-effects including vomiting, diarrhea, nosebleeds, racing pulse and more. Still, it has been used in herbal remedies for hundreds of years, often to treat physical ailments of the heart. Both roots and flowers are used.

My handy cream is a 10–per cent arnica extract applied to soothe sore muscles. I appreciate how it seeps in and quietly eases various aches and pains, in an amazingly short time. As with many other homeopathic or alternative treatments, there's no serious medical literature attesting to its effectiveness as a healing plant. You have to take it on faith….

(Do I hear you sniffing about how I can take a weed on faith but I can't take faith on faith? Yeah, I know, the irony isn't lost on me either.) Maybe I'm learning more about life through this humble weed – something about how even those things that seem useless to us have some benefit or message of value. Instead of trying to eradicate weeds/troubles from our lives, we need to learn to live with them, and to find – cherish – what is worthwhile or meaningful. It's like learning how to live with pain and gain from the experience, what the psychobabble crowd would call "soul work."

Have we been here before? I think so; I get the feeling I'm slowly circling back to acceptance and trying, once again, to assimilate its lessons. As Ron Hynes sings in the lovely ballad "No Change in Me" that he co-wrote with Murray McLauchlan, "This getting nowhere is getting to me / wondering where can you go to be all you can be? / …No change in the weather and no change in me / I don't want to leave but you can't live for free."

The other thing I've noted is how I weed when I'm in the garden now. I don't obsess over rooting out every single weed or foreign shoot anymore. As long as the "good" plants are dominant,

I'm content to leave some of the lesser-knowns. Often I'm just waiting, to see what they turn out to be. Maybe it will be a happy surprise, something helpful or wonderful in some unexpected way. What do you think?

There's an exceptional writer-photographer and motivational speaker I think I've mentioned to you before. Carl Hiebert stunned everyone when he roared back into life by opening a flight school just two years after the hang-gliding accident that broke his back and paralyzed him. He became Canada's first paraplegic flight instructor, then in 1986 he flew across the country in an open-cockpit ultralight aircraft to raise more than $100,000 for the Canadian Paraplegic Association.

Hiebert was raised in a Mennonite farming community in southern Ontario, with unswerving faith in God's love and the spiritual side of our existence. After he was injured, he said affirmations during his recovery period and the love and healing he received from friends pulled him through.

"Obviously, I was broken physically," he writes in *Gift of Wings*, the breathtaking coffee-table book that he later produced, "but that was only one dimension of existence. Neither my mind nor my spirit needed to be destroyed by what had happened." He was profoundly moved by the friends who stayed with him through it all: "Friendships are perhaps one of God's greatest gifts," he says.

The book has some amazing photographs that he took of this country, and convincing testaments to our strength and abilities as human beings. He philosophizes: "The adventure in life happens only when I break away from routine and explore the untried. Only in the success of having risked and triumphed can we build our security from within. It is the only security that can never be taken away…. We each walk a path that is uniquely ours. The capacity to dream, to risk and to live fully lies within each of us."

Much as I admire your faith, and Hiebert's, you know my trouble with it. Those protestations about God and goodness and the spirit that's always with you just don't ring true to me. Not on a level I can understand, anyway. With all the horror in this world, and all the hollow emptiness I feel so often in my heart,

I find it pretty hard to believe there's a bigger being out there somewhere with a master plan that makes it all okay. And I don't appreciate the ultra-churchy set telling me I don't get it because I haven't accepted Jesus into my heart or seen the light yet – that's just too easy.

Still, I suppose it's only human to wish there was *something* else, "something more," as the song says. It makes me feel infinitely better to know I'm not struggling alone, to think that maybe the "something more" is just people flailing and floating along, trying to make something decent of life, day by day and moment to moment.

Meanwhile, the best maxim I can think of for my life is Aristotle's: "We are what we repeatedly do." That seems valid, another way of expressing that old saw: "Actions speak louder than words."

I'm glad you are finding passion again, and hope that good fortune continues to flow your way. You're doing all the right things, concentrating on getting healthier and stronger and tossing all that negative baggage about the past. Here's a quote I've saved just for you, from the incomparable novelist/journalist Joan Barfoot. It accompanied her submission to *Dropped Threads: What We Aren't Told*, a collection of stories by women edited by Carol Shields and Marjorie Anderson: "People with friends are moderated by them, less likely to slice themselves on the real sharp edges that create extreme journalism or extreme fiction. In work, edges fascinate me; in life I like to know friends are holding the rope."

Thank you for sticking around to hold my rope. Now, come for a visit soon, to drink some fine wine with me and savour Maggie's ditzy humour, okay?

Anne

Dear Anne:

Sounds like neither of us can give up our sandals! My "rotten feet," as my surgeon calls them, protest in blood if I wear anything but my 15-year-old backless Birkenstocks. Oh, well!

Feet are the foot of my medical worries. I wish *Arnica* was the wonder weed to help me, as it's helped you. The last two weeks have been rough. My phone calls are testament to that. But it is time to put ink to paper. It has been a roller-coaster ride worthy of a major theme park. "No cancer – cancer – no cancer – cancer." The possibility of bladder cancer has returned. I await yet another specialist's appointment.

You mentioned Joan Barfoot's quote about friends who are "holding the rope." That rope has been the telephone cord for me. I don't know what I would do without family and friends who so willingly accept collect calls or simply talk with me and walk me through so many of the jolts on this trip.

Anne, you have no idea how it feels to have that Damocles sword of cancer hanging precariously over your soul. I'm sorry, but I don't think you do. So often my soul feels naked because I no longer have a parent to "protect" me. Strange, eh, from a 40-something woman? Maybe it is just that the child never really leaves the safety of a parent.

However, it is just me and death now with no one to say "Stop! She's my daughter and you can't have her!" You have parents, siblings – and a reason, Maggie – to see you through tough times. For me, it is loneliness and fear. That sounds selfish, doesn't it? Have I told you I'm afraid no one will attend my funeral so I've created a small invitation list? Weird, I know.

I'm afraid one of these latest cancer sneak attacks will catch me off guard. I haven't had the time to sift through my memories and decide which to discard, which to share and which to keep in the treasure chest of memories in my soul. "One has only a life of one's own," writes Barbara Kingsolver in *The Poisonwood Bible*. I hold the key to that treasure chest.

My breast expander pump-ups were finished this week. Wow! The expander sacks will be replaced with more permanent saline implants in a few months. I have had good fun telling girlfriends, nurses and physicians that it is interesting to go through menopause and puberty at the same time.

Annie, humour is one way I get through this. I hope you understand.

Breast reconstruction is a choice, as is the accompanying pain, a decision individual women make. For me, it is life-affirming to build permanently perky boobs. From this awkward angle, the pain seems worth the gain. However, this physical reconstruction is just an interlude, a kind of sideshow to my two main medical events – cancer and MS.

When I heard two weeks ago that the cancer had likely spread to my bladder, I arrived home desperately weary. My soul was empty. The well was dry. Jane Siberry wrote in "Calling All Angels" exactly how I felt. Here's the final chorus that made me weep – not heart-wrenching sobs, but quiet tears that inched down my cheeks. Someone understood. "Calling all angels calling all angels / walk me through this one / don't leave me all alone / callin' all angels callin' all angels / we're tryin' we're hopin' / we're hurtin' we're lovin' / we're cryin' we're callin' / because we're not sure how this goes."

I surely do not know how this will go. I feel like the Old Testament Job who wrestled with God about human suffering. I never ask God "why me?" but I cried, and I *damn* well called "why aren't you listening?"

You know what it is like to be crying so hard you can't catch your breath? I longed for someone to hold me during those gasps, but I only begged God for strength. The author of the book of Job writes, "For He wounds, but He also binds up" (Job 5:18, NIV). Sometime near dawn I heard a small voice. I had to stop crying to hear the words. Anne, I realized I did not need the strength to endure all of it, I just needed the strength to begin. I could breathe. So I could begin.

Where did the words come from? If from God, why isn't he listening to the cries of women, children and men in the Sudan or in Saigon or in Seattle?

"Your saviour doesn't come from outside; it comes from inside," writes Thich Nhat Hanh, in *Anger: Wisdom for Cooling the Flames*, one of my new favourite books. So where did those comforting words originate: outside or inside? It doesn't really matter, because I found some peace.

A beloved singer-songwriter is my cousin Chris Samson from northern California. A phrase from one song I heard when I was stateside this summer really spoke to me: "You can search forever for your peace and find it maybe if you have the time," he wrote in a piece titled "Snakes and Dust."

Maybe I finally had the time because once I listened, really listened, to that inner voice, I found some peace. I made a list of things I wanted to get done, from shredding old love letters to shedding clothes and material things. Shredding – it's such a feeling of finality to see yellowed love letters, kept for years, sliced so cleanly into narrow strips. But it is also freeing – I have the memories and they can't be shredded. They are kept intact in my heart's "treasure" chest.

As I checked my apartment bookshelves for any forgotten letters, I recognized how neglected my indoor plants were. The best going were old dried petals I found pressed in a King James Bible! Some gardener, eh? My mom's nineteenth-century flower cart, which takes up a large corner of my living room, is my only garden. I am ashamed to admit that even my hardy geraniums have bitten the dust. Literally. It is appalling.

Although a cousin resurfaced the cart years ago, it needs more work. Years of Canadian winters rusted the old ironwork as the cart sat outside, brightening one garden after another. This month my brother will remove the rust and paint my wagon! The colour must be Swedish: yellow or blue, honouring our mother's heritage. I think yellow looks better with real (or fake) plants. I do get a bit of afternoon sun in that corner so I hope to coax a few more indoor plants to grow. That said, you and I were never very good with houseplants, were we?

Thankfully, one of my mom's ivies is intact, and that humongous Christmas cactus survives even the kittens' hopscotch games. So they will live to see another day…I hope!

I haven't lived in the living room much. My time has been in or at the hospital, in my bedroom reading or in the back junk room with my computer. I guess my living needs more room.

Remember Audre Lorde? So much of her work resonates with me. She refused to be silenced at what she experienced with the loss of her breast in *The Cancer Journals*. She speaks words I wish I'd written:

> My visions of a future I can create have been honed by the lessons of my limitations…. Sometimes fear stalks me like another malignancy, sapping energy and power and attention from my work…. Those fears are most powerful when they are not given voice, and close upon their heels comes the fury that I cannot shake them. I am learning to live beyond fear by living through it, and in the process learning to turn fury at my own limitations into some more creative energy. I realize that if I wait until I am no longer afraid to act, write, speak, be, I'll be sending messages on a Ouija board, cryptic complaints from the other side.

She describes exactly what I feel at times. And, yes, I can hear you say we are all running out of time, but please read this: "When I dare to be powerful, to use my strength in the service of my vision, then it becomes less important whether or not I am unafraid."

I haven't been afraid since I realized I needed only the strength for today.

In the course of these past months, personal reconciliation has meant a whole bunch to me, like an entire Dutch polder of purple tulips. You know I lost a number of family and friends due to irresponsible behaviour in a personal relationship. But they have forgiven me.

Reconciliation and forgiveness. Big words and big thoughts. I think that is what the transcendent, numinous being and the gospel story is all about. And *that* is as close to preaching as I will ever get!

Is Maggie launched back into school? Did I hear you whisper a heartfelt "whew"? I imagine all parents are happy to have autumn roll around, even if the new clothes and school supply bills tumble in. Is Maggie into all that trendy girl stuff now?

And are you ready to continue your horticulture course? I am pleased you can do this one online. You need a break!

Next week I begin my course on the Psalms, the biblical book that praises the Creator, evokes all manner of human heartache but also comforts like no other. It's late, so I will sign off by "adjusting" a Psalm verse to thank you for your comfort and love.

"When I called, you answered me; you made me bold and stouthearted" (Psalm 138:3, NIV).

Let's tough out this next cancer scare, okay? Keep in touch? Always?

Liz

Permissions

Every effort has been made to determine whether previously published material required reprint permissions, and to contact current copyright holders. We apologize for any errors or omissions, and will make any necessary corrections that are brought to our attention in future editions of this book.

Marla Fletcher and Diane Sims

Poems by Cicely Mary Barker copyright © The Estate of Cicely Mary Barker, reproduced by permission of Frederick Warne & Co.

Several musicians, writers and publishing houses graciously allowed us to reprint phrases or excerpts from their works. Musically, our thanks go to:

- Bennett, Willie P., "The Lucky Ones," *The Lucky Ones*, ©1989, Duke Street Records.

- Bogle, Eric, "No Man's Land," ©1984, Larrikin Publishing

- Carpenter, Mary Chapin, "Stones in the Road," *Stones in the Road*, ©1992, EMI April Music Inc. and Getarealjob Music. Used by permission of EMI April Music Inc.

- Carter, Sydney, "Lord of the Dance," ©1963, Stainer & Bell Ltd. All rights reserved; used by permission of Hope Publishing Co.

- Cockburn, Bruce, "Trouble with Normal," written by Bruce Cockburn, ©1983 Golden Mountain Music Corp., courtesy of True North Records.

- Stephen Fearing, "Glory Train," written by Stephen Fearing, ©2002 Mummy Dust Music Ltd., courtesy of True North Records.

- Ferguson, Beth, "What Is Mine," *Dance on the Earth*, ©1997.

Selected Bibliography

We found many fertile sources for historical information, plant lore and inspirational quotations, including these favourites:

Garden Voices: Two Centuries of Canadian Garden Writing by Edwinna von Baeyer and Pleasance Crawford (Toronto: Random House of Canada, 1995).

Gardening from the Heart edited by Carol Olwell (Berkeley, CA: Antelope Island Press, 1990).

The Glory of the Garden edited by Kathleen Bronzert and Bruce Sherwin (New York: Avon Books, 1993).

The Harrowsmith Perennial Garden: Flowers for Three Seasons by Patrick Lima (Buffalo: Camden House, 1990).

Larousse Dictionary of World Folklore by Alison Jones (Edinburgh: Larousse PLC, 1996).

Rodale's Illustrated Encyclopedia of Herbs edited by William H. Hylton and Claire Kowalchik (Emmaus, PA: Rodale Press, 1987).

Wildflower Folklore by Laura C. Martin (Old Saybrook, CT: The Globe Pequot Press, 1984).

* * *

A Celebration of Sisters. Fort Worth, TX: Brownlow, 1996.

Abrams, Meyer Howard, ed. *The Norton Anthology of English Literature*, 3rd ed. New York: W.W. Norton, 1962.

Anderson, Bernard W. *Understanding the Old Testament*, 3rd ed. N.p.: Prentice-Hall, 1975.

Atwood, Mary Dean. *Spirit Healing: Native American Magic and Medicine*. New York: Sterling, 1991.

Baker, Jerry. *Jerry Baker's Fast, Easy Vegetable Garden*. New York: New American Library, 1985.

Selected Bibliography

Barfoot, Joan. *Charlotte and Claudia Keeping in Touch*. Toronto: Key Porter, 2002.

Barker, Cicely Mary. *Flower Fairies of the Garden*. 1923. Reprint, London: Penguin Group, 1990.

Barnes, Emilie. *Time Began in a Garden*. Eugene, OR: Harvest House, 1995.

Barnes, Emilie, with Anne Christian Buchanan. *Secrets of the Garden*. Eugene, OR: Harvest House, 1997.

Barrett, Marilyn. *Creating Eden: The Garden as a Healing Space*. San Francisco: Harper San Francisco, 1997.

Beebe Wilder, Louise. *The Fragrant Path*. Point Roberts, WA: Hartley and Marks, 1996.

Bennett, Jennifer, and Turid Forsyth. *The Harrowsmith Annual Garden*. N.p.: Camden House, 1990.

Berger, Terry, ed. *Garden Proverbs*. Philadelphia: Running Press, 1984.

Binetti, Marianne. *Tips for Carefree Landscapes*. Pownal, VT: Storey Communications, 1990.

Boggs, Jean Sutherland. *Degas, 1834–1917*. Ottawa: National Gallery of Canada, 1988.

Bondar, Roberta. *Touching the Earth*. Toronto: Key Porter Books, 1994.

Breathnach, Sarah Ban. *Simple Abundance: A Daybook of Comfort and Joy*. New York: Warner Books, 1995.

Brickell, Christopher, and Trevor Cole, eds. *Practical Guide to Gardening in Canada*. Westmount, QC: Dorling Kindersley Books, 1993.

Bronzert, Kathleen, and Bruce Sherwin, eds. *The Glory of the Garden*. New York: Avon Books, 1993.

Bryant, M. Darrol. *Religion in a New Key*. Kitchener, ON: Pandora Press, 2001.

Buckley, A.R. *Canadian Garden Perennials*. Saanichton, BC: Hancock House, 1977.

Burnett, Frances Hodgson. *The Secret Garden*. 1910. Reprint, London: The Folio Society, 1986.

Burrell, C. Colston, ed. *Woodland Gardens: Shade Gets Chic*. New York: Brooklyn Botanic Garden, Handbook #145, 1995.

Carter, Bernard F. *The Floral Birthday Book*. London: Bloomsbury Books, 1990.

Chan, Wing-tsit. *The Great Asian Religions: An Anthology*. New York: Macmillan, 1969.

Cloninger, Claire. *Postcards for People Who Hurt*. Dallas: Word Publishing, 1995.

Cousins, Norman. *The Healing Heart: Antidotes to Panic and Helplessness*. Boston: G.K. Hall, 1984.

Cox, Jeff. *Landscaping with Nature: Using Nature's Designs to Plan Your Yard*. Emmaus, PA: Rodale Press, 1991.

Crozier, Lorna. *The Garden Going on Without Us*. Toronto: McClelland & Stewart, 1985.

Cruden, Loren. *Medicine Grove: A Shamanic Herbal*. Rochester, VT: Destiny Books, 1997.

Cullen, Mark. *The All Seasons Gardener*. Toronto: Viking, Penguin Books Canada, 1995.

Dickens, Charles. *The Personal History of David Copperfield*. Garden City, NJ: Nelson Doubleday, n.d.

Dirr, Michael. *Manual of Woody Landscape Plants: Their Identification, Ornamental Characteristics, Culture, Propagation and Uses*. Champaign, IL: Stipes Publishing, 1990.

Duerck, Judith. *Circle of Stones: Woman's Journey to Herself*. Philadelphia: Innisfree Press, 1989.

Ellwood, Robert S., Jr., ed. *Readings on Religion from Inside and Outside*. Englewood Cliffs, NJ: Prentice-Hall, 1978.

Erikson, Erik H. *Gandhi's Truth*. New York: W.W. Norton, 1969.

Estes, Clarissa Pinkola. *Women Who Run with the Wolves: Myths and Stories of the Wild Woman Archetype*. New York: Ballantine Books, 1992.

Favorite Poems of Emily Dickinson. New York: Avenel Books, 1978.

Fell, Derek. *Essential Perennials*. New York: Michael Friedman Publishing, 1989.

Fell, Derek. *New Ideas in Flower Gardening*. N.p.: Countryside Books, 1976.

Ferguson, Mary, and Richard M. Saunders. *Canadian Wildflowers Through the Seasons*. N.p.: Discovery Books, 1982.

Foley, Denise, Eileen Nechas, and the editors of *Prevention* magazine. *Women's Encyclopedia of Health and Emotional Healing: Top Women Doctors Share Their Unique Self-Help Advice on Your Body, Your Feelings and Your Life*. Emmaus, PA: Rodale Press, 1993.

Frankl, Viktor E. *Man's Search for Meaning*. Boston: Beacon Press, 1959.

Frazer, James George. *The Illustrated Golden Bough*. N.p.: George Rainbird, 1978.

Fulton, Robert, ed. *Death and Dying: Challenge and Change*. San Francisco: Boyd and Fraser, 1978.

Gardner, Jo Ann. *The Heirloom Garden: Selecting and Growing Over 300 Old-Fashioned Ornamentals*. Pownal, VT: Storey Communications, 1992.

Gibran, Kahlil. *The Prophet*. New York: Alfred A. Knopf, 1972.

Glyck, Vivian Elisabeth. *12 Lessons on Life I Learned from My Garden: Spiritual Guidance from the Vegetable Patch.* Emmaus, PA: Daybreak Books, 1997.

Handbook on Herbs. Special Printing of *Plants and Gardens*, Vol. 14, No 2; Brooklyn Botanic Garden, 13th printing, Ann Arbor, MI: Edwards Bros., 1978.

Handford, S. A., trans. *Caesar the Conquest of Gaul*, rev. ed. London: Penguin Books, 1982.

Hansen, Rick, and Jim Taylor. *Rick Hansen: Man in Motion.* Vancouver: Douglas and McIntyre, 1987.

Harpur, Tom. *For Christ's Sake.* Toronto: Oxford University Press, 1986.

Harpur, Tom. *Would You Believe?* Toronto: McClelland & Stewart, 1996.

Harris, Marjorie. *The Canadian Gardener: A Guide to Gardening in Canada.* Toronto: Random House of Canada, 1990.

Harris, Marjorie. *Ecological Gardening: Your Path to a Healthy Garden.* Toronto: Random House of Canada, 1996.

Harris, Marjorie. *Favorite Garden Tips.* Toronto: Harper Perennial, 1994.

Harris, Marjorie. *The Healing Garden: Nature's Restorative Powers.* N.p.: HarperCollins, 1996.

Harvey, Gail, ed. *A Host of Angels.* New York: Gramercy Books, 1992.

Harvey, Gail. *The Language of Flowers.* New York: Gramercy Books, 1995.

Hill, Lewis, and Nancy Hill. *Lawns, Grasses and Groundcovers.* Emmaus, PA: Rodale Press, 1995.

Hillesum, Etty. *Etty: The Letters and Diaries of Etty Hillesum 1941–1943.* Ottawa: Novalis, 2002.

Hole, Lois. *Lois Hole's Northern Flower Gardening*. Edmonton: Lone Pine Publishing, 1994.

Hole, Lois. *Lois Hole's Perennial Favorites*. Edmonton: Lone Pine Publishing, 1995.

Holmes, Sally, and Tracey Williamson. *An English Cottage Year*. New York: Hearst, 1993.

Hosie, R.C. *Native Trees of Canada*. Ottawa: Canadian Forestry Service, 1975.

Hyde, Gertrude. *Seeds from a Secret Garden*. White Plains, NY: Peter Pauper Press, 1997.

Jahns, Marsha, ed. *Step-by-Step Successful Gardening: Ornamental Grasses*. Des Moines: Better Homes and Gardens Books, 1995.

James, Wilma. *Gardening with Biblical Plants: Handbook for the Home Gardener*. Chicago: Nelson-Hall, 1983.

Jeffares, A. Norman. *W.B. Yeats: Man and Poet*. London: Routledge and Kegan Paul, 1949.

Jones, Pamela. *Just Weeds: History, Myths and Uses*. Shelbourne: Chapters Publishing, 1994.

Kingsolver, Barbara. *The Poisonwood Bible*. New York: HarperPerennial, 1999.

Kirk, G.S. *The Nature of Greek Myths*. Harmondsworth: Penguin Books, 1974.

Knitter, Paul F. *One Earth, Many Religions: Multifaith Dialogues and Global Responsibility*. Maryknoll, NY: Orbis Books, 1995.

Kruger, Anna. *Canadian Nature Guides – Herbs*. New York: Smithmark Publishers, 1992.

Kübler-Ross, Elisabeth. *Death: The Final Stage of Growth*. Englewood Cliffs, NJ: PrenticeHall, 1975.

Kundera, Milan. *The Unbearable Lightness of Being*. New York: HarperPerennial, 1984.

Küng, Hans. *Does God Exist? An Answer for Today*. Trans. Edward Quinn. New York: Doubleday, 1980.

Kushner, Harold S. *When Bad Things Happen to Good People*. N.p.: Avon, 1981.

Lannoy, Richard. *The Speaking Tree*. New York: Oxford University Press, 1971.

Laurence, Margaret. *Dance on the Earth: A Memoir*. Toronto: McClelland & Stewart, 1989.

Le Garsmeur, Alain, and Bernard McCabe. *W.B. Yeats: Images of Ireland*. New York: Macmillan, 1991.

Leddy, Mary Jo. *Say to the Darkness, We Beg to Differ*. Toronto: Lester & Orpen Dennys, 1990.

Lewis, C.S. *A Grief Observed*. New York: Bantam Books, 1976.

Little, Jean. *Look Through My Window*. Toronto: Harper Collins, 1970.

Little, Jean. *Stars Come Out Within*. Toronto: Viking, 1990.

Lorde, Audre. *The Cancer Journals*. San Francisco: aunt lute books, 1997.

The Macmillan Book of Proverbs, Maxims and Famous Phrases. New York: Macmillan, 1948.

Magnusson, Magnus, ed. *Chambers Biographical Dictionary*. Edinburgh: W&R Chambers, 1990.

Masson, Jeffrey Moussaieff, and Susan McCarthy. *When Elephants Weep: The Emotional Lives of Animals*. New York: Dell, 1995.

May, Hal, and Susan Trotsky, eds. *Contemporary Authors*, vols. 77–80 and 123. Detroit: Gale Research, 1979 and 1988.

Mayle, Peter. *A Year in Provence*. New York: First Vintage Edition, 1991.

Selected Bibliography

Miller, James E. *Winter Grief, Summer Grace: Returning to Life After a Loved One Dies.* N.p.: Augsburg, 1995.

Milne, A.A. *The World of Pooh.* London: E.P. Dutton, 1957.

Montgomery, L.M. *Anne of Windy Poplars.* 1936. Reprint, Toronto: McClelland & Stewart/Seal Books, 1981.

Morford, Mark P.O., and Robert J. Lenardon. *Classical Mythology.* New York: Longman, 1977.

Nhat Hanh, Thich. *Anger: Wisdom for Cooling the Flames.* New York: Riverhead Books, 2001.

Nhat Hanh, Thich. *Be Still and Know.* New York: Riverhead Books, 1996.

Nhat Hanh, Thich. *Zen Keys.* New York: Doubleday, 1973.

Oakes, A.J. *Ornamental Grasses and Grasslike Plants.* Malabar, FL: Krieger, 1993.

Osborne, Robert. *Roses for Canadian Gardens: A Practical Guide to Varieties and Techniques.* Toronto: Key Porter Books, 1991.

Paterson, John, and Katherine Paterson. *Consider the Lilies: Plants of the Bible.* New York: Thomas Y. Crowell, 1986.

Peterson, Richard F. *William Butler Yeats.* Boston: Twayne Publishers, 1982.

Potter, Beatrix. *The Tale of Squirrel Nutkin.* 1903. Reprint, London: William Clowes, 1986.

Radner, Gilda. *It's Always Something.* New York: Simon and Schuster, 1989.

Reinhardt, Thomas, Martina Reinhardt, and Mark Moscowitz. *Ornamental Grass Gardening.* New York: Michael Friedman Publishing Group, 1989.

Richter's Herb Catalogue 1998. Goodwood, ON: Richters, The Herb Specialists, 1998.

Riotte, Louise. *Carrots Love Tomatoes: Secrets of Companion Planting for Successful Gardening*. Vancouver: Storey Communications, 1975.

Riotte, Louise. *Roses Love Garlic*. N.p.: Garden Way Publishing, Storey Communications, 1983.

Robbins, Tom. *Still Life with Woodpecker*. New York: Bantam Books, 1980.

Robertson, Laurel, Carol Flinders, and Bronwen Godfrey. *Laurel's Kitchen: A Handbook for Vegetarian Cookery and Nutrition*. N.p: Bantam Books, 1976.

Rose, Jeanne. *Jeanne Rose's Herbal Guide to Inner Health*. New York: Grosset and Dunlap, 1979.

Roses. Alexandria, VA: Time-Life, 1996.

Russell, Edward C. *Customs and Traditions of the Canadian Armed Forces*. N.p: Minister of Supply and Services Canada, 1980.

Sackville-West, Vita. *A Joy of Gardening*. New York: Harper and Row, 1958.

Saint-Exupéry, Antoine de. *The Little Prince*. New York: Harcourt Brace Jovanovich, 1943.

Scrivener, Leslie. *Terry Fox: His Story*. 1981.

Seuss, Dr. (Geisel, Theodore S.) *How the Grinch Stole Christmas*. New York: Random House, 1957.

Sheehy, Gail. *The Silent Passage*. Toronto: Random House, 1991.

Shields, Carol, and Marjorie Anderson, eds. *Dropped Threads: What We Aren't Told*. Toronto: Random House, 2001.

Shields, Dinah, and Edwinna von Baeyer. *The Reluctant Gardener: A Beginner's Guide to Gardening in Canada*. Toronto: Random House of Canada, 1992.

Siegel, Bernie S. *How to Live Between Office Visits*. New York: HarperCollins, 1993.

Siegel, Bernie S. *Love, Medicine and Miracles*. New York: HarperCollins, 1986.

Silverstein, Shel. *A Light in the Attic*. New York: HarperCollins, 1981.

Simpson, D.P. *Cassell's New Latin Dictionary*. New York: Funk and Wagnalls, 1960.

Still, Steven. *Manual of Herbaceous Ornamental Plants*, 4th ed. Champaign, IL: Stipes Publishing, 1994.

Stone, I.F. *The Trial of Socrates*. Boston: Little, Brown and Company, 1988.

Strong, James H. *Strong's Exhaustive Concordance*. Grand Rapids, MI: Baker Book House, 1992.

Stuckey, Charles, ed. *Monet: A Retrospective*. Hong Kong: Hugh Lauter Levin Associates, 1985.

Swenson, Allan A. *Your Biblical Garden: Plants of the Bible and How to Grow Them*. Garden City, NY: Doubleday, 1981.

Tagore, Rabindranath. *Collected Poems and Plays*. New York: Macmillan, 1958.

Thompson, H.C., and Fred Bonnie. *Growing Flowers*. Birmingham: Oxmoor House, 1975.

Thorpe, Patricia. *Growing Pains: Time and Changes in the Garden*. Orlando, FL: Harcourt Brace, 1994.

Tierra, Michael. *The Way of Herbs*. New York: Pocket Books, 1990.

Tolle, Eckhart. *Practicing the Power of Now*. Novato, CA: New World Library, 2001.

Tyler, Anne. *Ladder of Years*. New York: Alfred A. Knopf, 1995.

Unterecker, John, ed. *Yeats: A Collection of Critical Essays*. Englewood Cliffs, NJ: Prentice-Hall, 1963.

Vanier, Jean. *Tears of Silence*. New York: Paulist Press, 1970.

Vardey, Lucinda, comp. *Mother Teresa: A Simple Path*. New York: Ballantine Books, 1995.

Visser, Margaret. *Much Depends on Dinner*. Toronto: McClelland & Stewart, 1986.

von Baeyer, Edwinna, and Pleasance Crawford, eds. *Garden Voices: Two Centuries of Canadian Garden Writing*. Toronto: Random House of Canada, 1995.

Wallace, Bronwen. *The Stubborn Particulars of Grace*. Toronto: McClelland & Stewart, 1987.

Westberg, Granger E. *Good Grief*. Philadelphia: Fortress Press, 1962.

Williams, Penelope. *That Other Place: A Personal Account of Breast Cancer*. Toronto: Dundurn Press, 1993.

Winokur, Jon, ed. *The Portable Curmudgeon*. New York: Penguin Group, 1987.

Woodson, Meg. *Making It Through the Toughest Days of Grief*. New York: Harper, 1994.

Woolaver, Lance, and Bob Brooks. *The Illuminated Life of Maud Lewis*. Halifax: Nimbus Publishing, 1998.

Wydra, Nancilee. *Feng Shui in the Garden*. Chicago: Contemporary Books, 1997.

Zachner, R.C. *Hinduism*. N.p.: Oxford University Press, 1966.

Other References

Adam, Judith. "Scent and Sentiment: Symbols of Nostalgia and Renewal, Lilacs Spring to Life in Cold-climate Gardens." *Gardening Life*, Vol. 2, No. 2 (Spring 1997), 50-56.

Cole, Trevor. "Consider Oaks to Replace Storm-ravaged Trees." *Ottawa Citizen*, February 28, 1998, 1-9.

Cole, Trevor. "Dancing Fairies Good Name for Swaying Columbines." *Ottawa Citizen*, December 19, 1997, I-4.

Cole, Trevor. "Consider Biennials for Colour and Variety." *Ottawa Citizen*, January 10, 1998, L-6.

Dyhouse, Tim. "Keeping Faith Through the Buddy Poppy." *VFW*, May 1997, 12-13.

Farina, Richard. "The Swallow Song."

Grieve, Maude. *A Modern Herbal*, Internet site: www. botanical.com/botanical/mgmh

Hardy, Eric. "The Vanishing Poppy." *The Legionary*, November 1937, 37.

MacGregor, Tom. "Liberation Celebration." *Legion Magazine*, August 1995, 6.

Mallett, Dave. "Garden Song."

Martin, Carl. "Barnyard Dance."

Microsoft. *Encarta 97 Encyclopedia*, CD-ROM. ©Microsoft 1993–96.

Rogers, Stan. *Songs from Fogarty's Cove: A Collection of the Words, Music and Spirit of the Songs from Fogarty's Cove, Turnaround, Between the Breaks… Live! and Northwest Passage* (Ottawa: OFC Publications, 1982).

von Baeyer, Edwinna. "The Horticultural Odyssey of Isabella Preston." *Canadian Horticultural History: An Interdisciplinary Journal*, Vol. 1, No. 3, 1987 (Centre for Canadian Historical Horticultural Studies, Royal Botanical Gardens).

1997 CKCU Ottawa Folk Festival Lucky Program, "Colleen Peterson In Memoriam."

Index

English, 97-98
Garry, 97
pin, 95-96
red, 69, 94, 95, 96, 97
swamp, 95
white, 96-97
Oenothera biennis, 74;
    see also Evening primrose
onion, 72-73, 101, 134, 135;
    see also Allium
    Egyptian self-seeding,
    72-73, 77
Origanum majorana, 172;
    see also Marjoram

Papaver, see also Poppy
    P. commutatum, 117-18
    P. orientale, 120
    P. rhoeas, 120
    P. somniferum, 120
peppermint, 136, 137-38, 178
periwinkle, 156-58, 174
    Madagascar, 156
    rosy, 156
phlox, summer, 125
pine, Eastern white, 96
poplar, 21, 53, 58-60;
    see also Aspen, Populus
    Balm-of-Gilead, 60
    balsam, 60
    Japanese, 58
    Lombardy black, 60
    white, 58
poppy, 117; see also Papaver
    corn, 120
    Flanders, 117-20

opium, 120
Oriental, 120
Shirley, 120
Populus, 58; see also Aspen,
    Poplar
    P. alba, 58
    P. balsamifera, 60
    P. candicans, 60
    P. deltoides, 59
    P. maximowiczii, 58
    P. trichocarpa, 60
primrose, 37, 132
primula, 9, 56
pyrethrum, 101;
    see also Tanacetum

Quaking grass, 42-43, 58;
    see also Briza
Quercus; see also Oak
    Q. alba, 96
    Q. garryana, 97
    Q. macrocarpa, 95
    Q. muehlenbergii, 95
    Q. palustris, 95
    Q. robur, 97-98
    Q. rubra, 96
    Q. velutina, 95

radicchio, 100
radish, 72, 101
rose, 37, 38, 57, 78, 80, 110,
    111, 134-35, 148-52, 165
    French apothecary, 150-51
Rosa gallica officinalis, 150